NEW CONSTRUCTION

ALSO BY SAM ALDEN:

IT NEVER HAPPENED AGAIN
HAUNTER
WICKED CHICKEN QUEEN
LYDIAN

DESIGN: TOM KACZYNSKI + SAM ALDEN
PRODUCTION ASSIST: ANDREW GEORGE

UNCIVILIZED BOOKS
P.O. BOX 6434
MINNEAPOLIS, MN 55406
USA
UNCIVILIZEDBOOKS.COM

FIRST EDITION, OCTOBER 2015

10 9 8 7 6 5 4 3 2 1

ISBN 978-1-941250-03-7

DISTRIBUTED TO THE TRADE BY:

CONSORTIUM BOOK SALES & DISTRIBUTION, LLC
34 THIRTEENTH AVE NE
SUITE 101 MINNEAPOLIS, MN
55413-1007
ORDERS: (800) 283-3572

PRINTED IN USA

NEW CONSTRUCTION

SAM ALDEN

UNCIVILIZED BOOKS, PUBLISHER

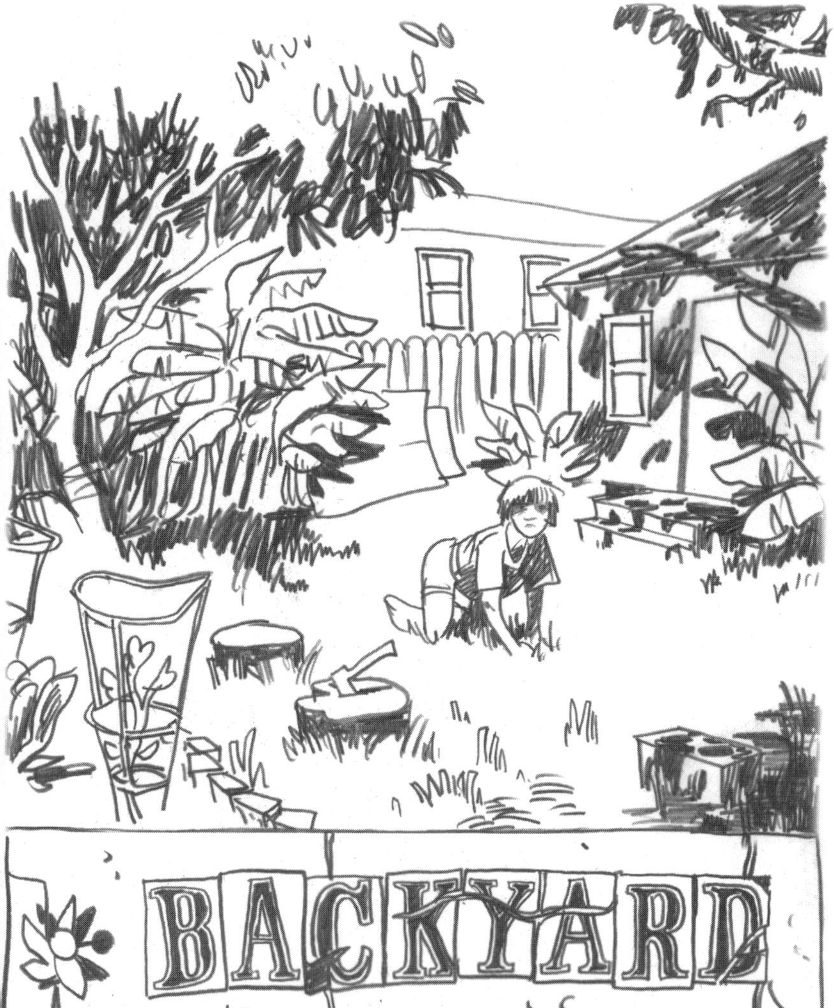
BACKYARD

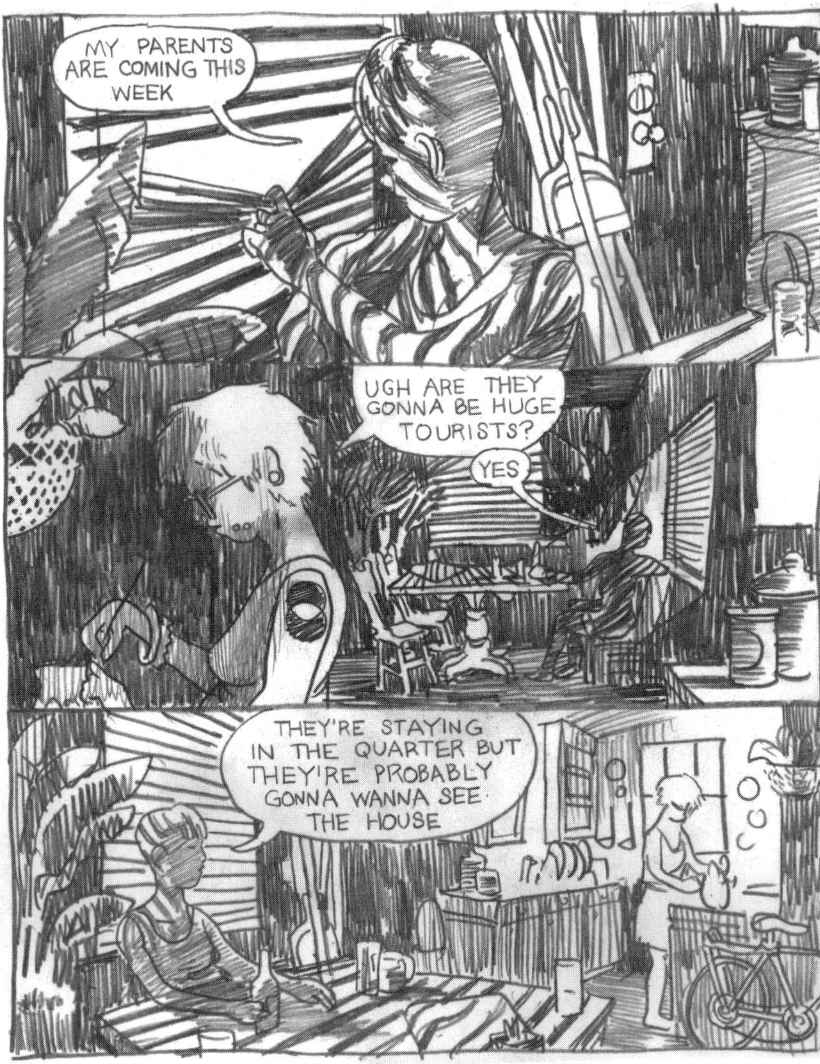
MY PARENTS ARE COMING THIS WEEK
UGH ARE THEY GONNA BE HUGE TOURISTS?
YES
THEY'RE STAYING IN THE QUARTER BUT THEY'RE PROBABLY GONNA WANNA SEE THE HOUSE

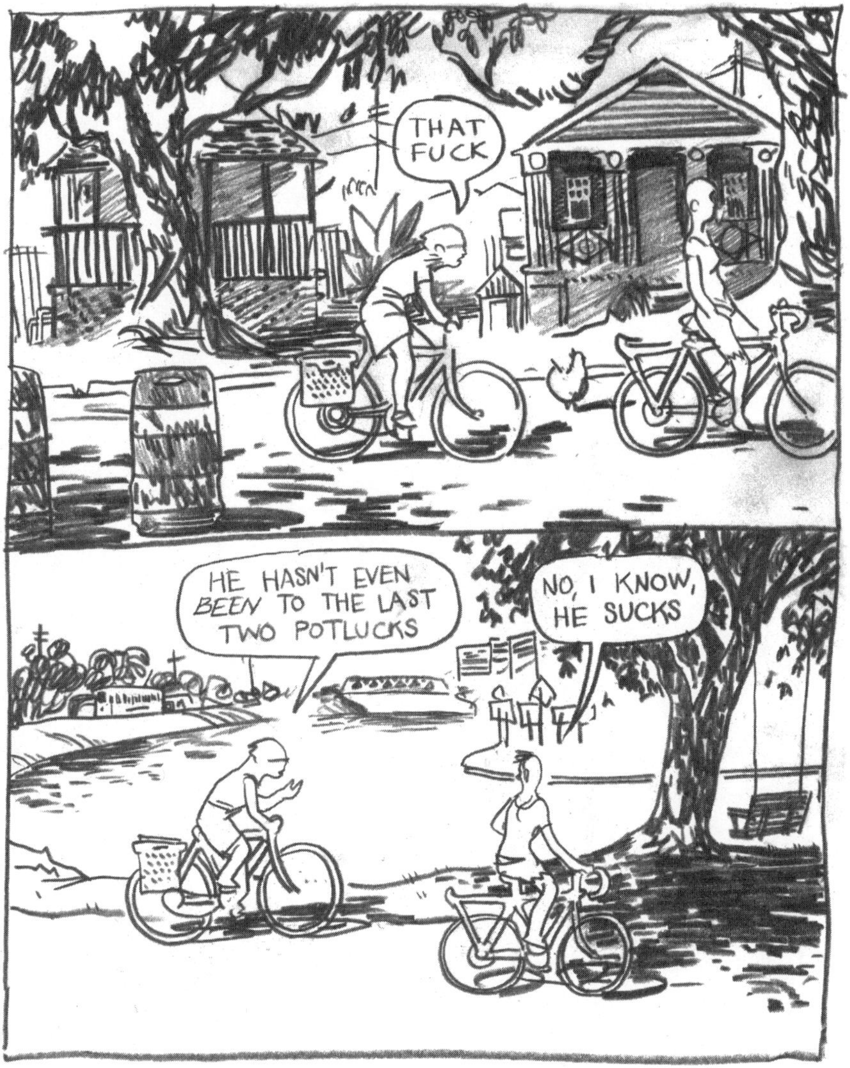
THAT FUCK
HE HASN'T EVEN BEEN TO THE LAST TWO POTLUCKS
NO, I KNOW, HE SUCKS

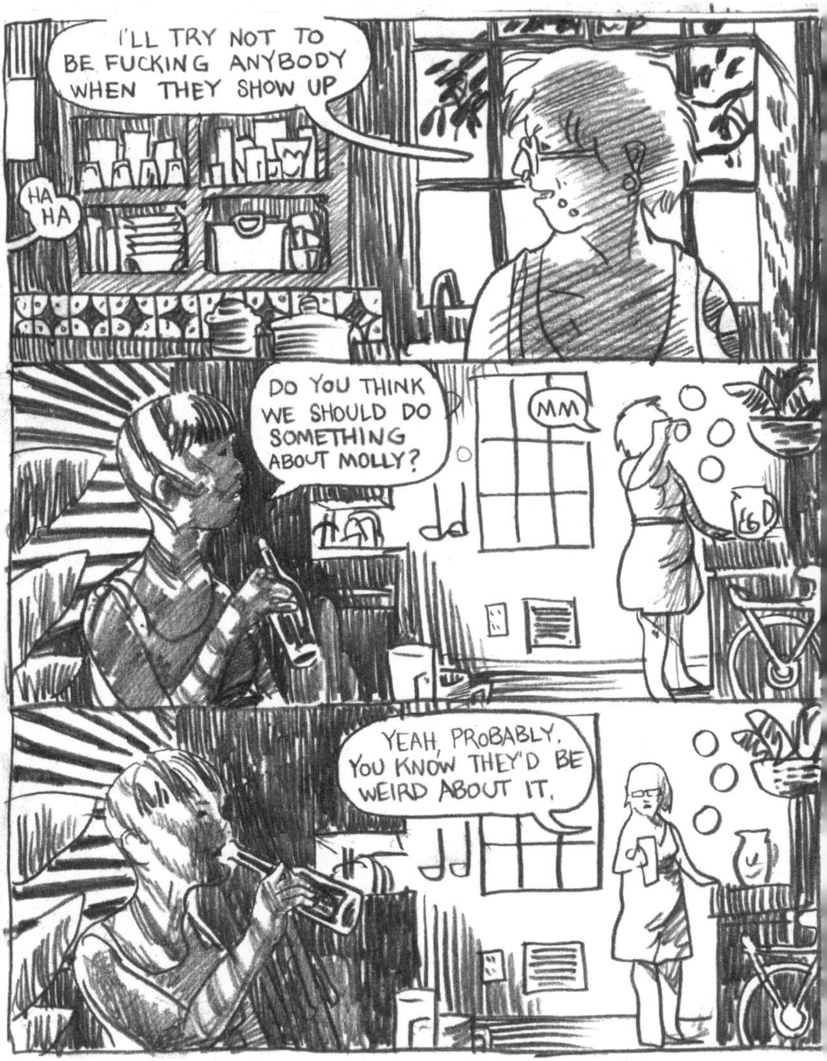
I'LL TRY NOT TO BE FUCKING ANYBODY WHEN THEY SHOW UP
HA HA
DO YOU THINK WE SHOULD DO SOMETHING ABOUT MOLLY?
MM
YEAH, PROBABLY. YOU KNOW THEY'D BE WEIRD ABOUT IT.

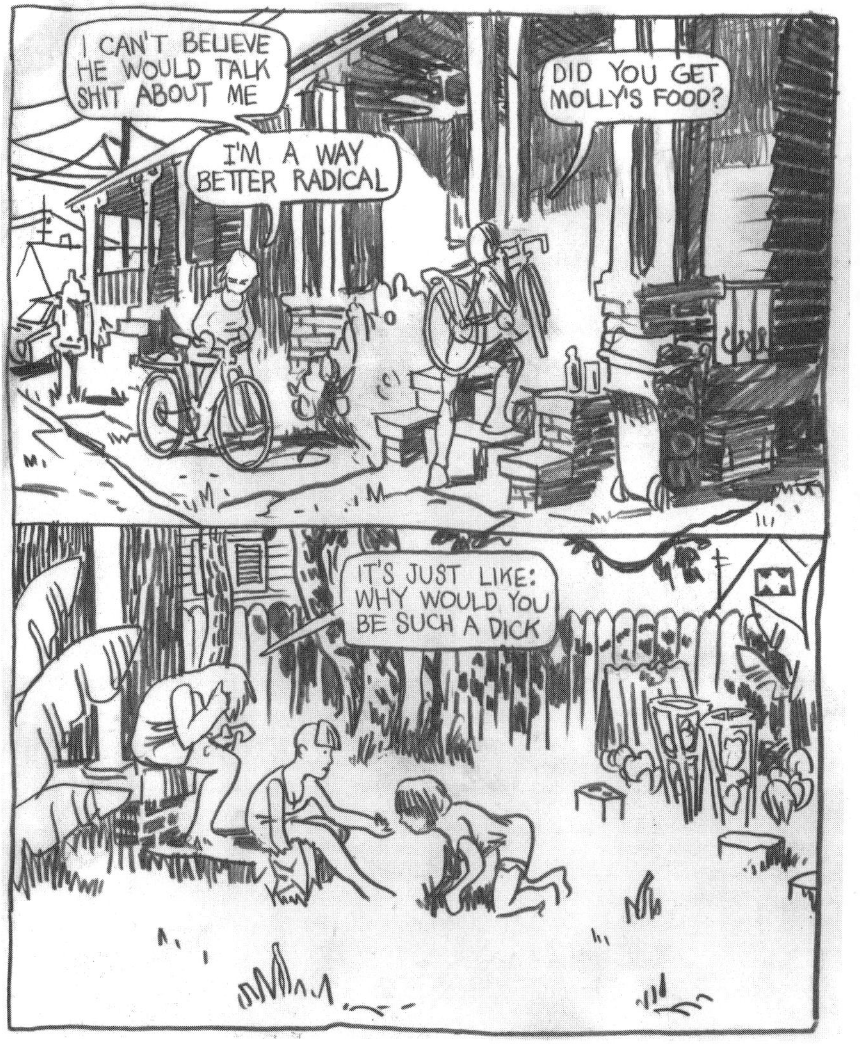
I CAN'T BELIEVE HE WOULD TALK SHIT ABOUT ME
I'M A WAY BETTER RADICAL
DID YOU GET MOLLY'S FOOD?
IT'S JUST LIKE: WHY WOULD YOU BE SUCH A DICK

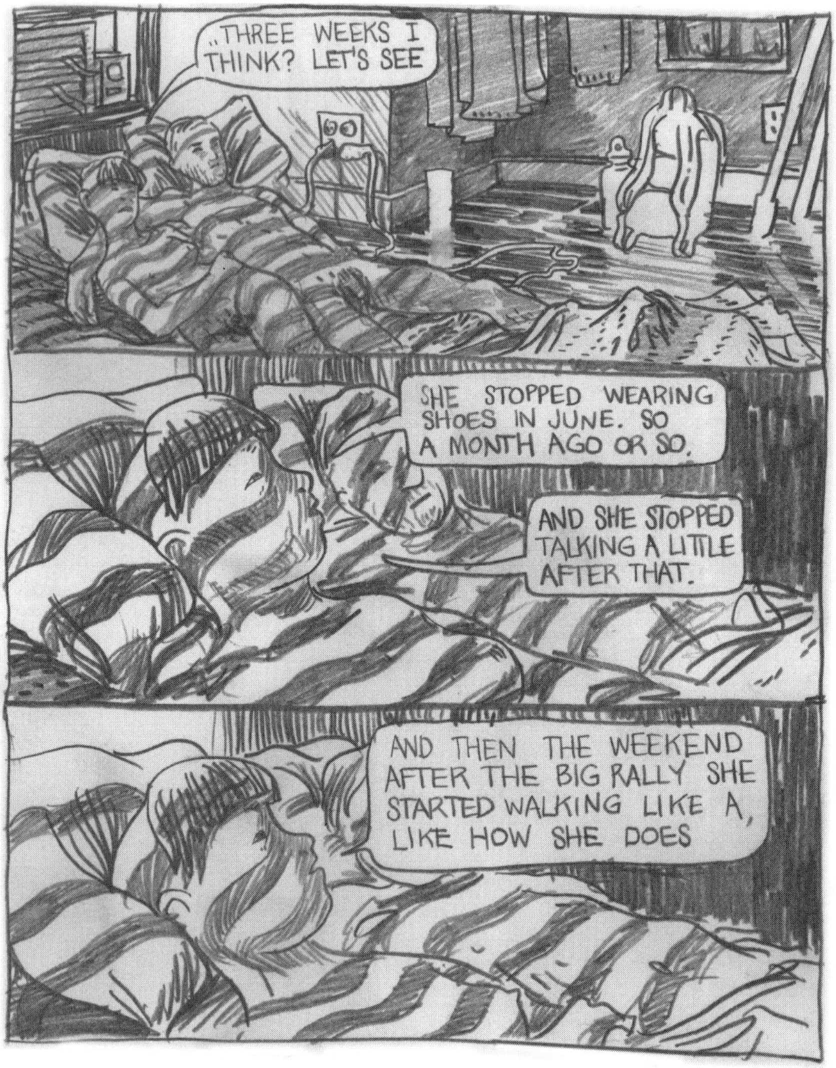
..THREE WEEKS I THINK? LET'S SEE
SHE STOPPED WEARING SHOES IN JUNE. SO A MONTH AGO OR SO.
AND SHE STOPPED TALKING A LITTLE AFTER THAT.
AND THEN THE WEEKEND AFTER THE BIG RALLY SHE STARTED WALKING LIKE A, LIKE HOW SHE DOES

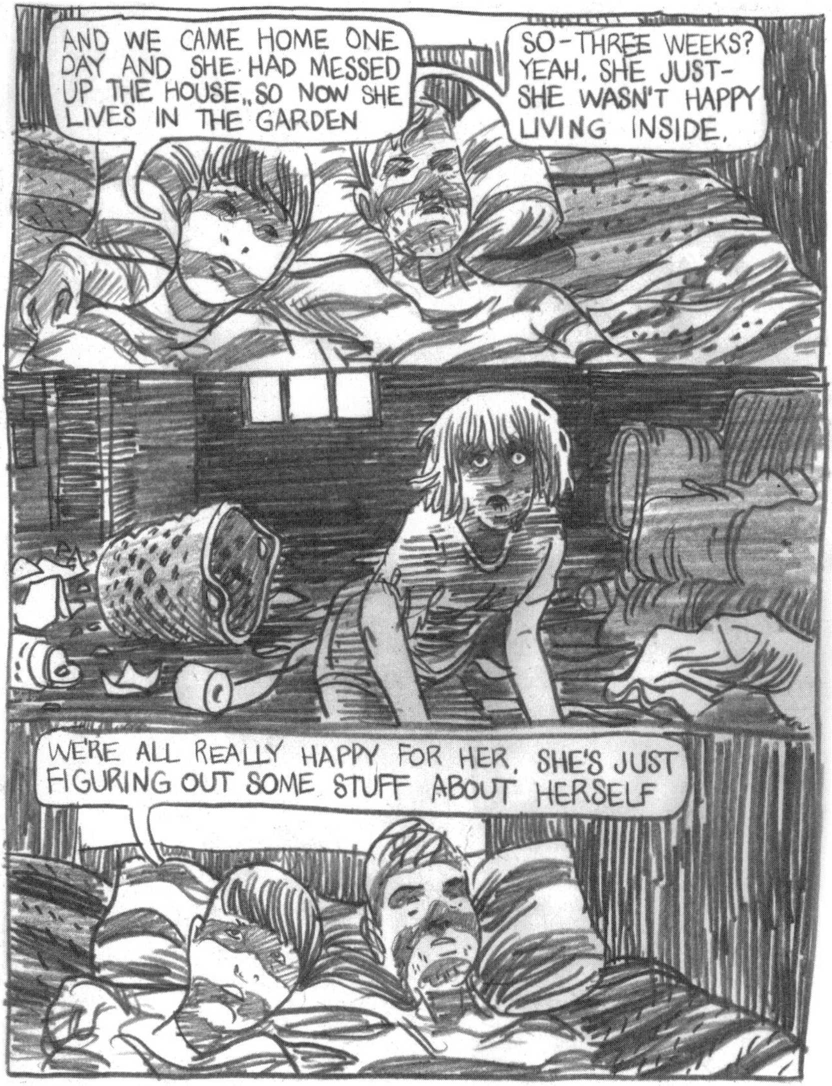
AND WE CAME HOME ONE DAY AND SHE HAD MESSED UP THE HOUSE,, SO NOW SHE LIVES IN THE GARDEN
SO-THREE WEEKS? YEAH, SHE JUST- SHE WASN'T HAPPY LIVING INSIDE.
WE'RE ALL REALLY HAPPY FOR HER. SHE'S JUST FIGURING OUT SOME STUFF ABOUT HERSELF

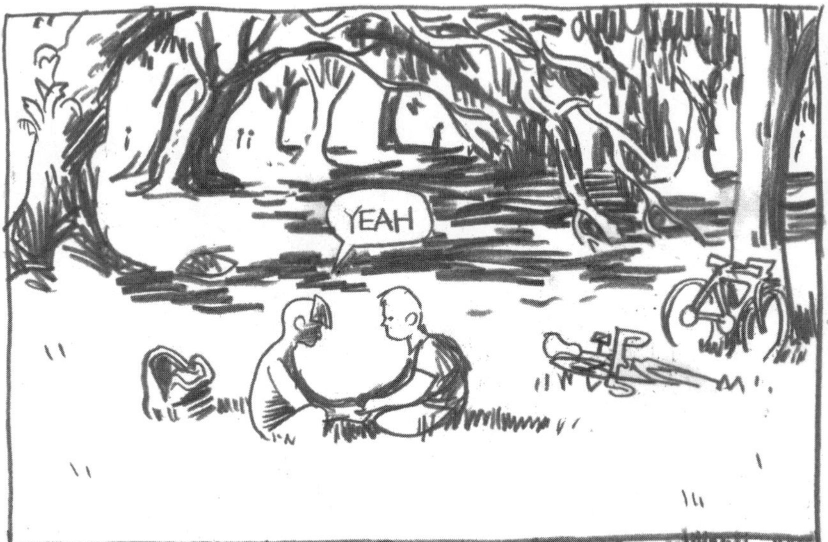
YEAH

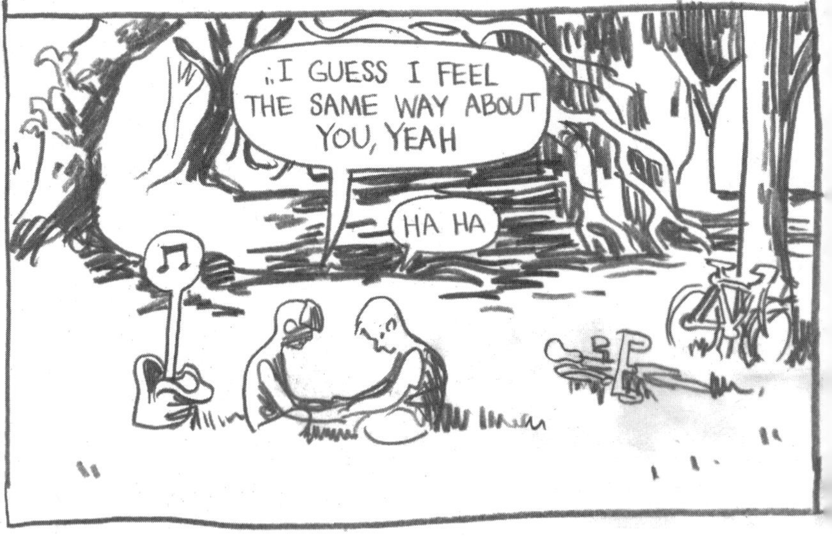
...I GUESS I FEEL THE SAME WAY ABOUT YOU, YEAH
HA HA

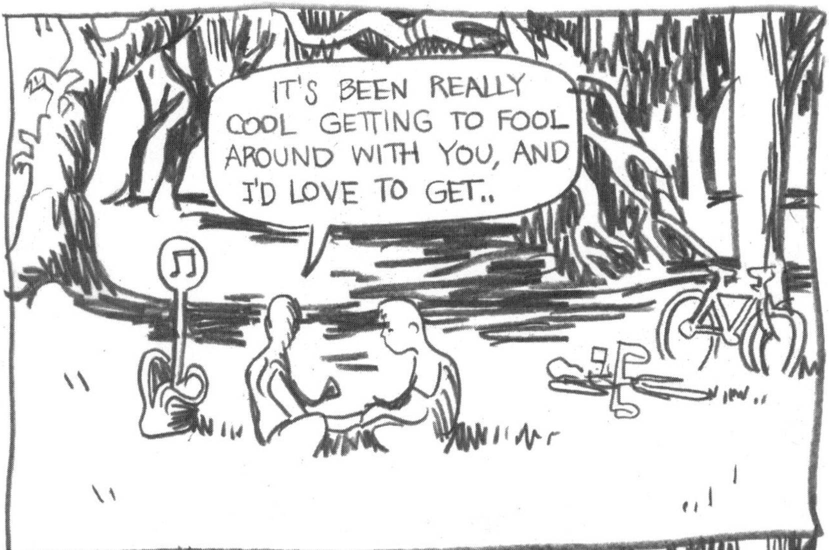
IT'S BEEN REALLY COOL GETTING TO FOOL AROUND WITH YOU, AND I'D LOVE TO GET..

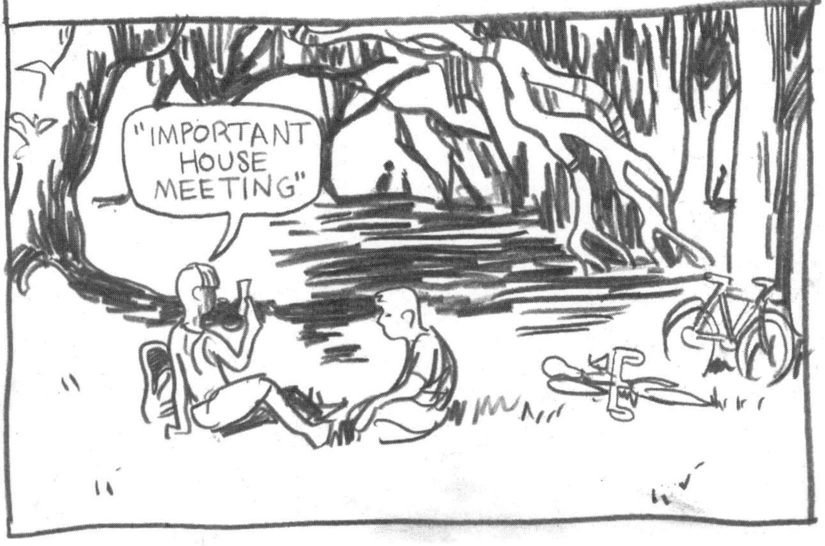
"IMPORTANT HOUSE MEETING"

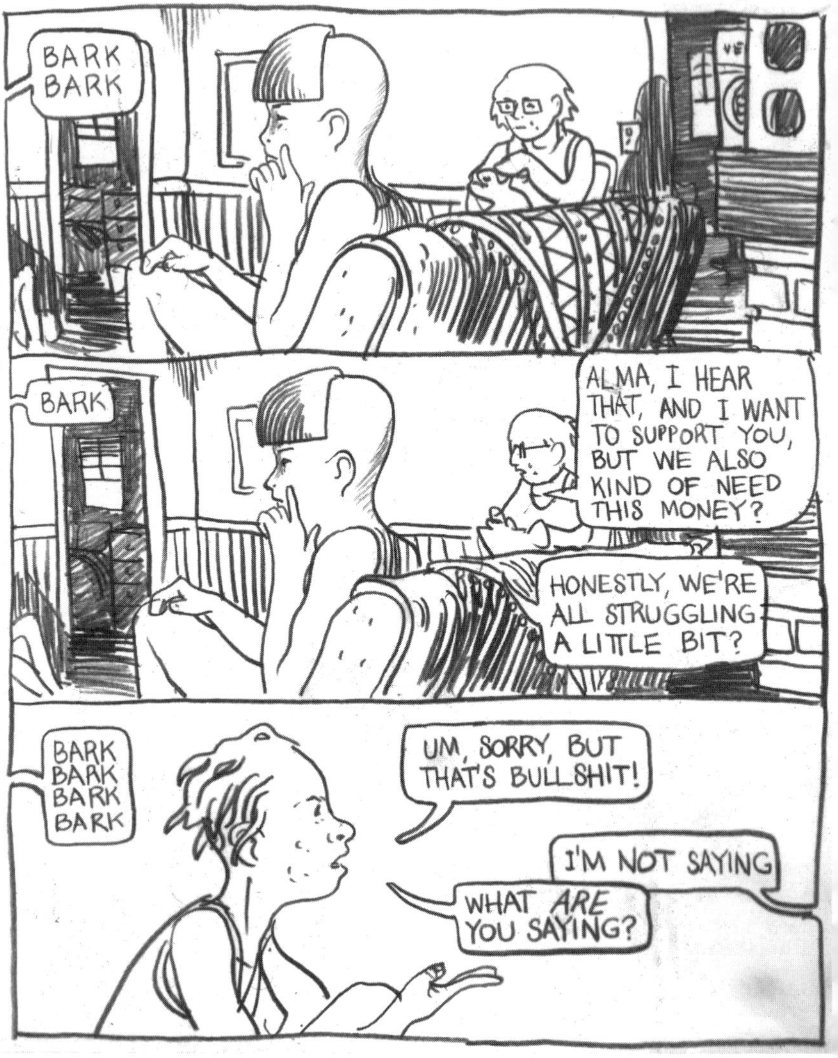
BARK BARK
BARK
ALMA, I HEAR THAT, AND I WANT TO SUPPORT YOU, BUT WE ALSO KIND OF NEED THIS MONEY?
HONESTLY, WE'RE ALL STRUGGLING A LITTLE BIT?
BARK BARK BARK BARK
UM, SORRY, BUT THAT'S BULLSHIT!
I'M NOT SAYING
WHAT ARE YOU SAYING?

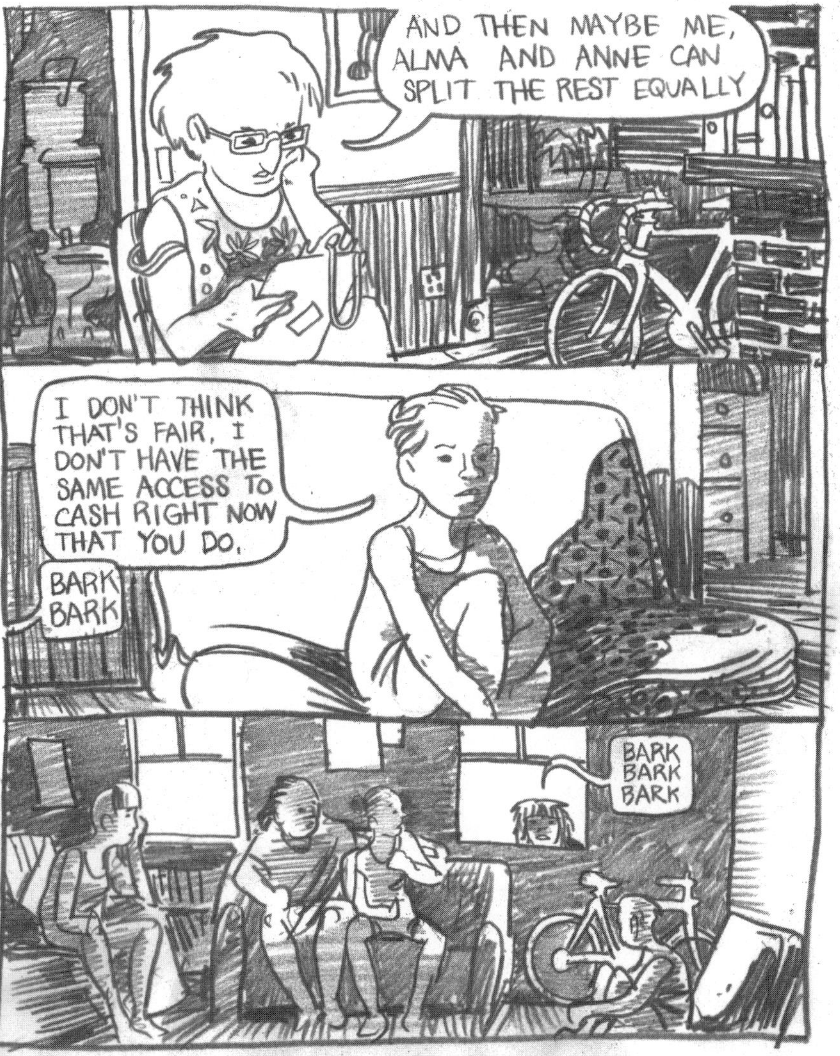
AND THEN MAYBE ME, ALMA AND ANNE CAN SPLIT THE REST EQUALLY
I DON'T THINK THAT'S FAIR, I DON'T HAVE THE SAME ACCESS TO CASH RIGHT NOW THAT YOU DO.
BARK BARK
BARK BARK BARK

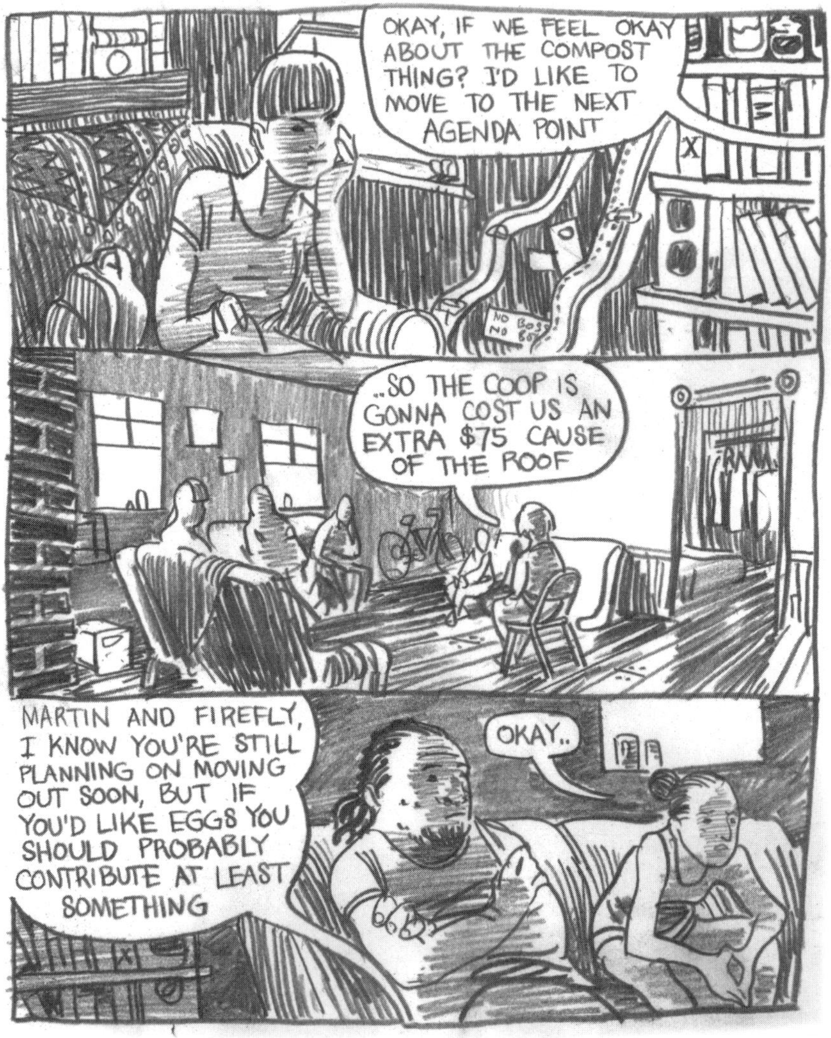
OKAY, IF WE FEEL OKAY ABOUT THE COMPOST THING? I'D LIKE TO MOVE TO THE NEXT AGENDA POINT
..SO THE COOP IS GONNA COST US AN EXTRA $75 CAUSE OF THE ROOF
MARTIN AND FIREFLY, I KNOW YOU'RE STILL PLANNING ON MOVING OUT SOON, BUT IF YOU'D LIKE EGGS YOU SHOULD PROBABLY CONTRIBUTE AT LEAST SOMETHING
OKAY..

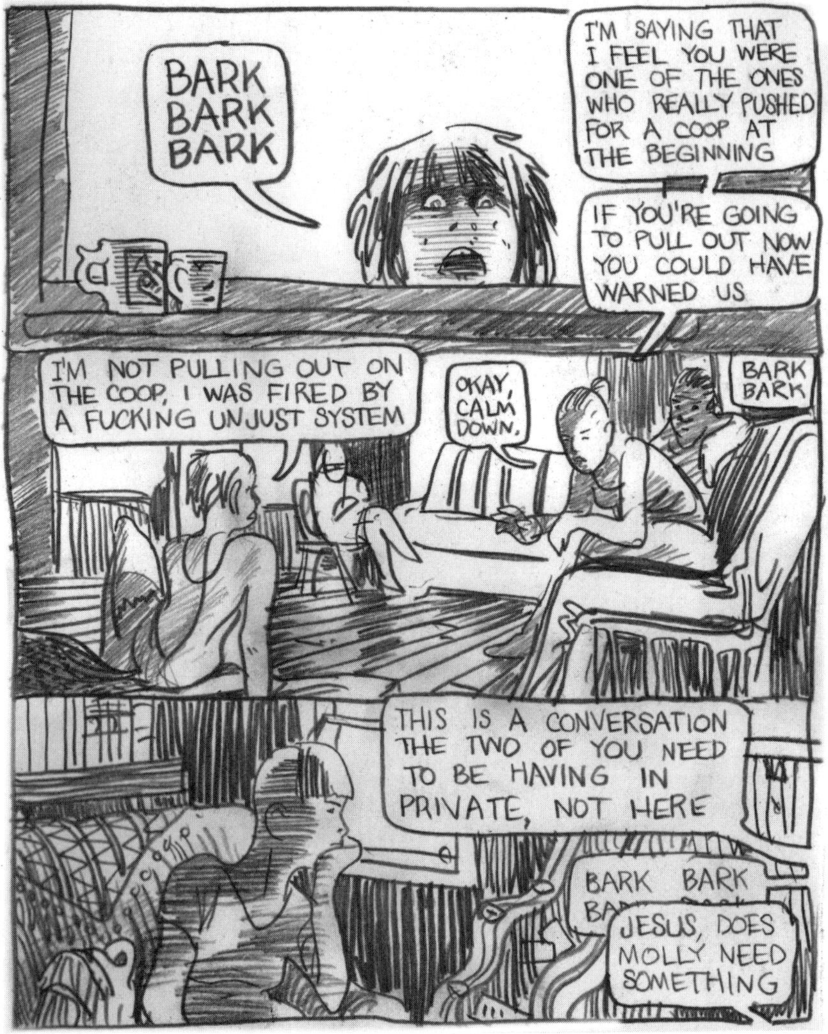
BARK BARK BARK
I'M SAYING THAT I FEEL YOU WERE ONE OF THE ONES WHO REALLY PUSHED FOR A COOP AT THE BEGINNING
IF YOU'RE GOING TO PULL OUT NOW YOU COULD HAVE WARNED US
I'M NOT PULLING OUT ON THE COOP, I WAS FIRED BY A FUCKING UNJUST SYSTEM
OKAY, CALM DOWN,
BARK BARK
THIS IS A CONVERSATION THE TWO OF YOU NEED TO BE HAVING IN PRIVATE, NOT HERE
BARK BARK
JESUS, DOES MOLLY NEED SOMETHING

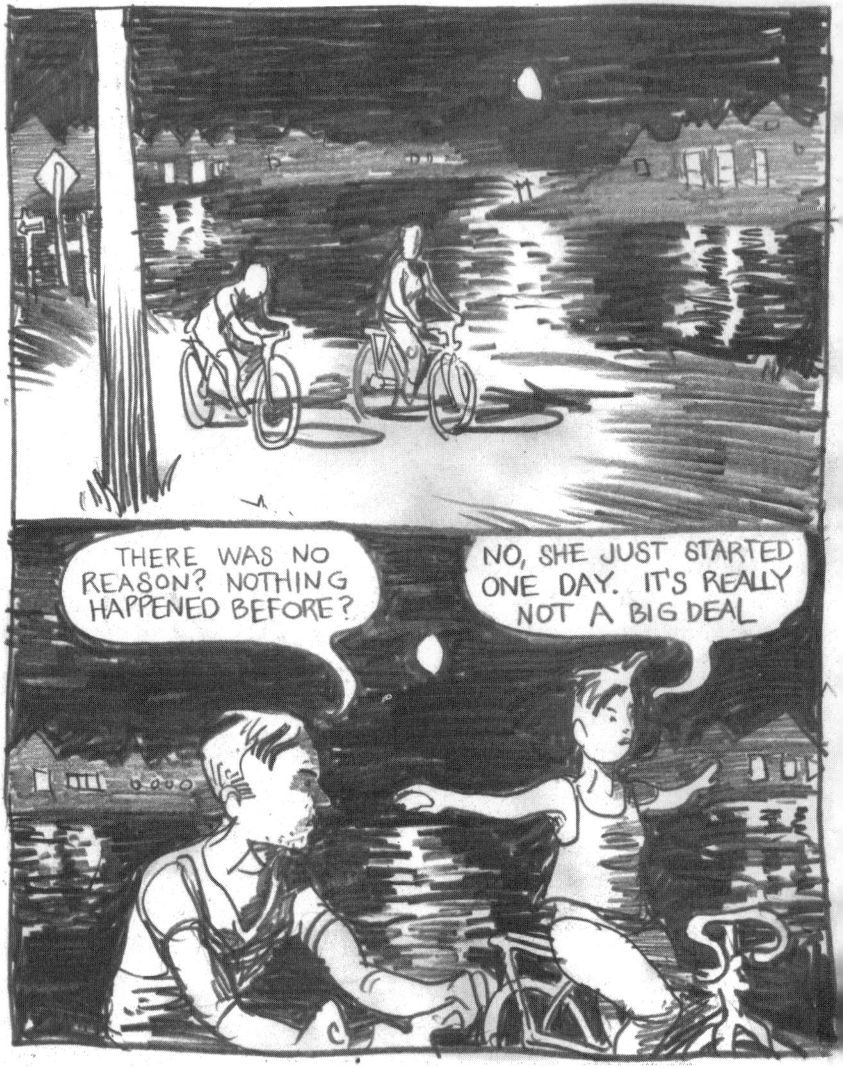
THERE WAS NO REASON? NOTHING HAPPENED BEFORE?
NO, SHE JUST STARTED ONE DAY. IT'S REALLY NOT A BIG DEAL

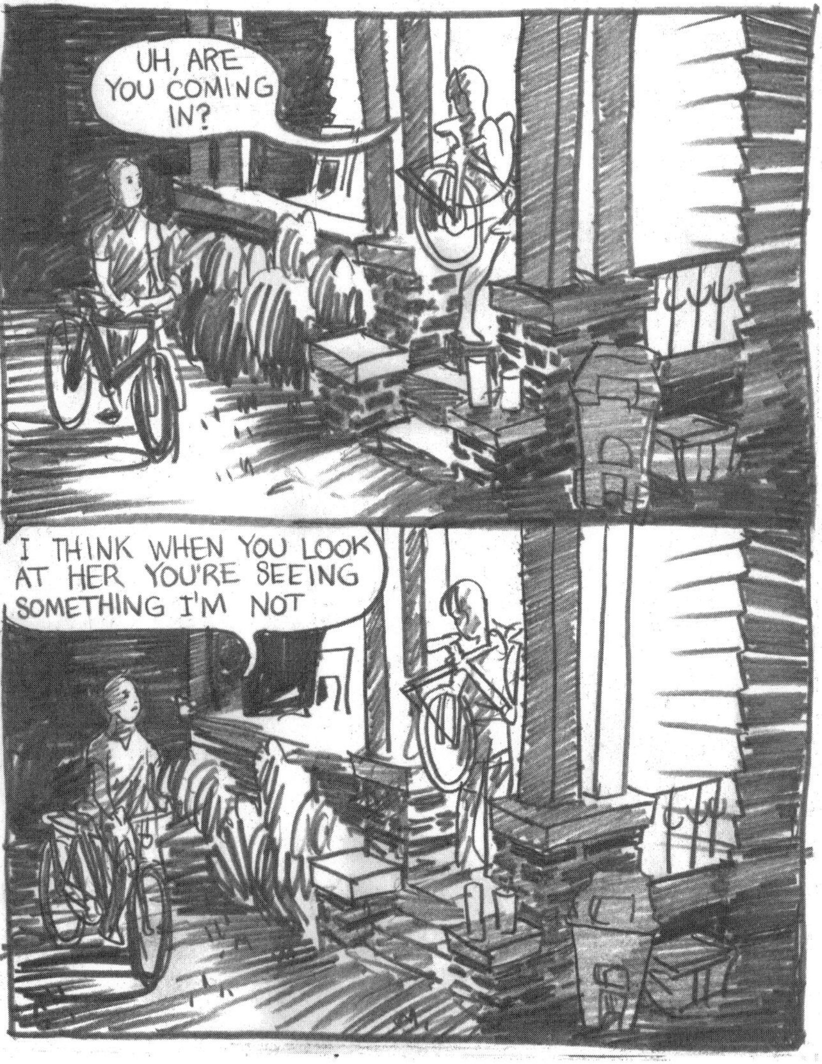
UH, ARE YOU COMING IN?
I THINK WHEN YOU LOOK AT HER YOU'RE SEEING SOMETHING I'M NOT

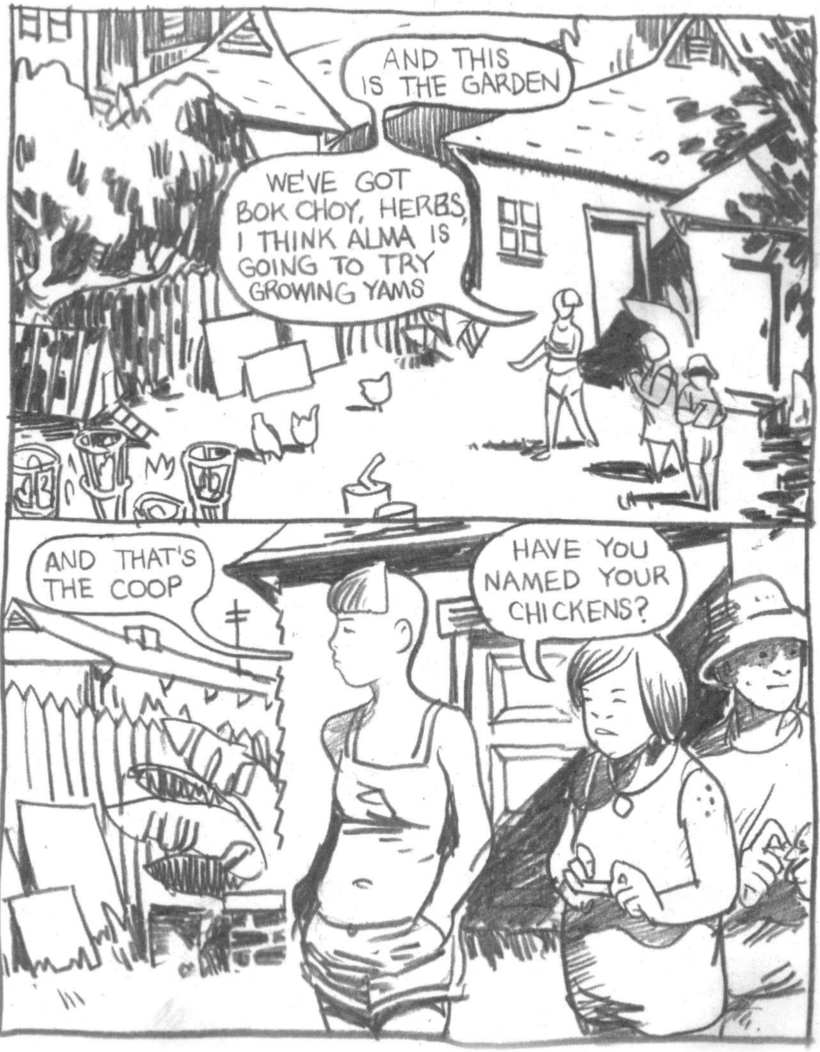
AND THIS IS THE GARDEN
WE'VE GOT BOK CHOY, HERBS, I THINK ALMA IS GOING TO TRY GROWING YAMS
AND THAT'S THE COOP
HAVE YOU NAMED YOUR CHICKENS?

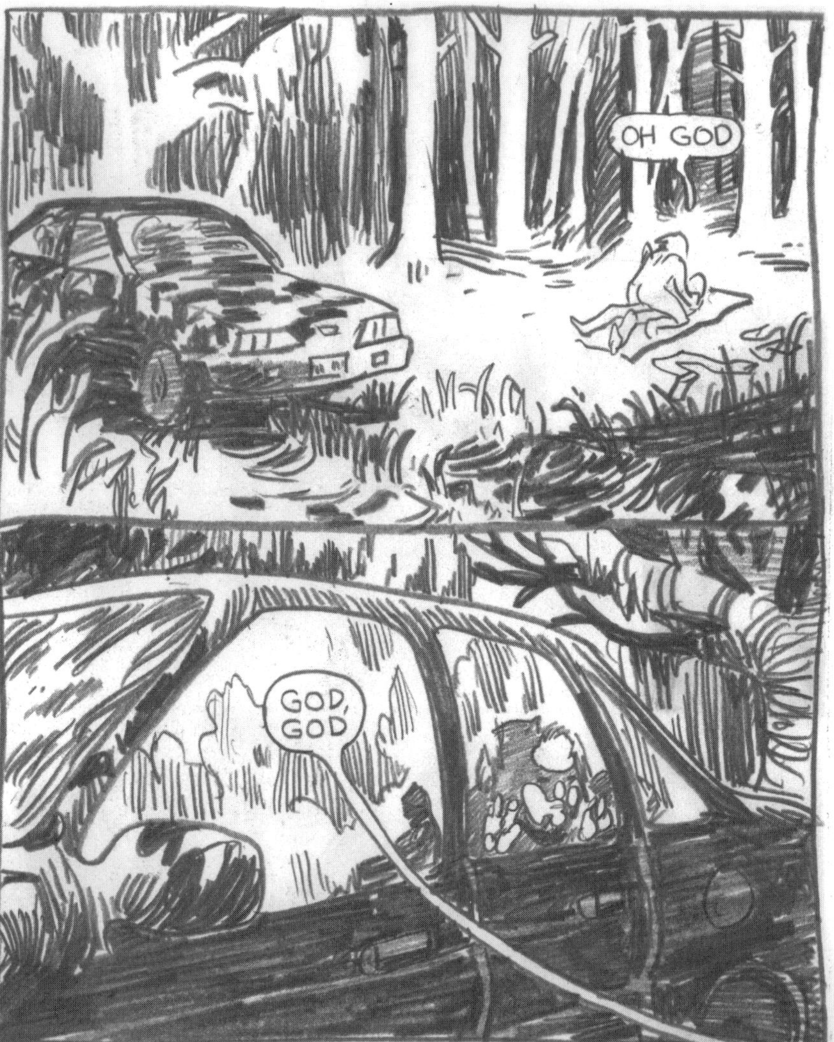
OH GOD
GOD, GOD

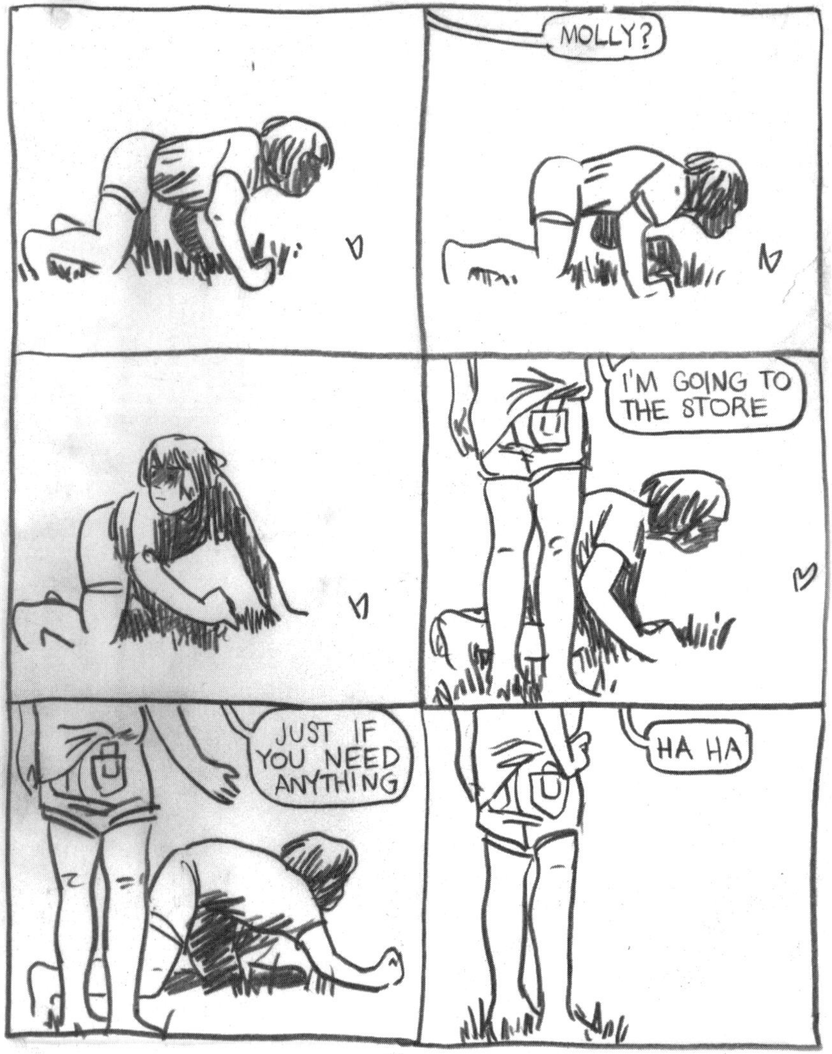
MOLLY?
I'M GOING TO THE STORE
JUST IF YOU NEED ANYTHING
HA HA

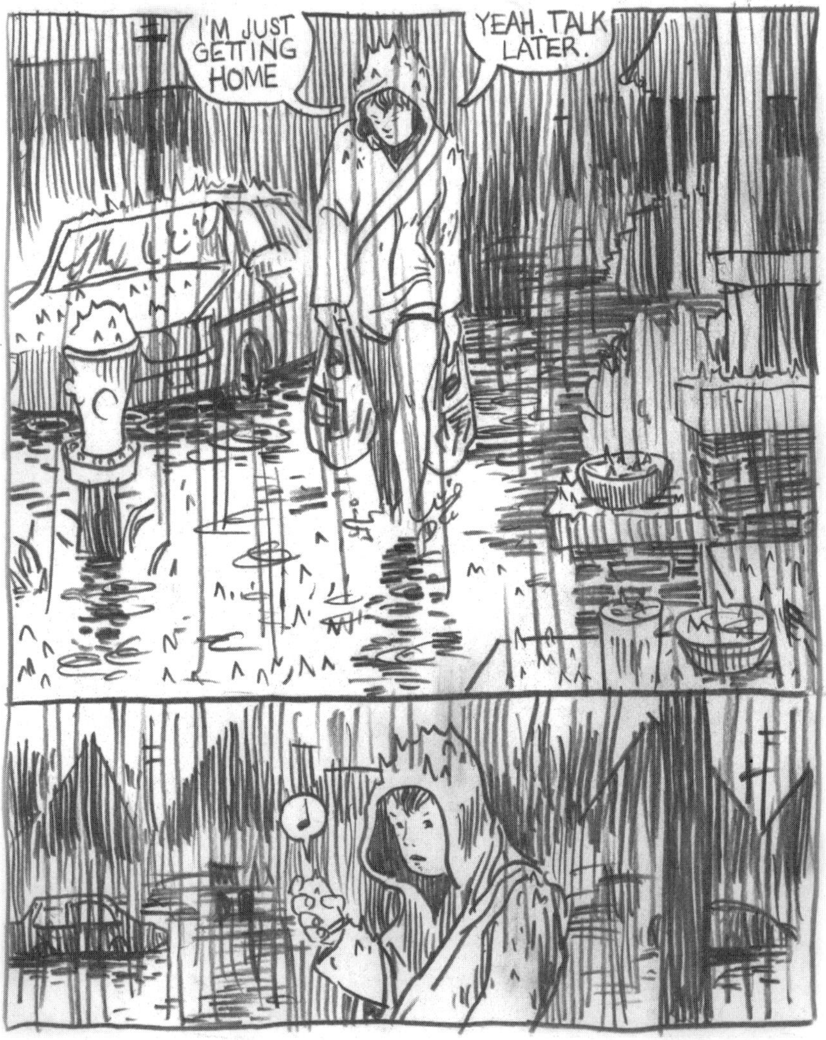
I'M JUST GETTING HOME
YEAH. TALK LATER.

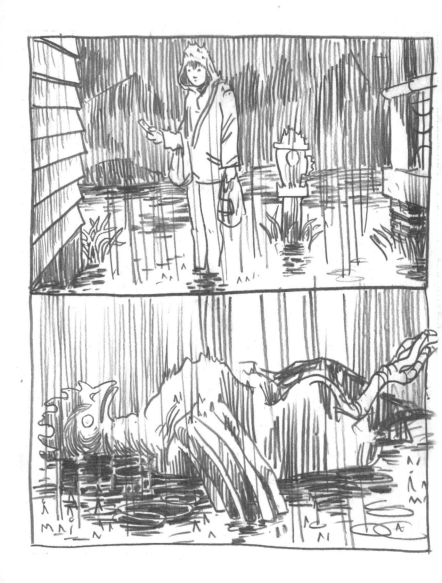

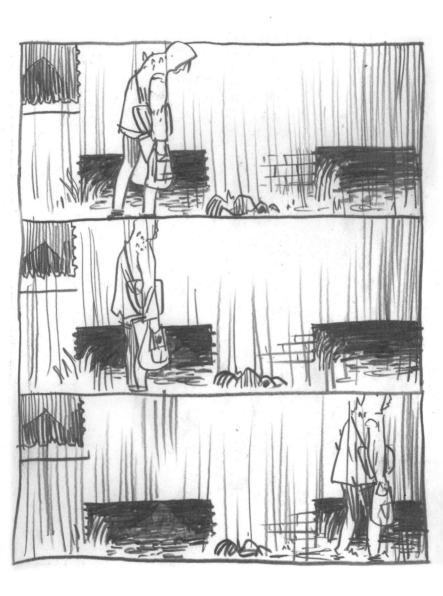

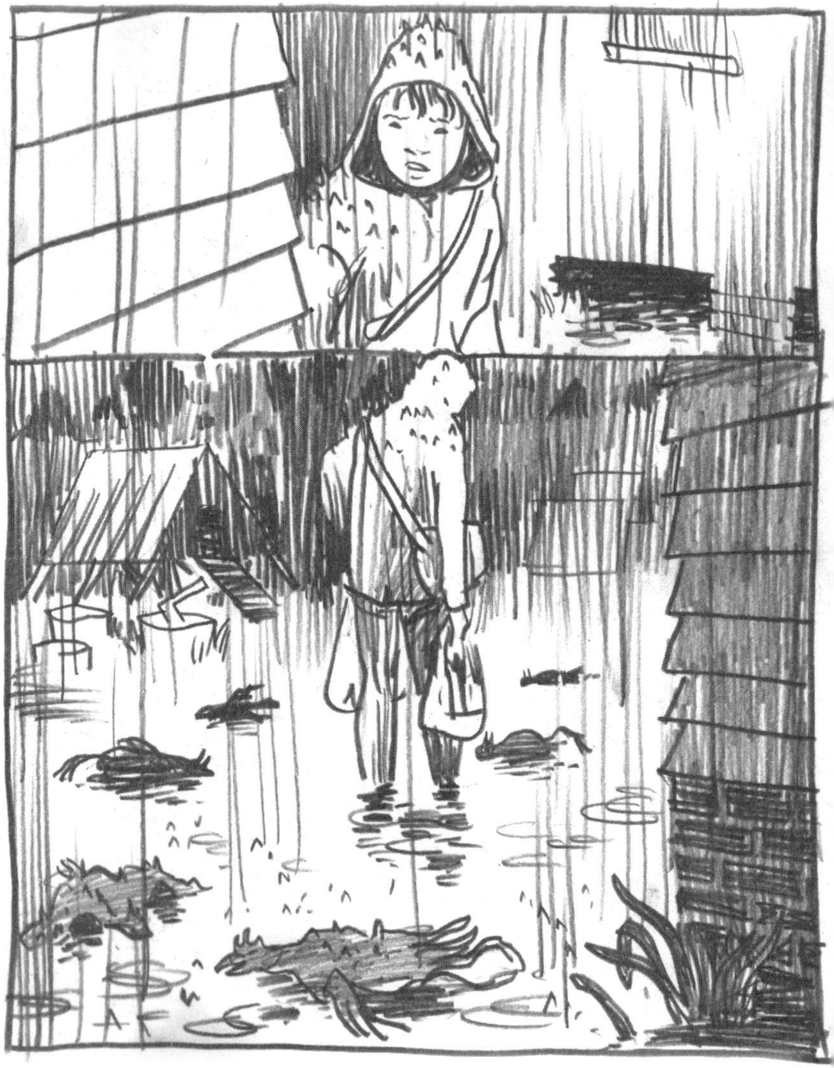

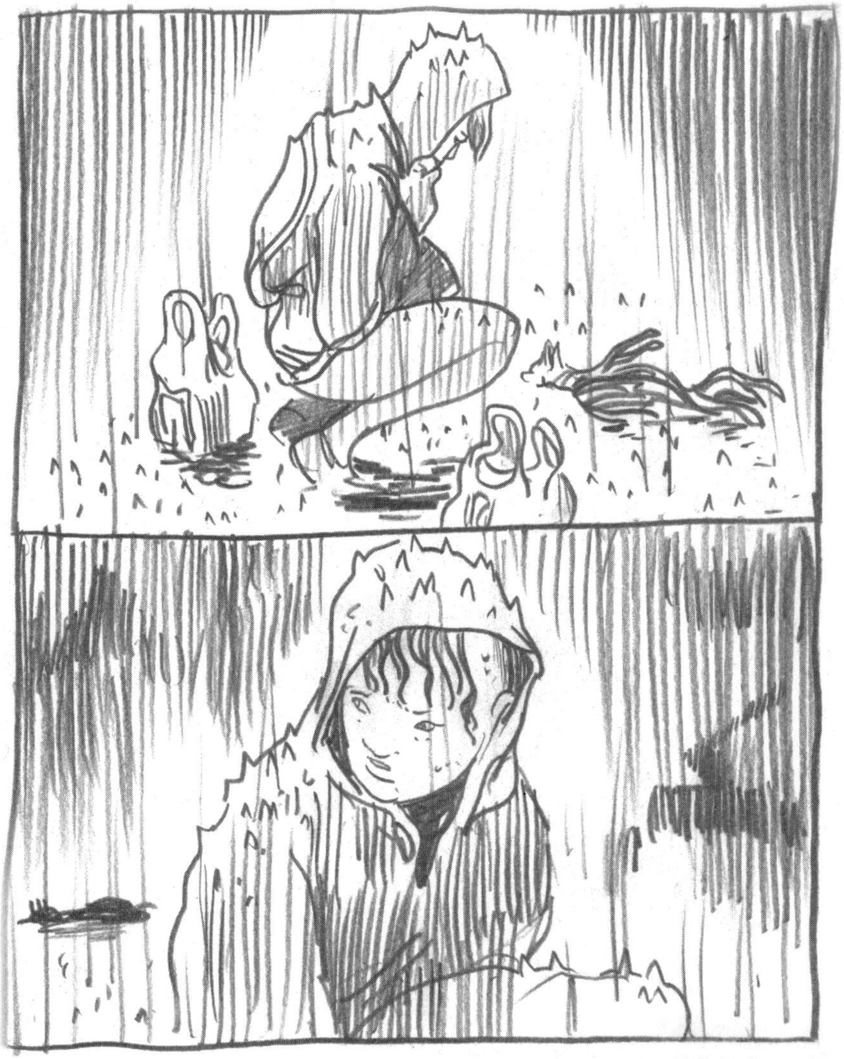

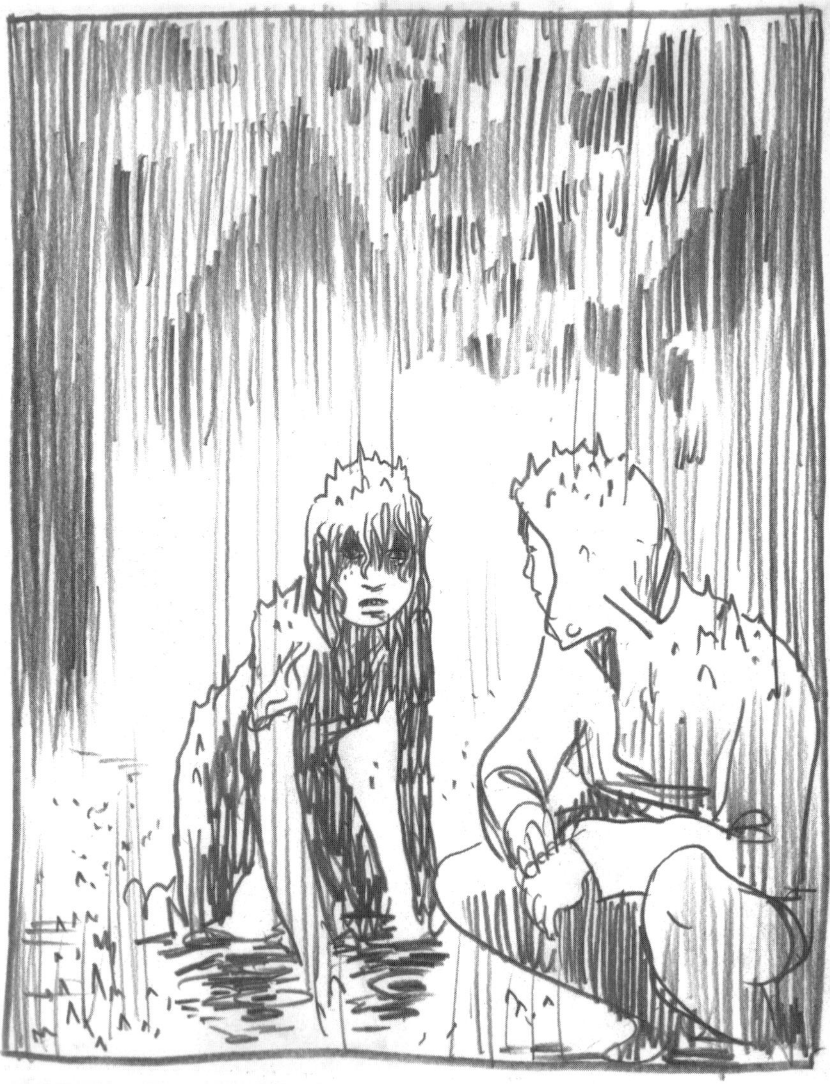

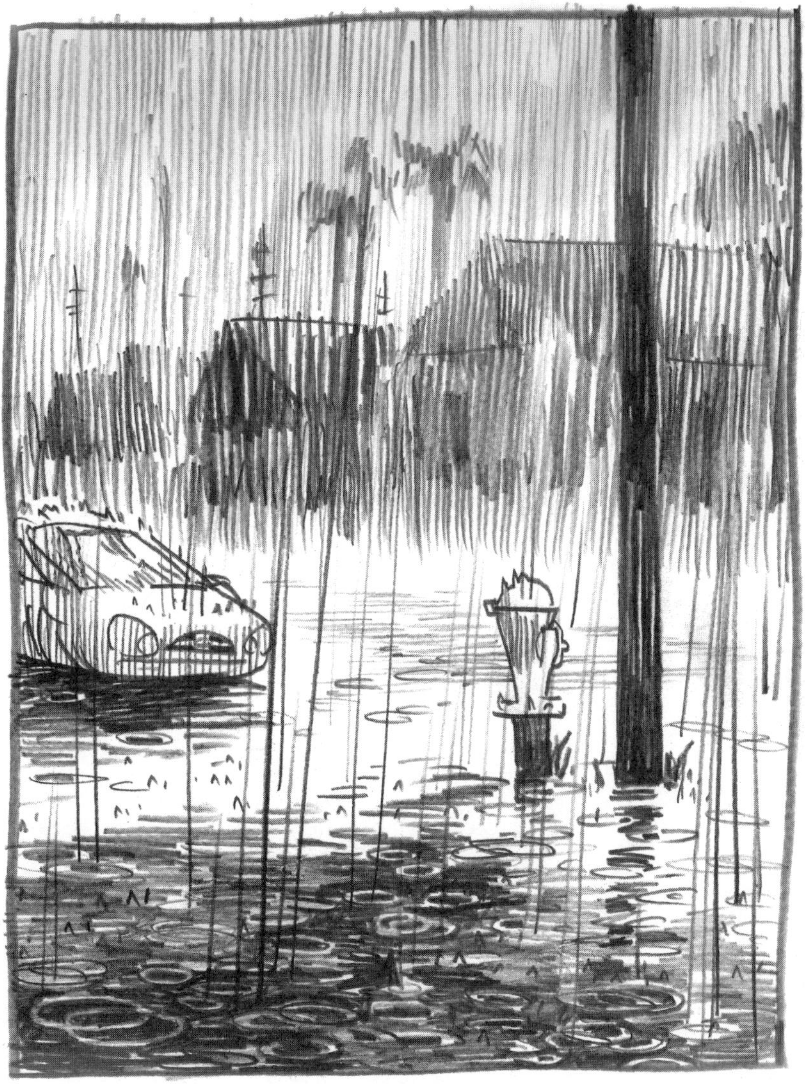

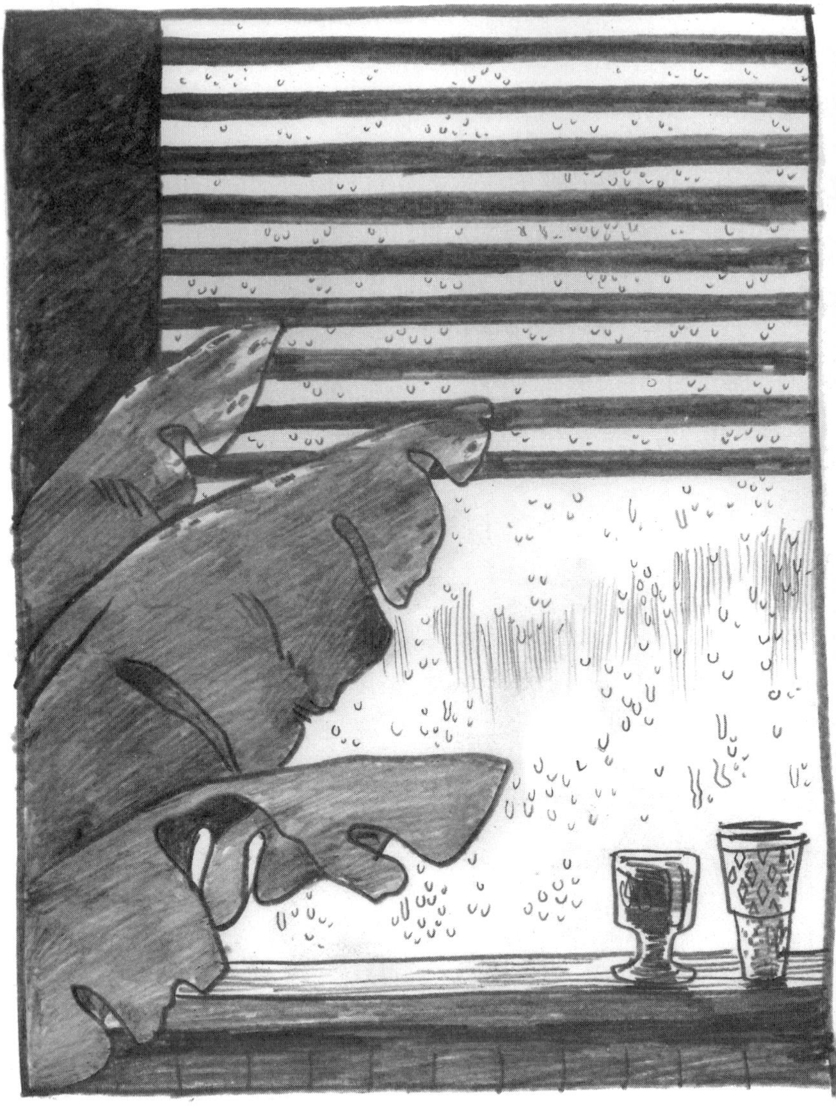

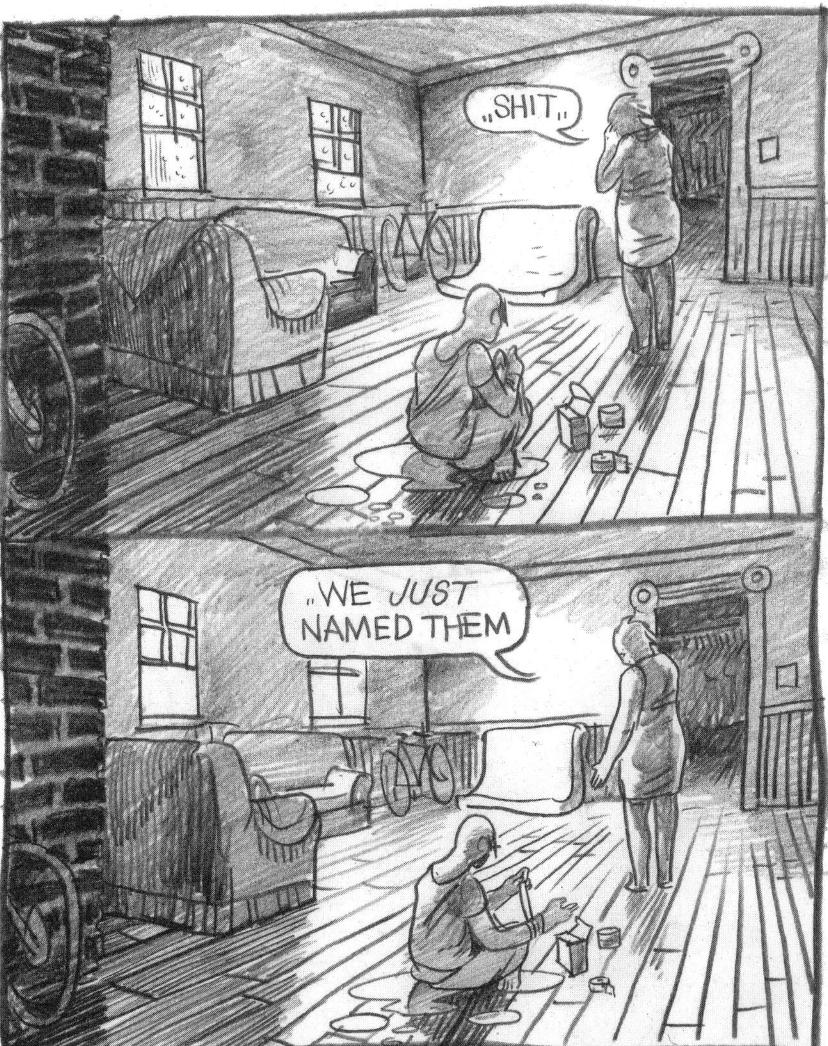
„SHIT„
„WE JUST NAMED THEM

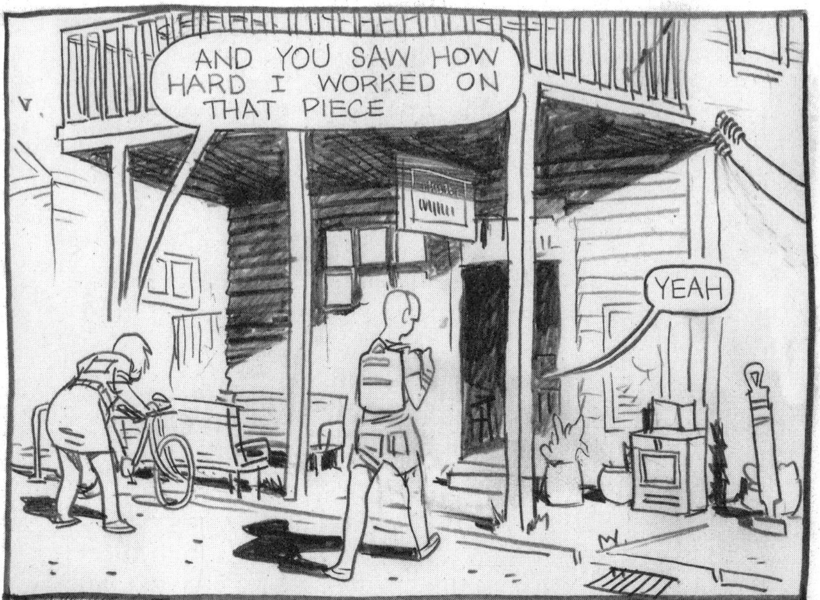
AND YOU SAW HOW HARD I WORKED ON THAT PIECE
YEAH

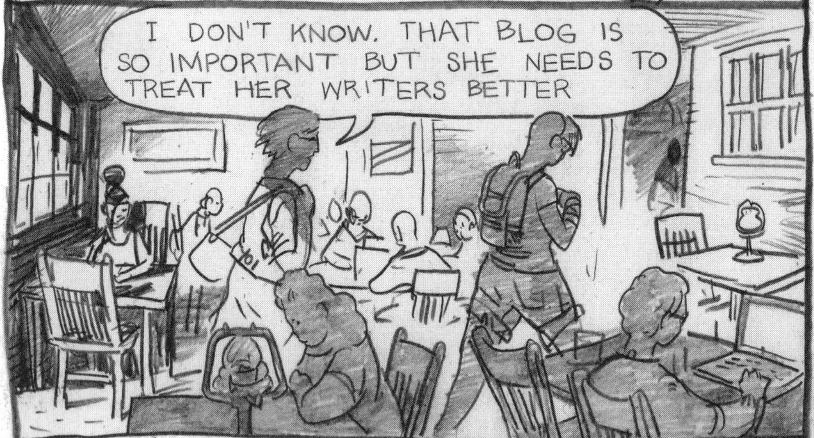
I DON'T KNOW. THAT BLOG IS SO IMPORTANT BUT SHE NEEDS TO TREAT HER WRITERS BETTER

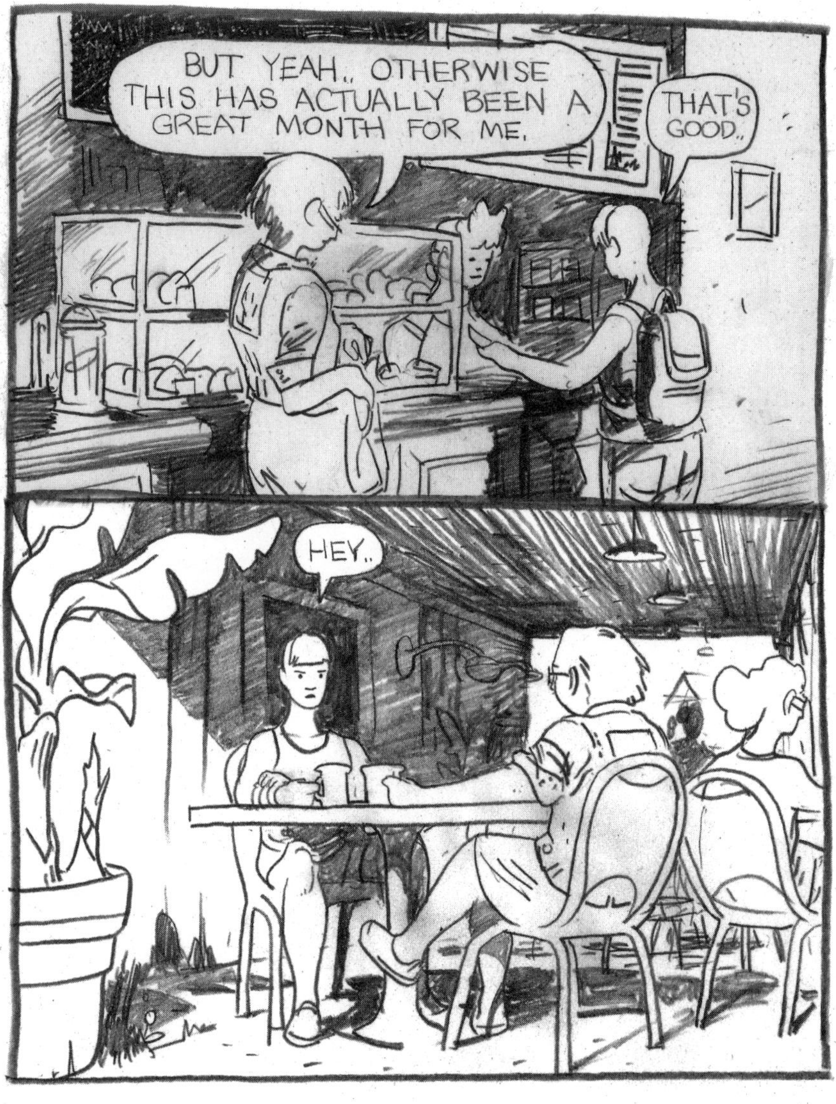
BUT YEAH.. OTHERWISE THIS HAS ACTUALLY BEEN A GREAT MONTH FOR ME.
THAT'S GOOD..
HEY..

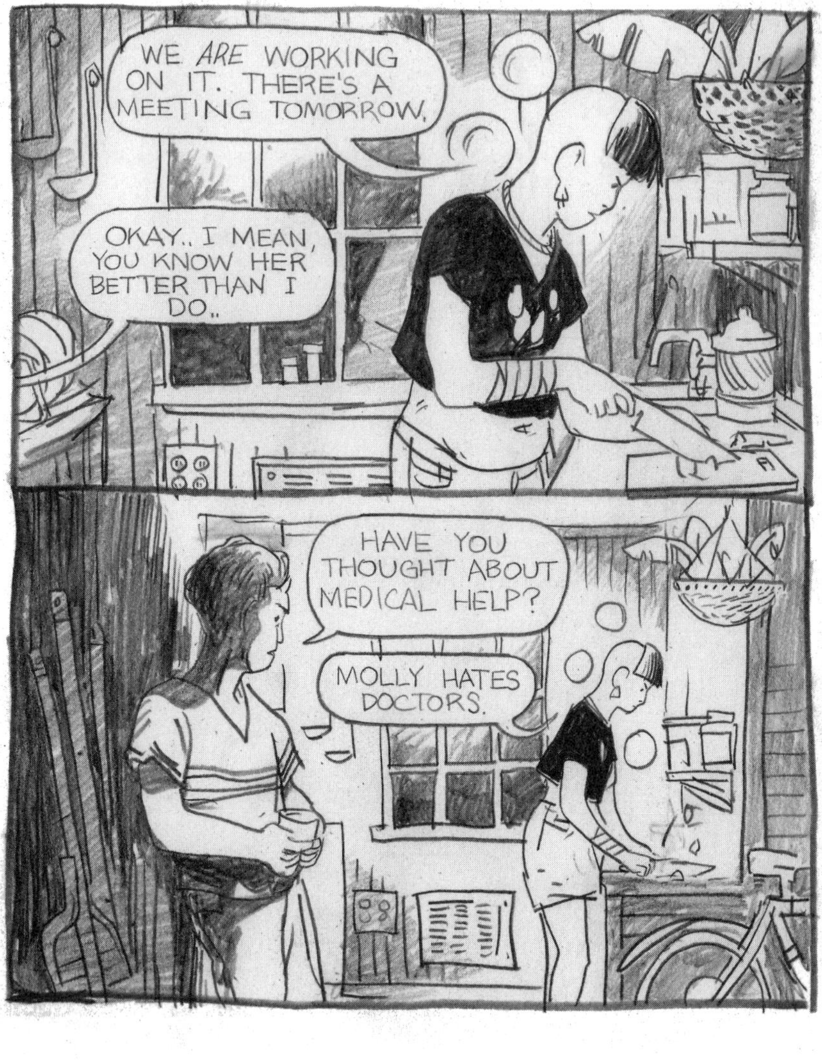
WE *ARE* WORKING ON IT. THERE'S A MEETING TOMORROW.
OKAY.. I MEAN, YOU KNOW HER BETTER THAN I DO..
HAVE YOU THOUGHT ABOUT MEDICAL HELP?
MOLLY HATES DOCTORS.

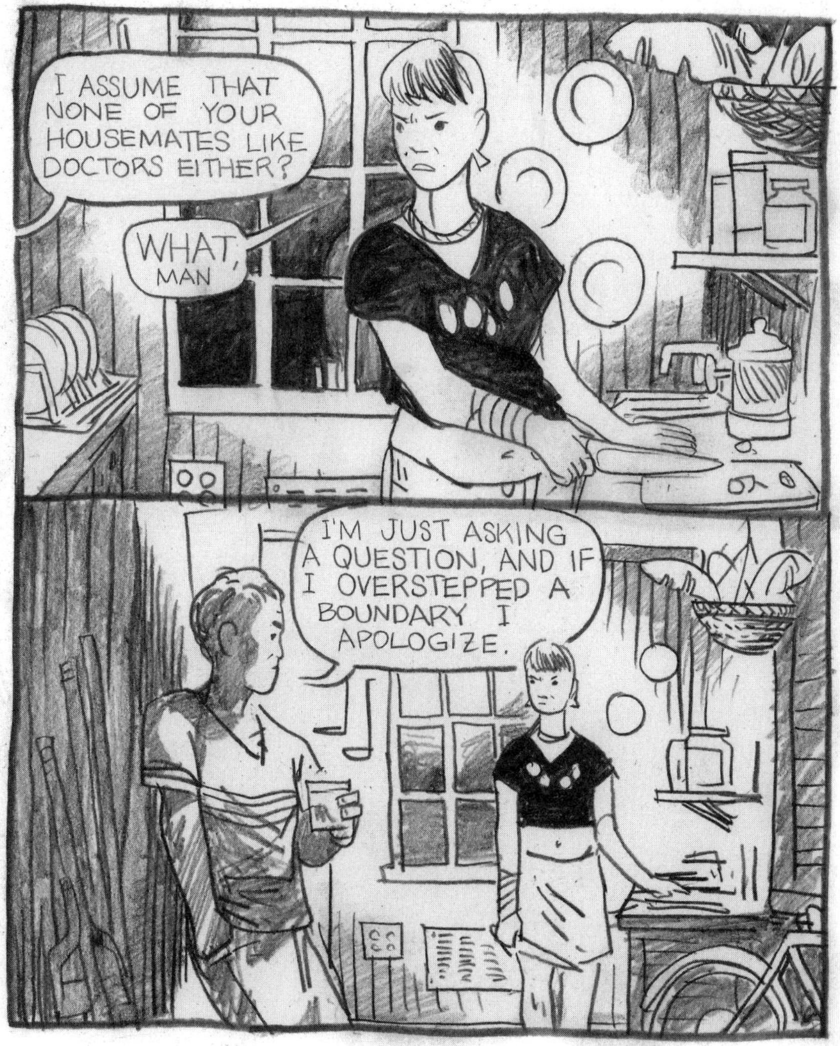
I ASSUME THAT NONE OF YOUR HOUSEMATES LIKE DOCTORS EITHER?
WHAT, MAN
I'M JUST ASKING A QUESTION, AND IF I OVERSTEPPED A BOUNDARY I APOLOGIZE.

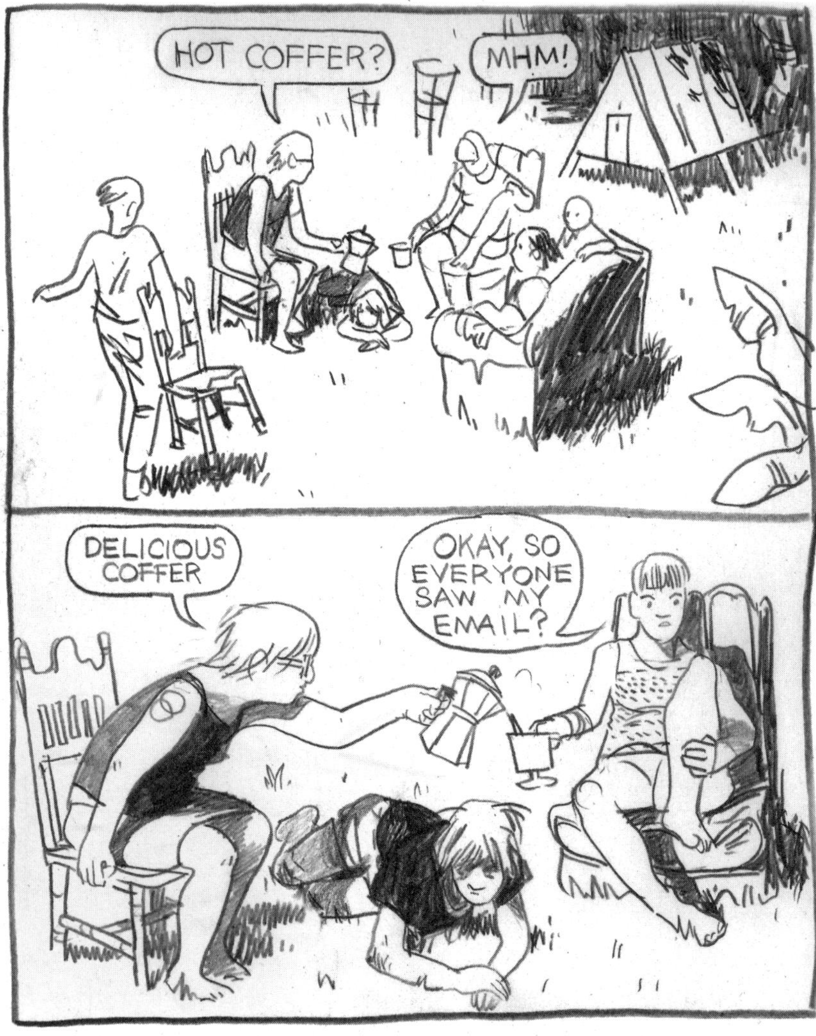
HOT COFFER?
MHM!
DELICIOUS COFFER
OKAY, SO EVERYONE SAW MY EMAIL?

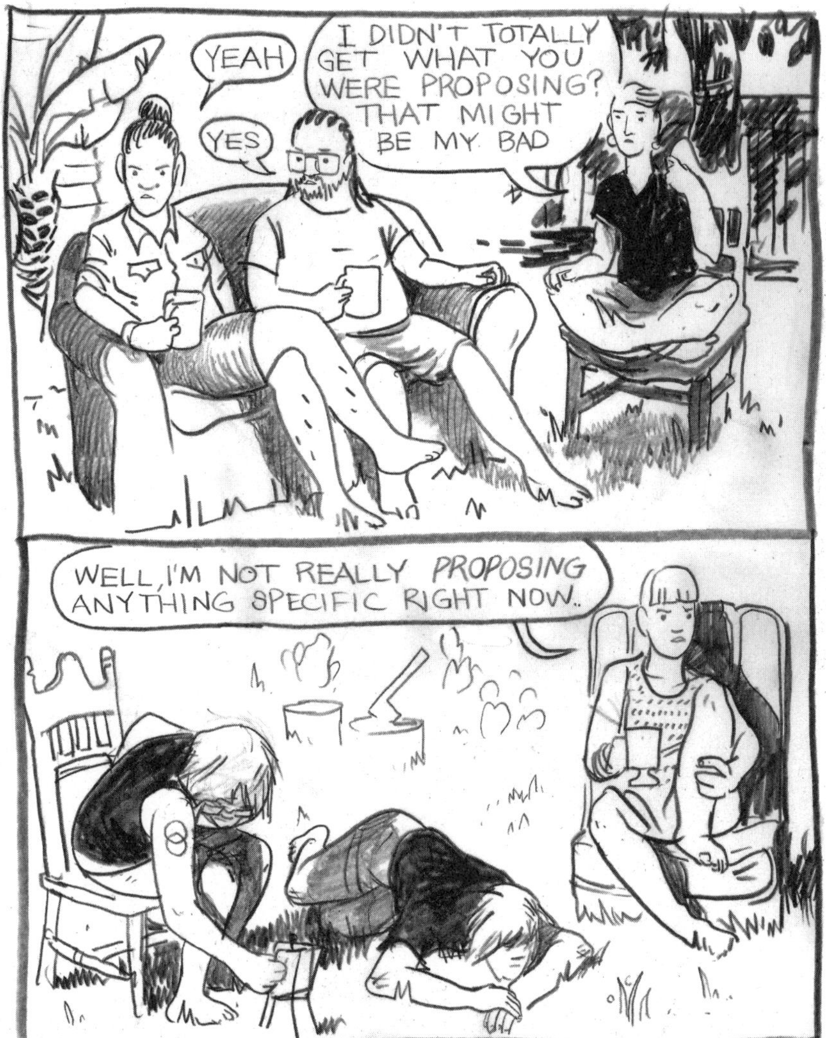
YEAH
YES
I DIDN'T TOTALLY GET WHAT YOU WERE PROPOSING? THAT MIGHT BE MY BAD
WELL, I'M NOT REALLY *PROPOSING* ANYTHING SPECIFIC RIGHT NOW..

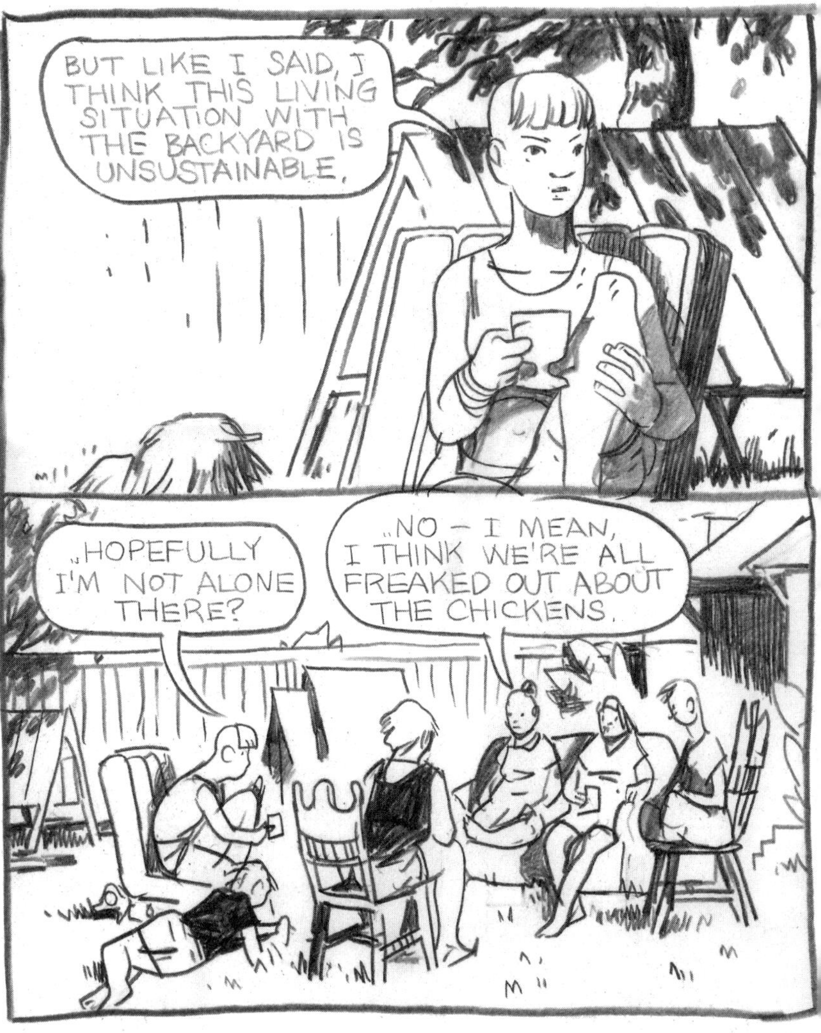
BUT LIKE I SAID, I THINK THIS LIVING SITUATION WITH THE BACKYARD IS UNSUSTAINABLE.
..HOPEFULLY I'M NOT ALONE THERE?
..NO — I MEAN, I THINK WE'RE ALL FREAKED OUT ABOUT THE CHICKENS.

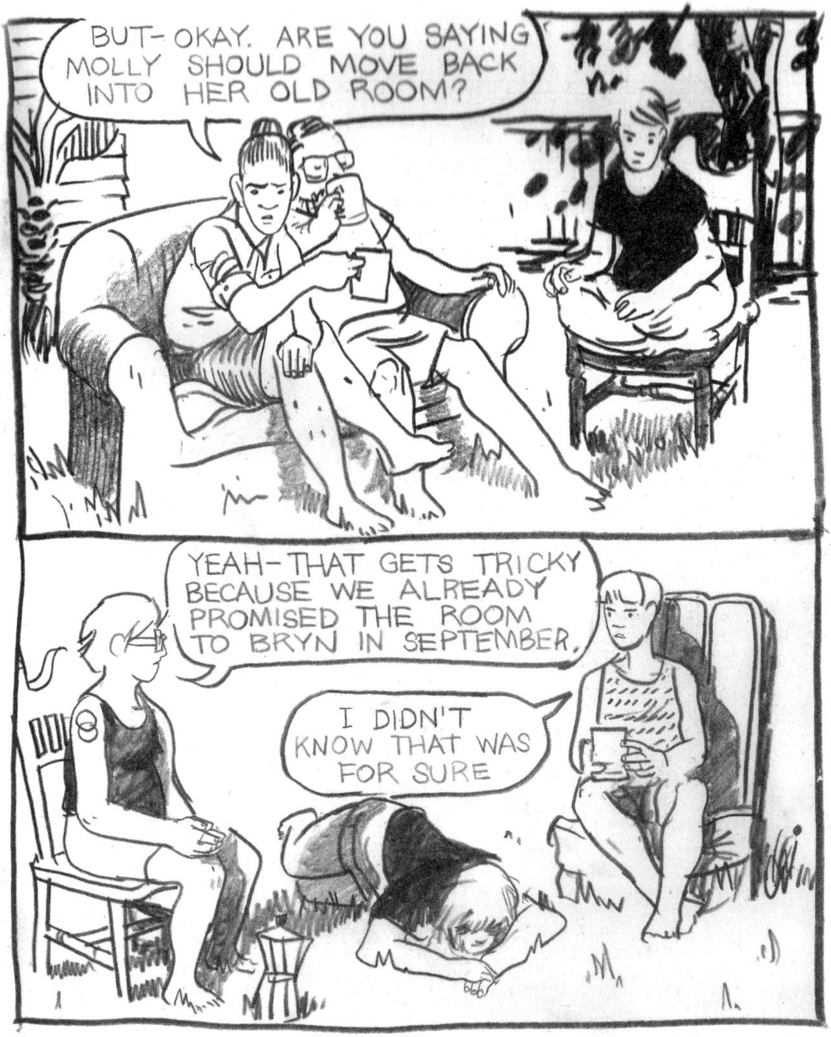
BUT- OKAY. ARE YOU SAYING MOLLY SHOULD MOVE BACK INTO HER OLD ROOM?
YEAH- THAT GETS TRICKY BECAUSE WE ALREADY PROMISED THE ROOM TO BRYN IN SEPTEMBER.
I DIDN'T KNOW THAT WAS FOR SURE

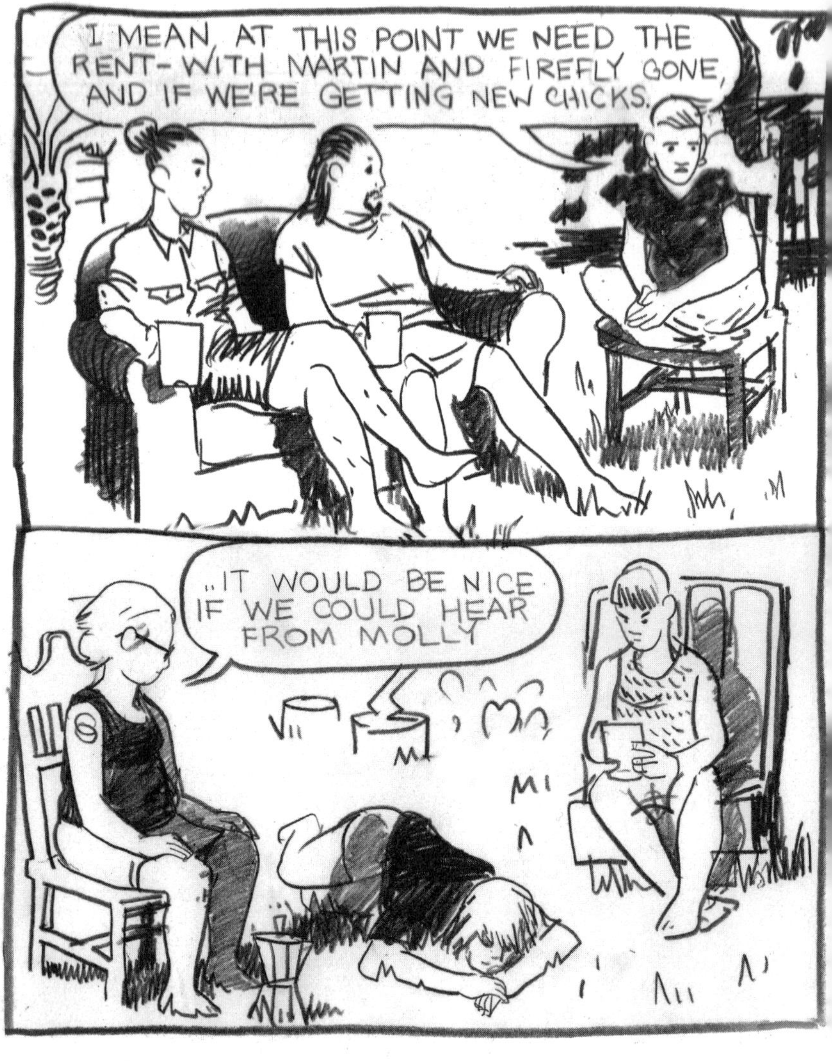
I MEAN, AT THIS POINT WE NEED THE RENT- WITH MARTIN AND FIREFLY GONE, AND IF WE'RE GETTING NEW CHICKS.
..IT WOULD BE NICE IF WE COULD HEAR FROM MOLLY

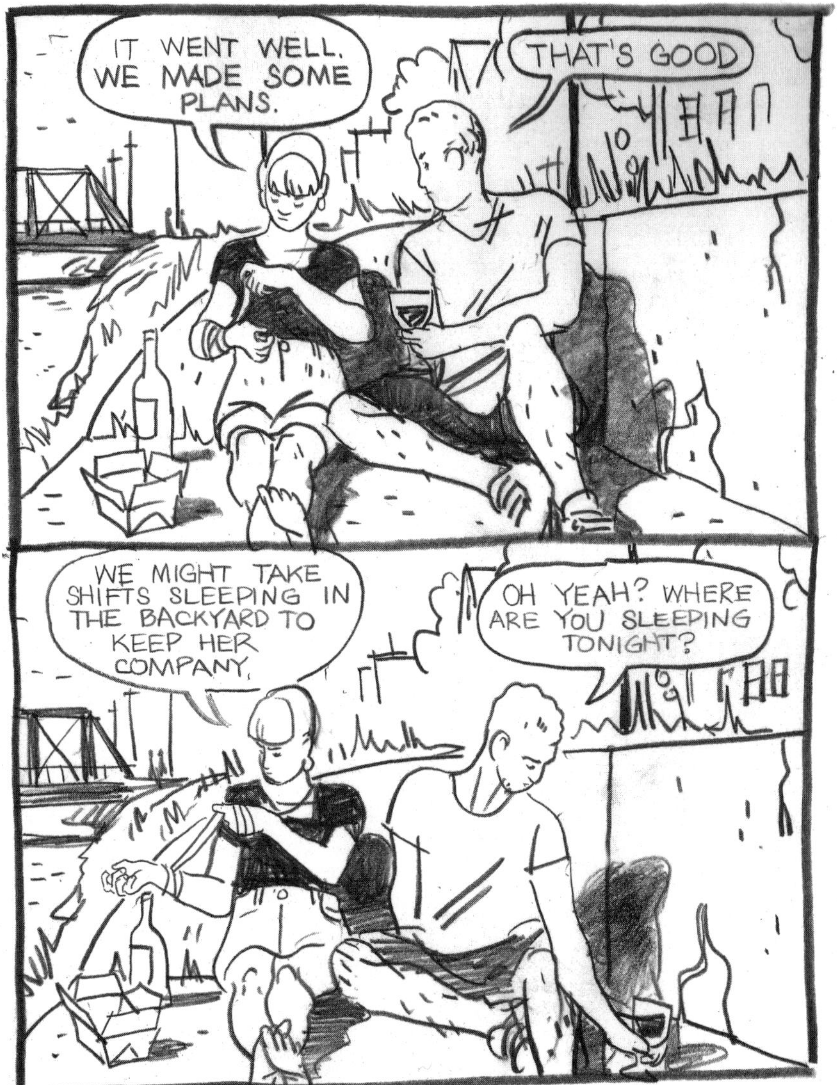
IT WENT WELL. WE MADE SOME PLANS.
THAT'S GOOD
WE MIGHT TAKE SHIFTS SLEEPING IN THE BACKYARD TO KEEP HER COMPANY.
OH YEAH? WHERE ARE YOU SLEEPING TONIGHT?

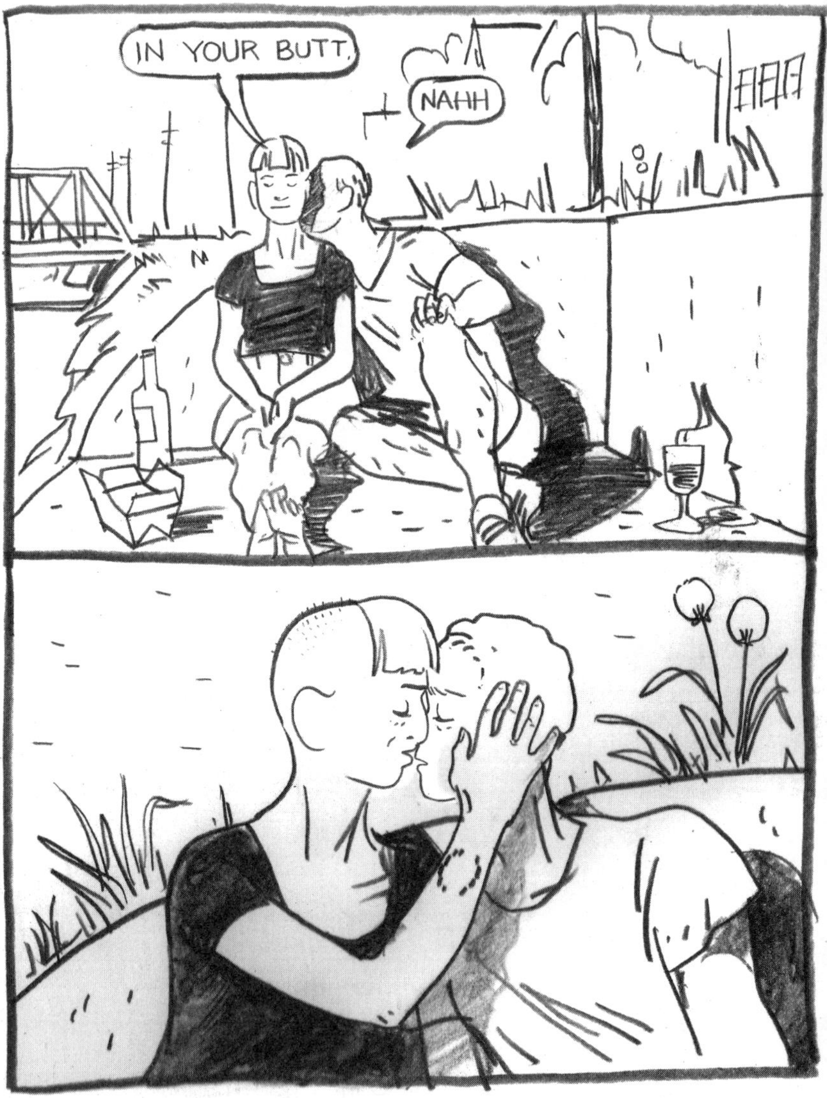
IN YOUR BUTT.
NAHH

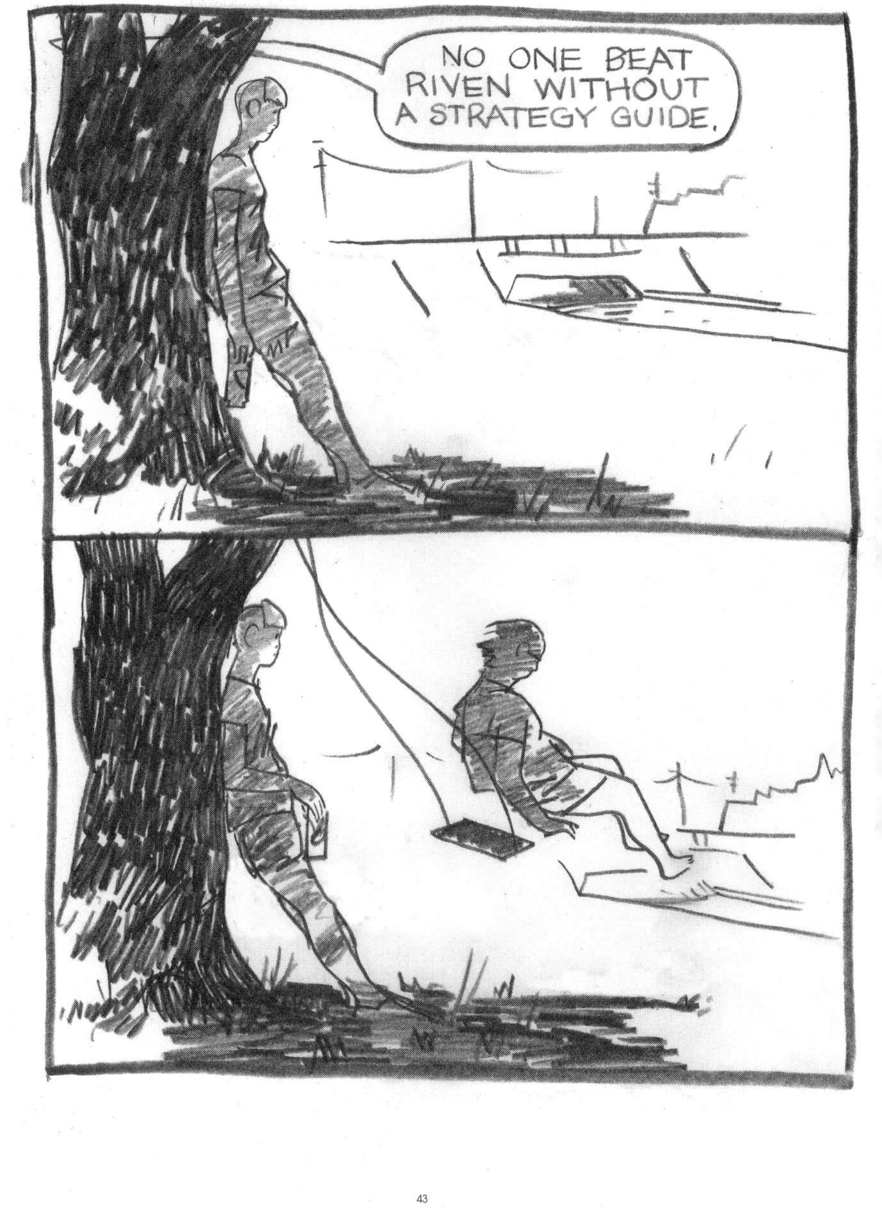
NO ONE BEAT RIVEN WITHOUT A STRATEGY GUIDE.

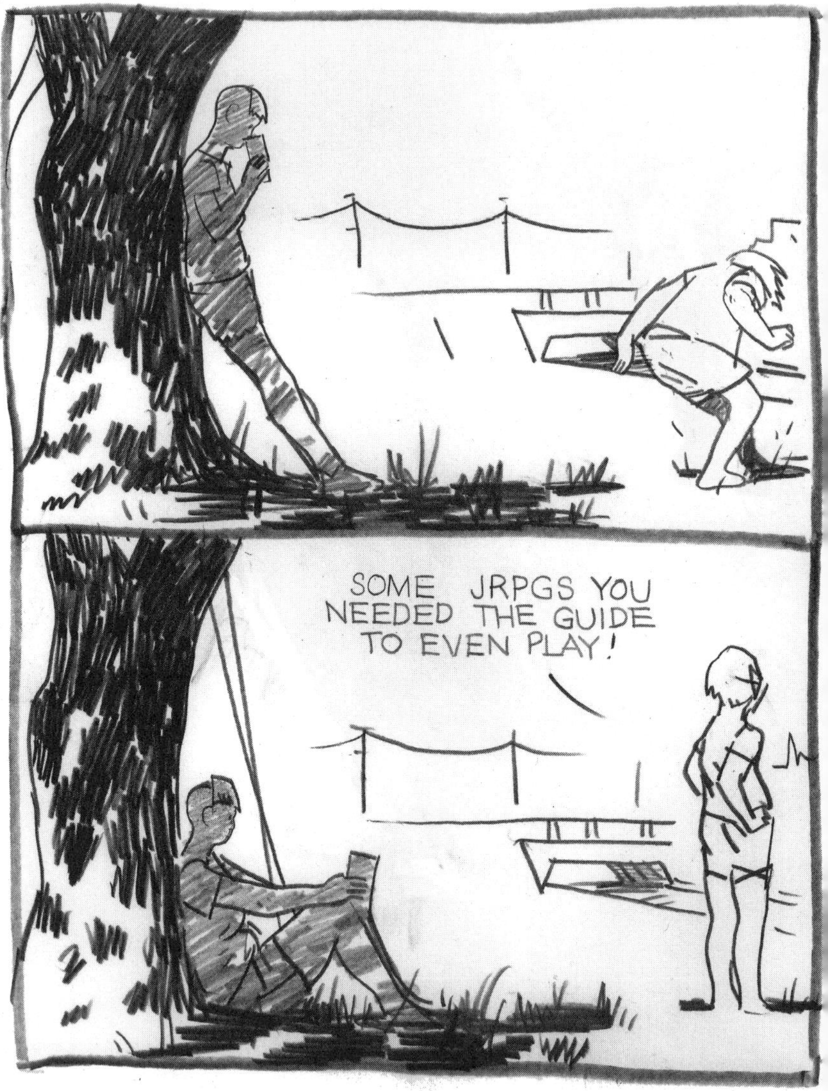
SOME JRPGS YOU NEEDED THE GUIDE TO EVEN PLAY!

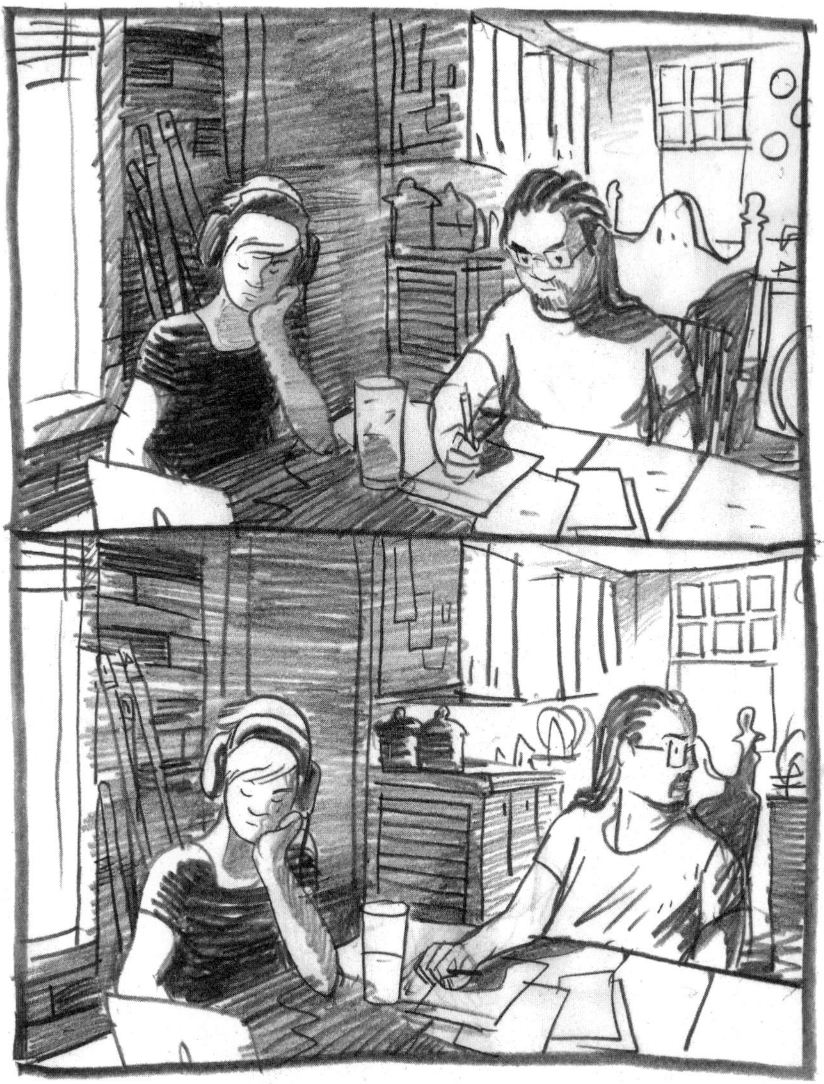

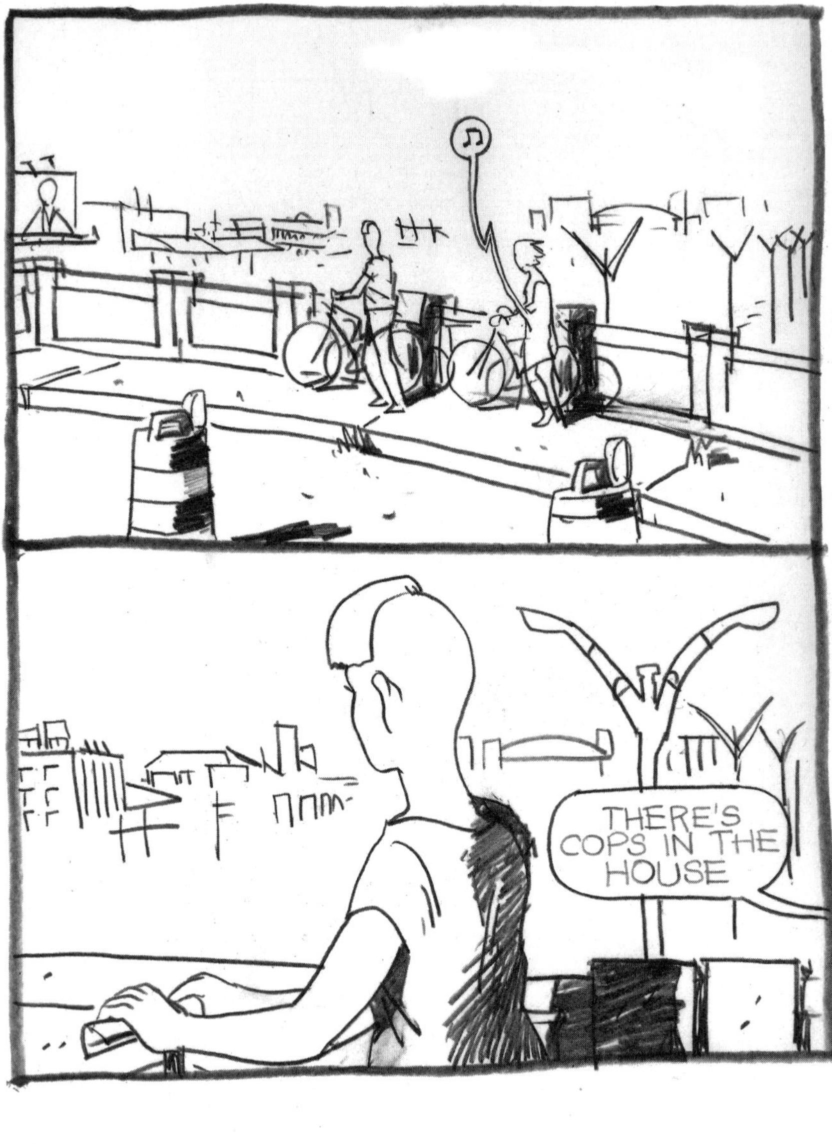
♫
THERE'S COPS IN THE HOUSE

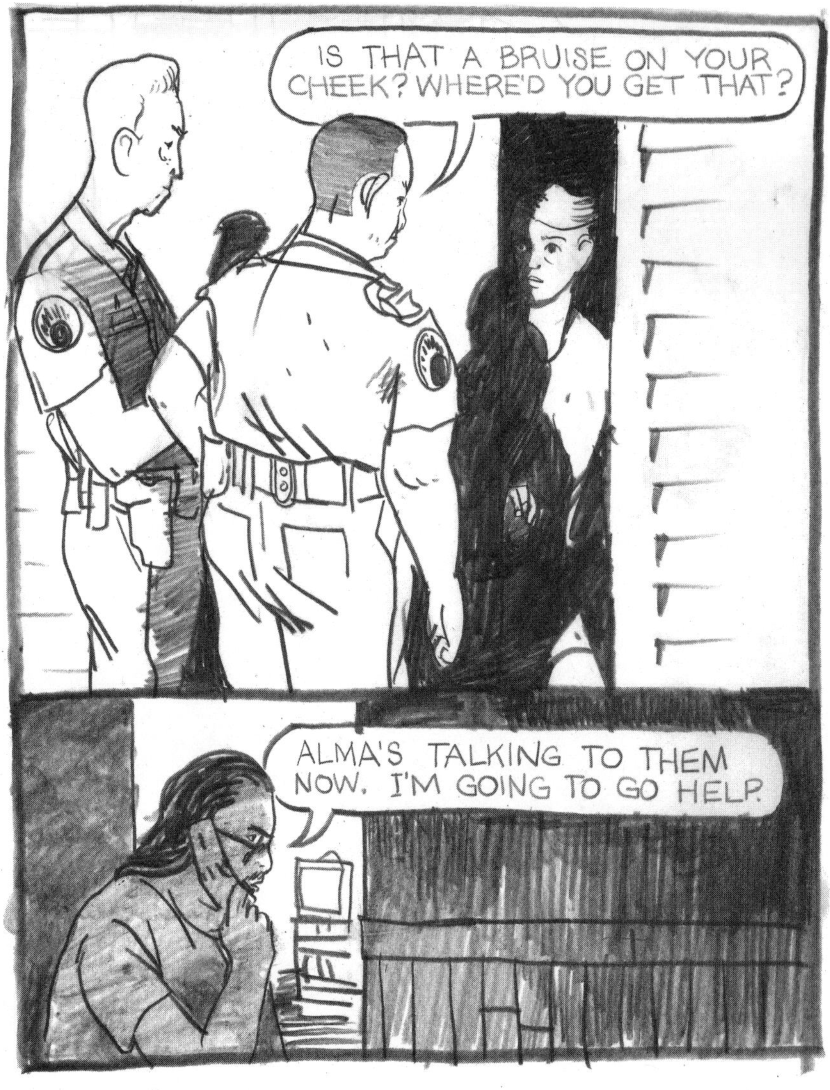
IS THAT A BRUISE ON YOUR CHEEK? WHERE'D YOU GET THAT?
ALMA'S TALKING TO THEM NOW. I'M GOING TO GO HELP.

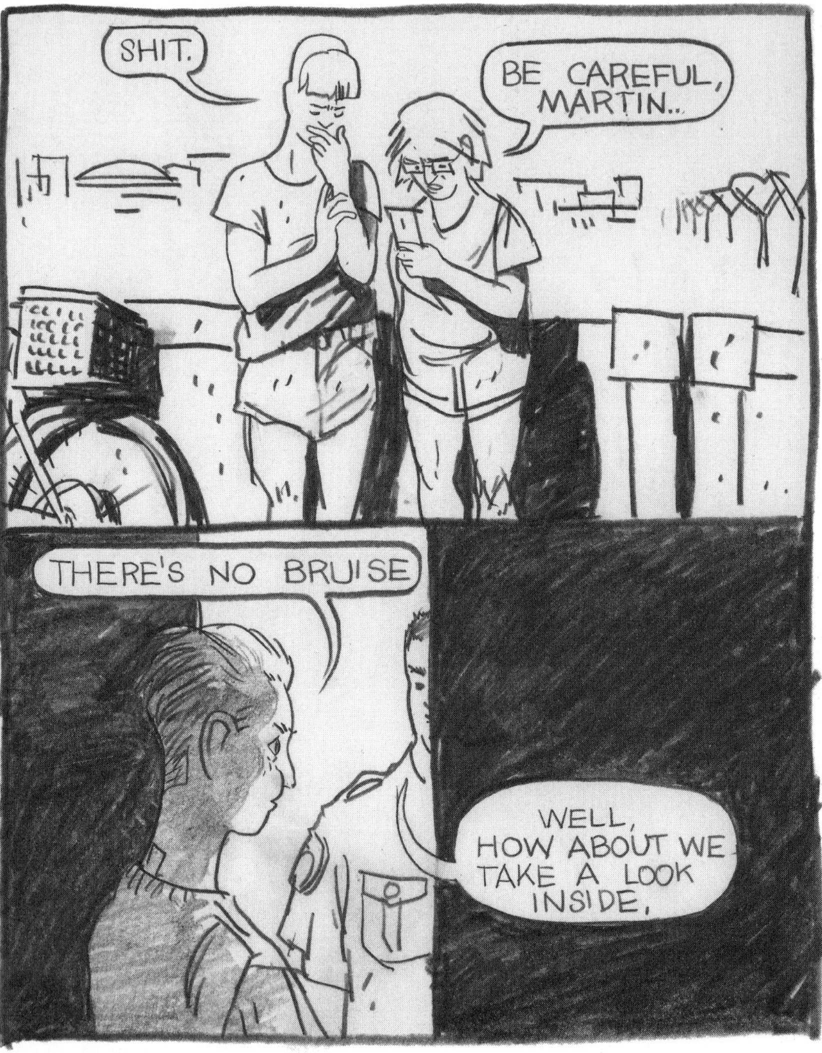
SHIT.
BE CAREFUL, MARTIN..
THERE'S NO BRUISE
WELL, HOW ABOUT WE TAKE A LOOK INSIDE,

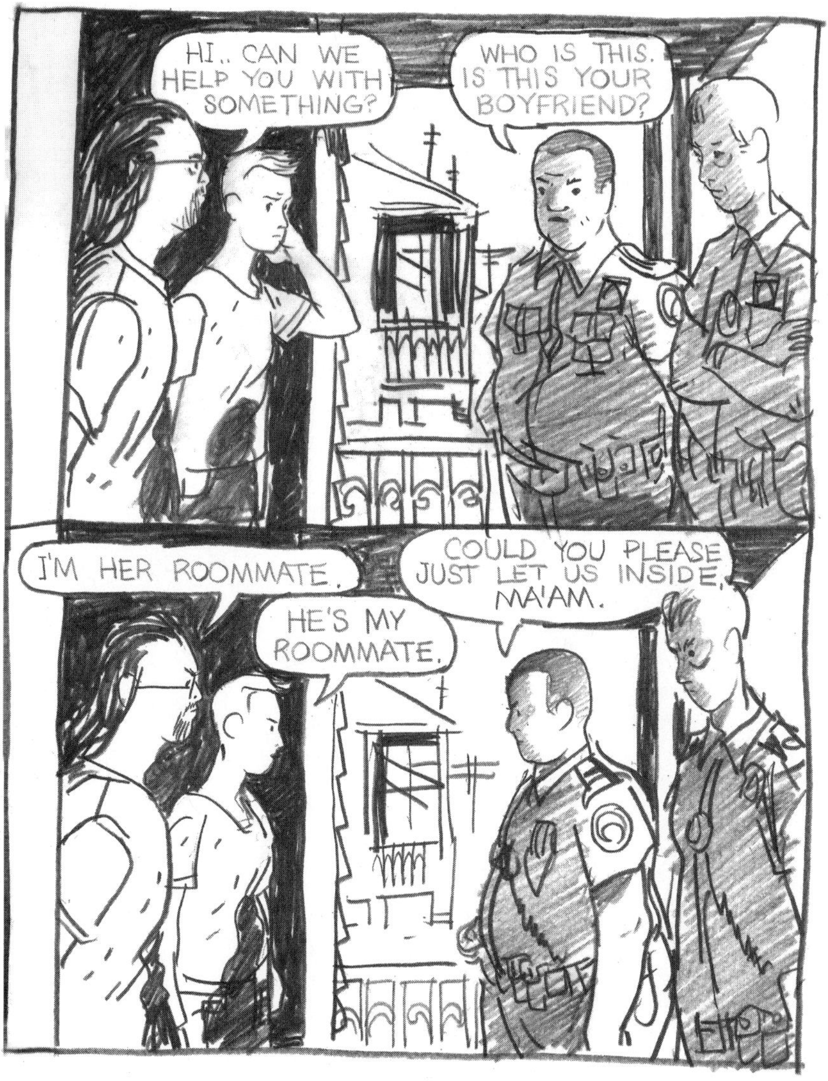
HI.. CAN WE HELP YOU WITH SOMETHING?
WHO IS THIS. IS THIS YOUR BOYFRIEND?
I'M HER ROOMMATE.
HE'S MY ROOMMATE.
COULD YOU PLEASE JUST LET US INSIDE, MA'AM.

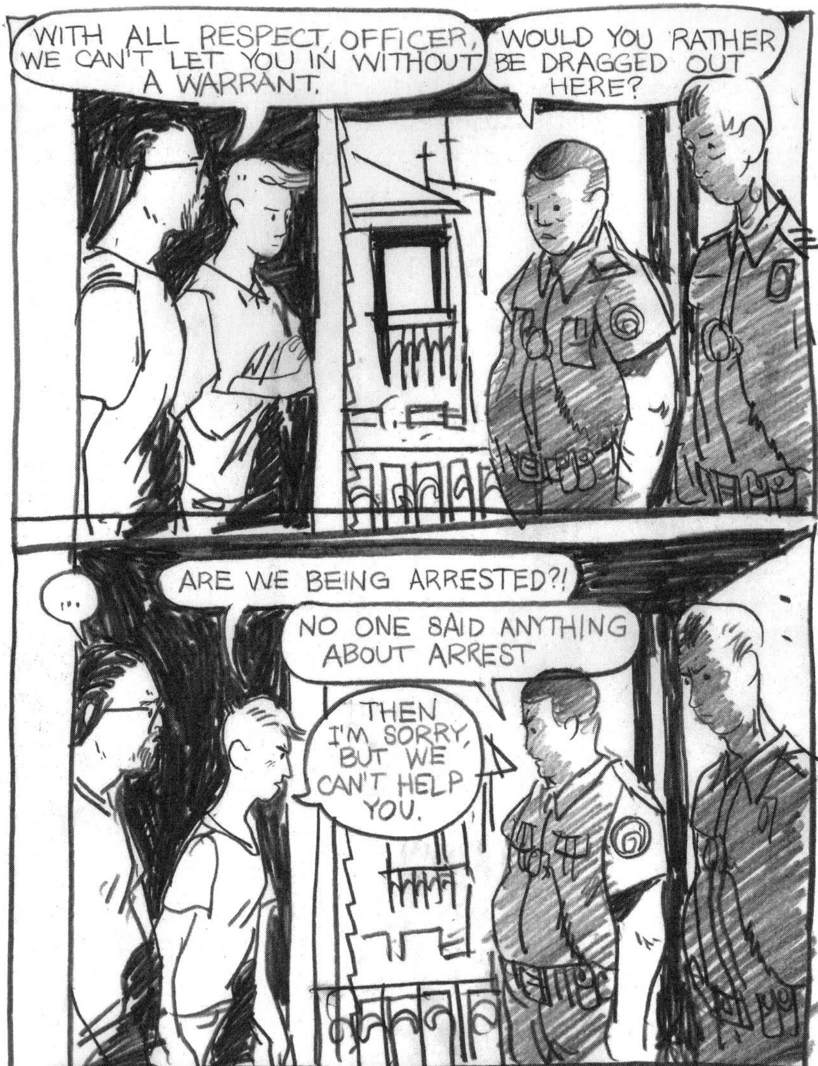
WITH ALL RESPECT, OFFICER, WE CAN'T LET YOU IN WITHOUT A WARRANT.
WOULD YOU RATHER BE DRAGGED OUT HERE?
...
ARE WE BEING ARRESTED?!
NO ONE SAID ANYTHING ABOUT ARREST
THEN I'M SORRY, BUT WE CAN'T HELP YOU.

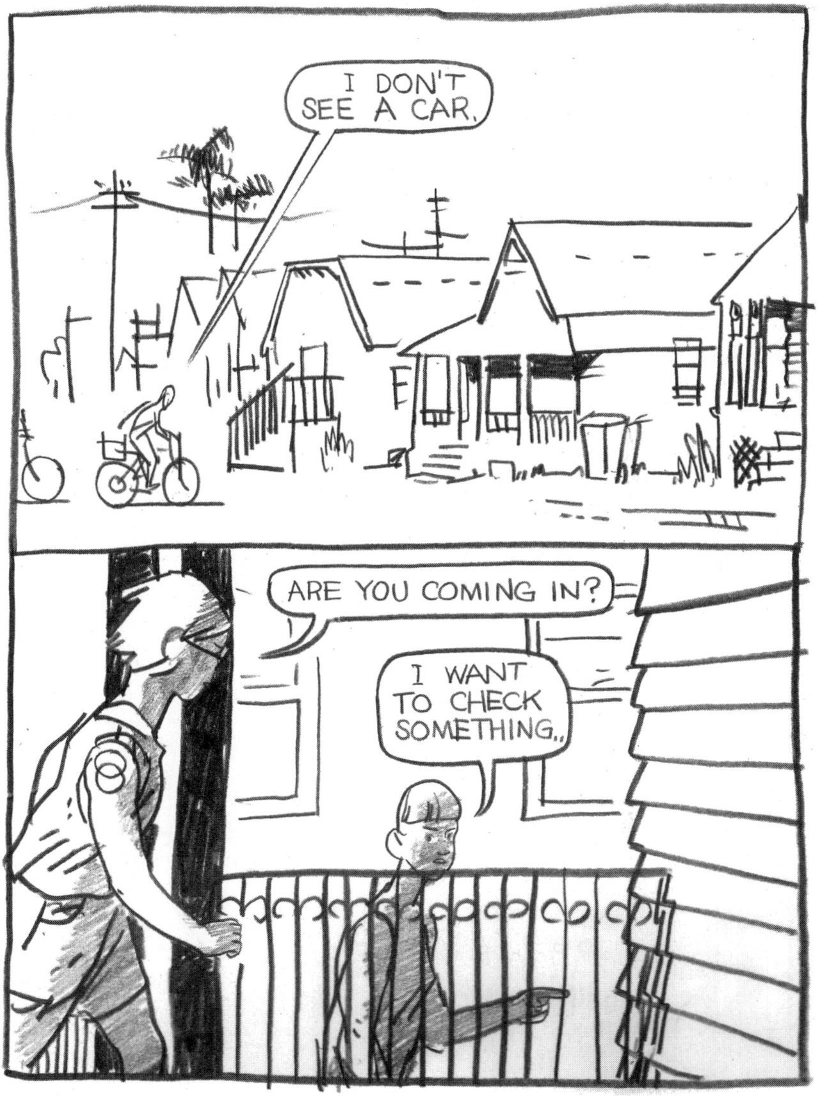
I DON'T SEE A CAR.
ARE YOU COMING IN?
I WANT TO CHECK SOMETHING..

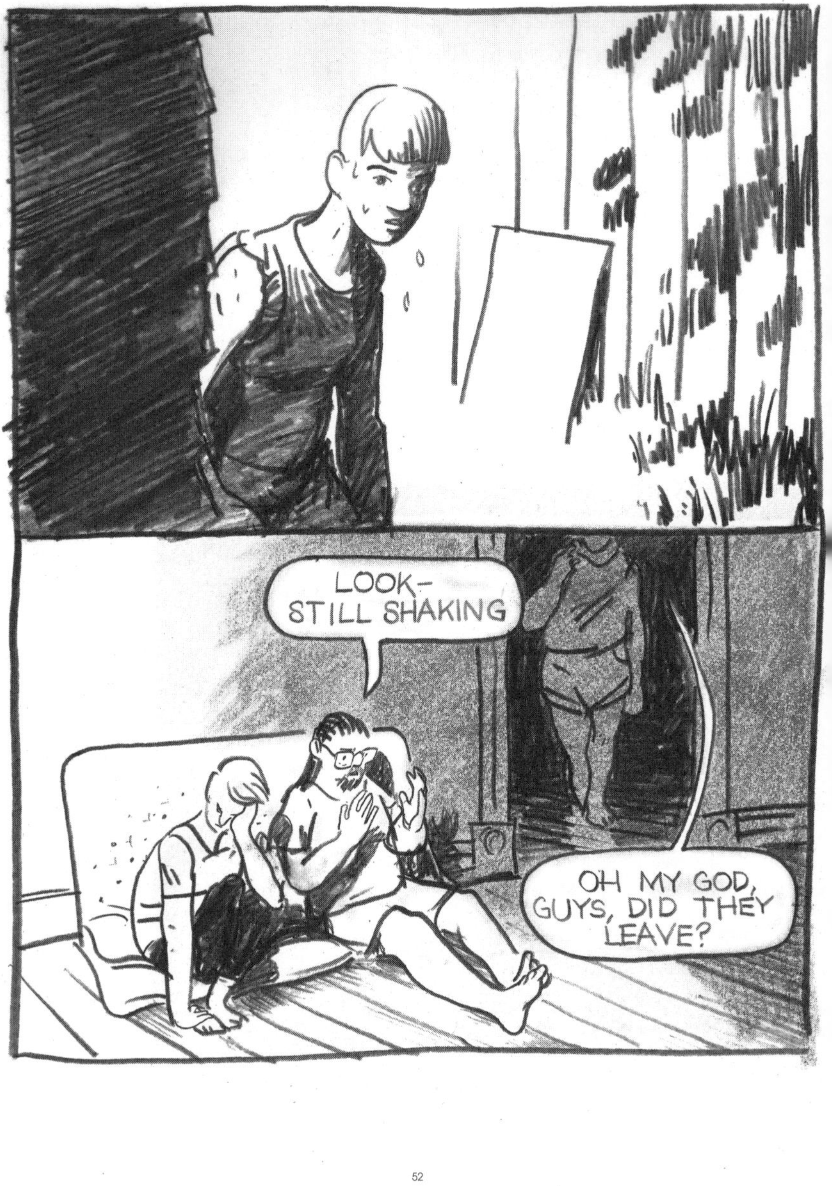
LOOK-
STILL SHAKING
OH MY GOD,
GUYS, DID THEY
LEAVE?

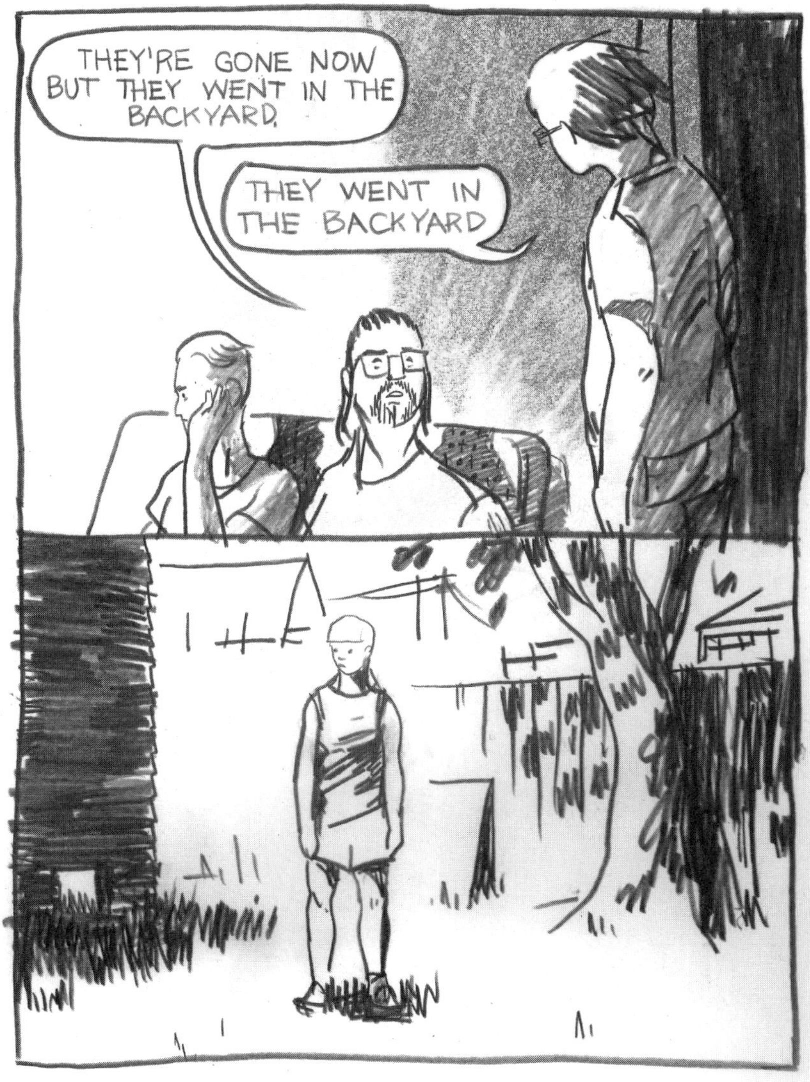
THEY'RE GONE NOW BUT THEY WENT IN THE BACKYARD.
THEY WENT IN THE BACKYARD

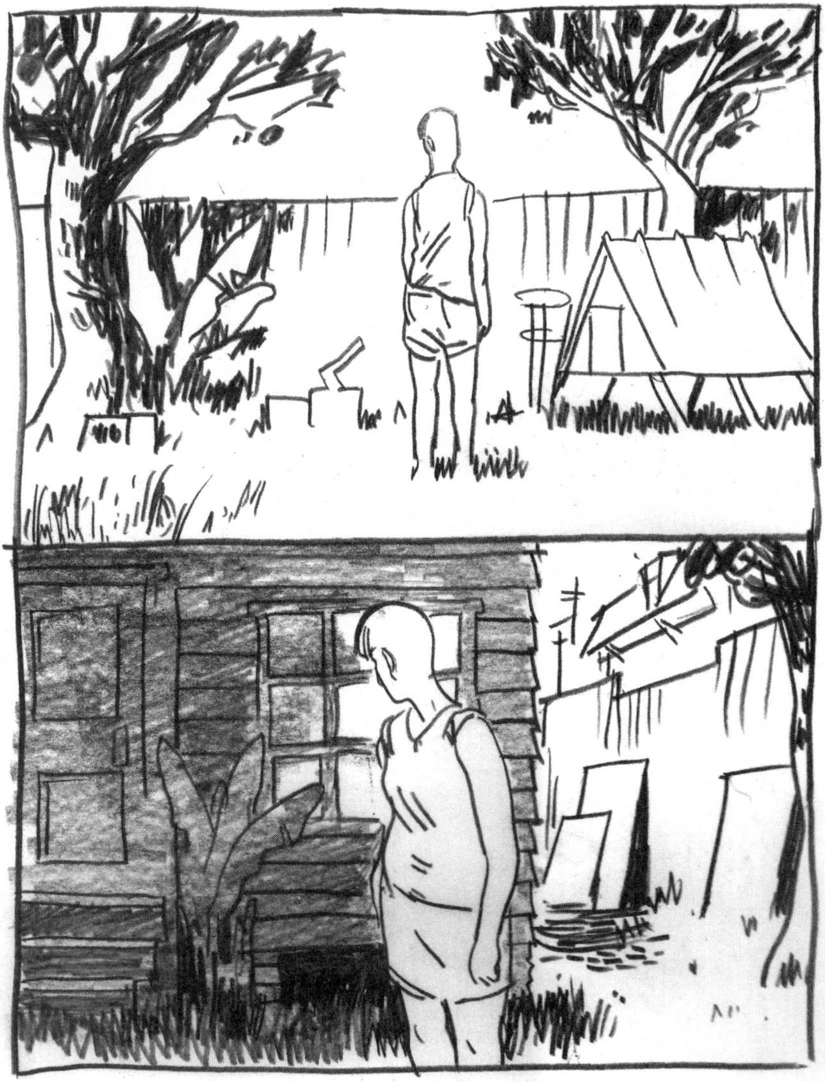

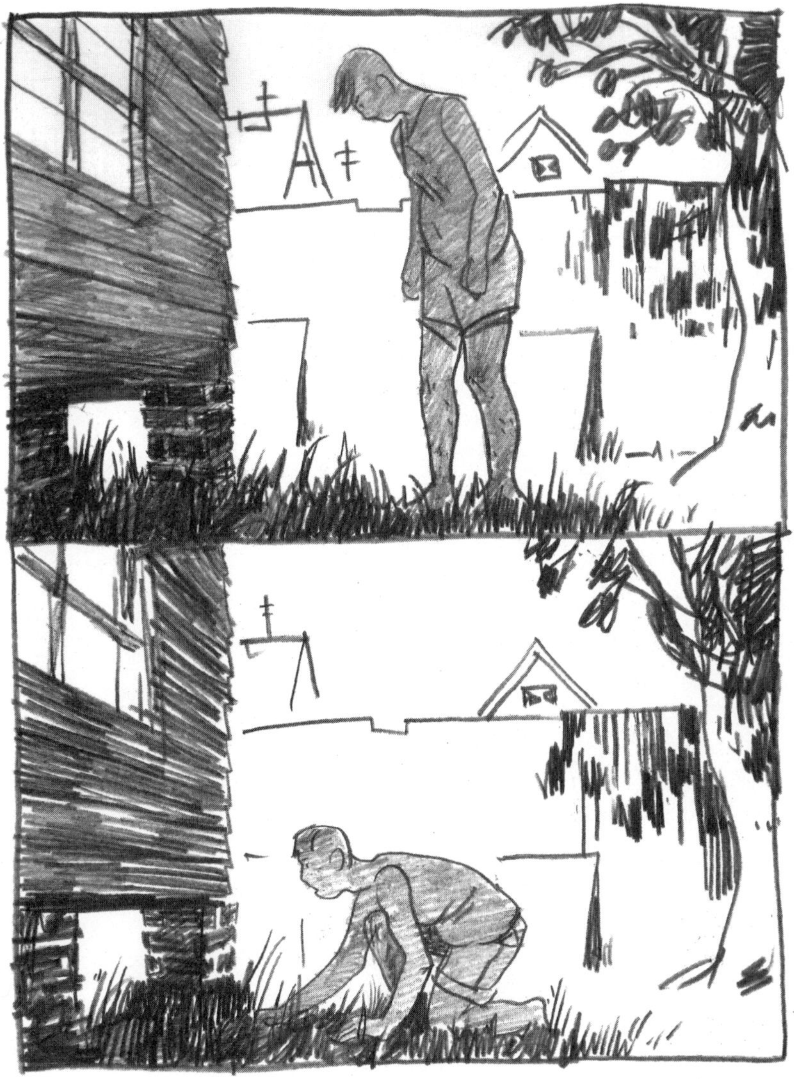

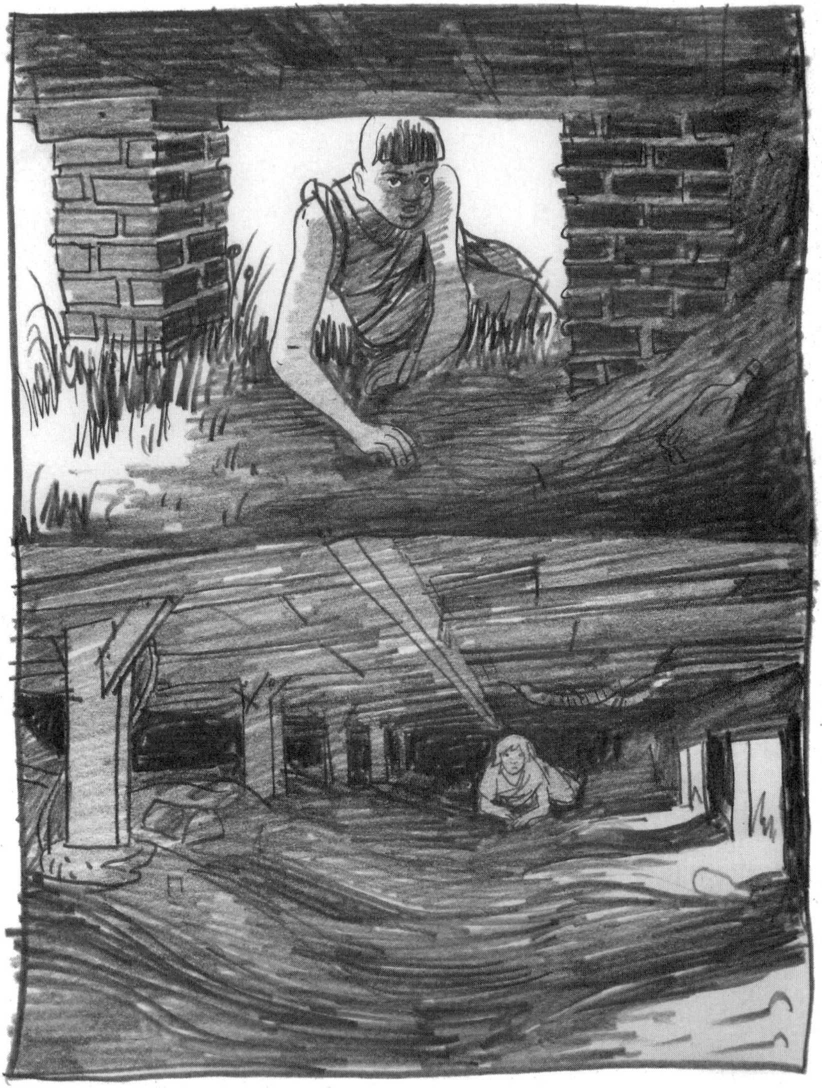

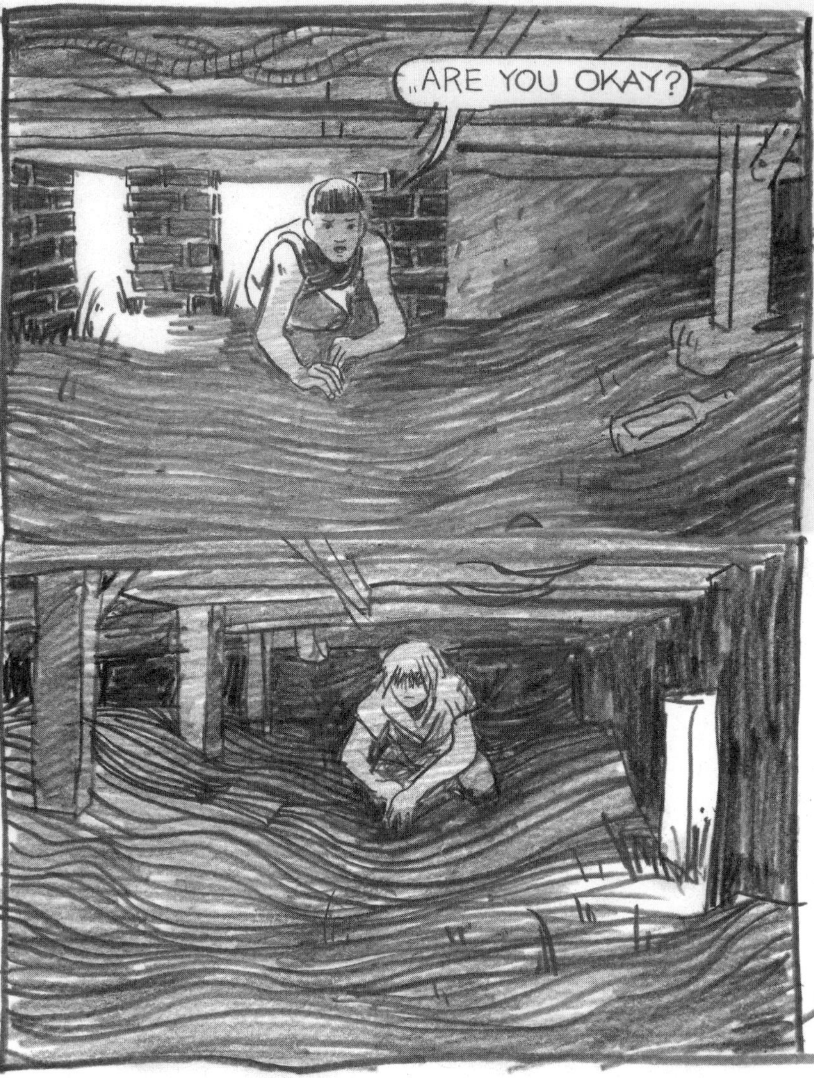
„ARE YOU OKAY?

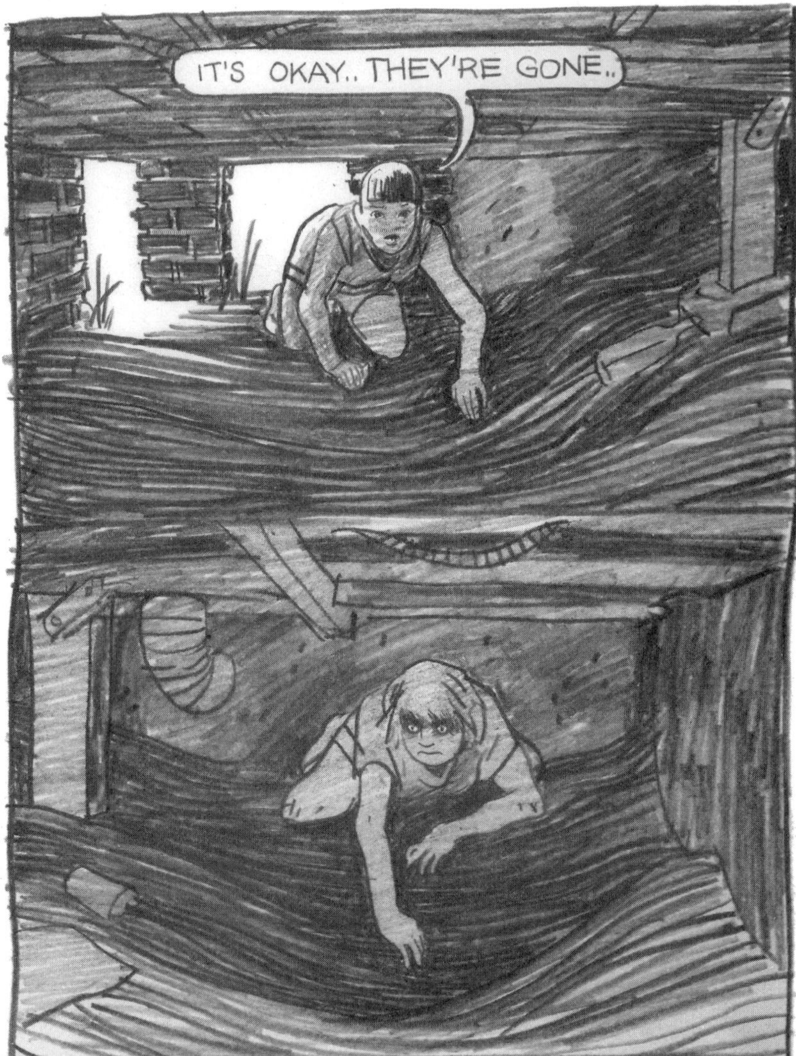
IT'S OKAY.. THEY'RE GONE..

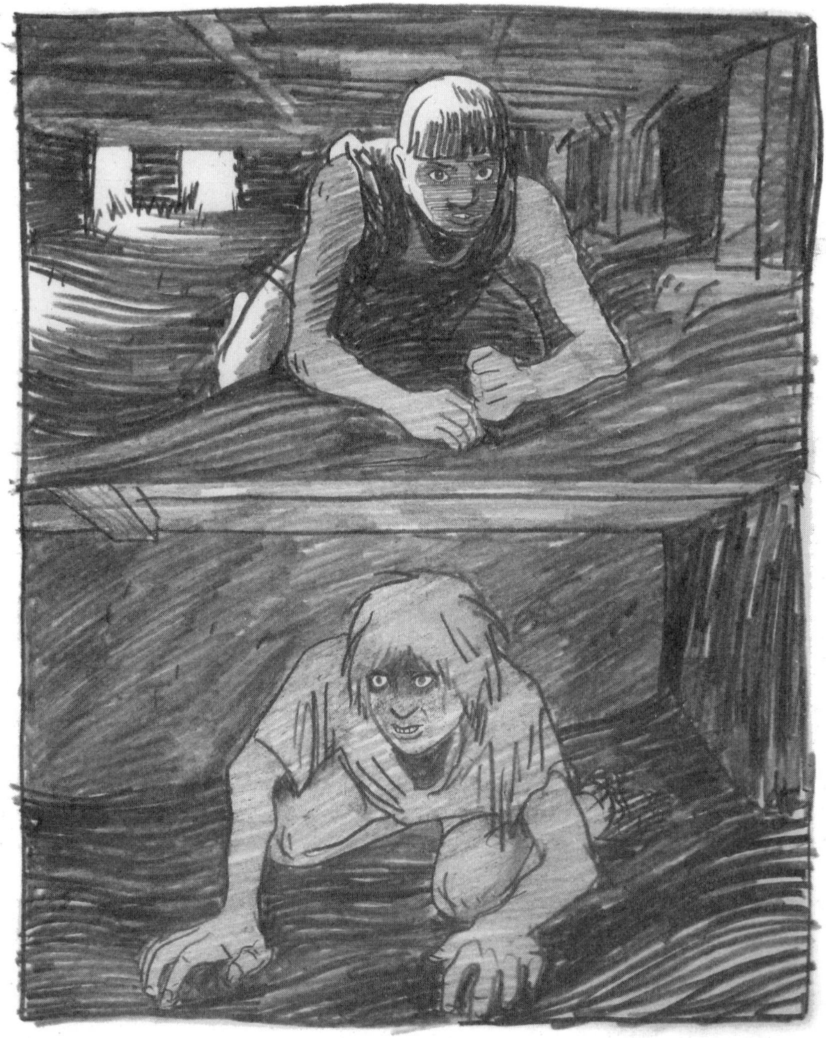

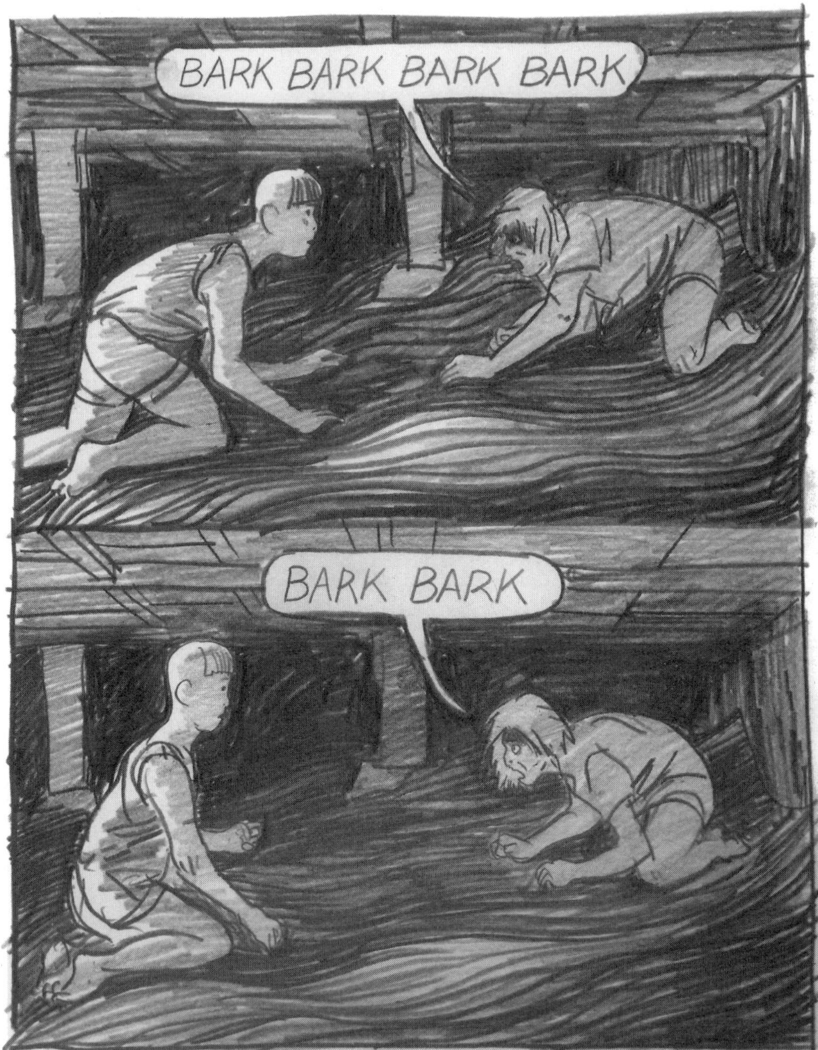
BARK BARK BARK BARK
BARK BARK

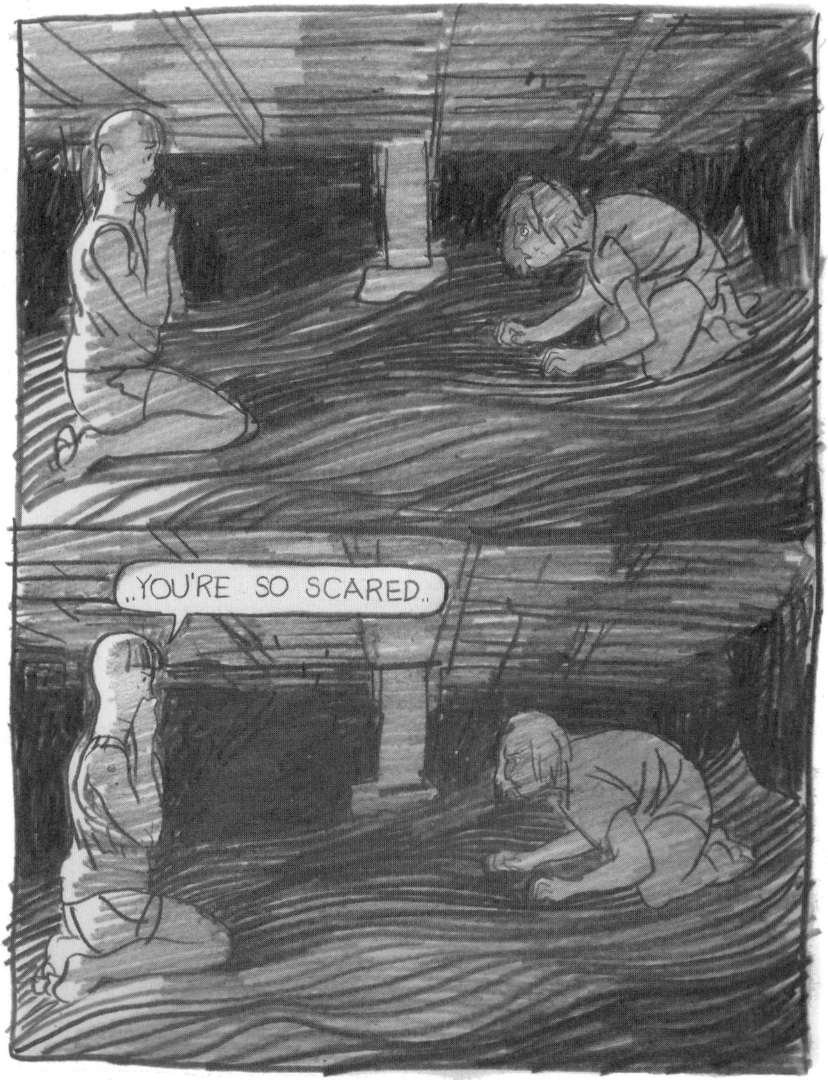
..YOU'RE SO SCARED..

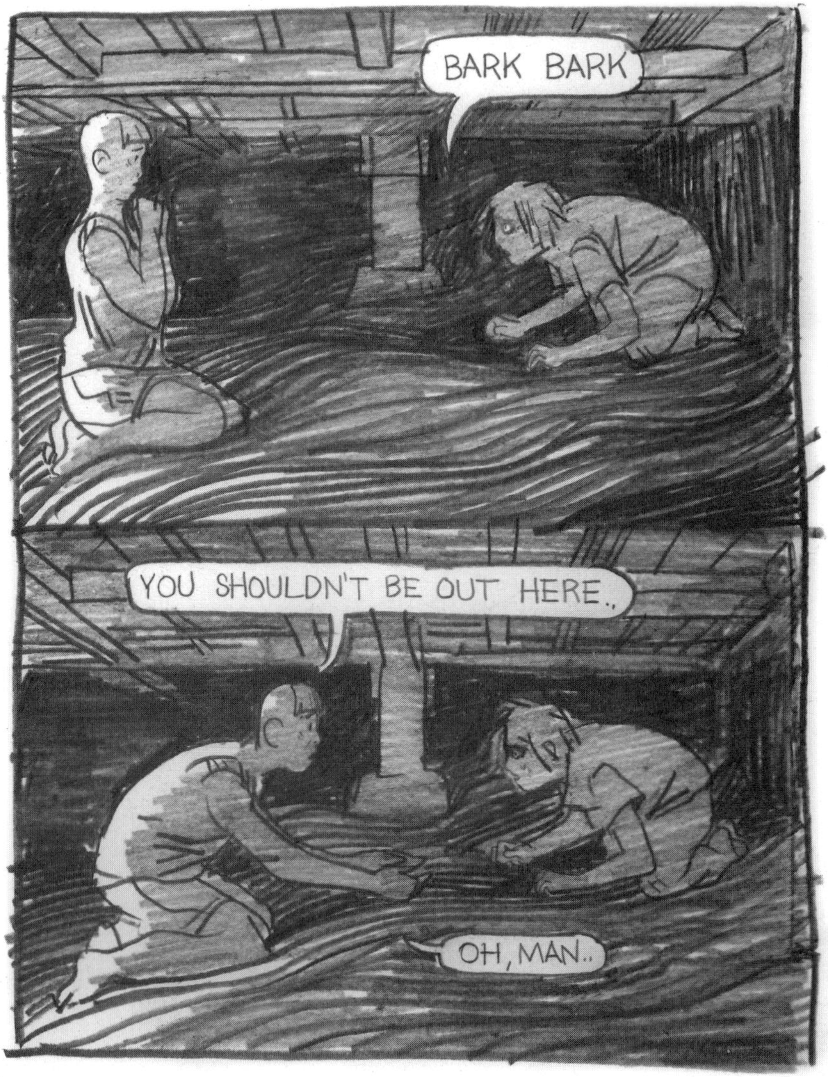
BARK BARK
YOU SHOULDN'T BE OUT HERE..
OH, MAN..

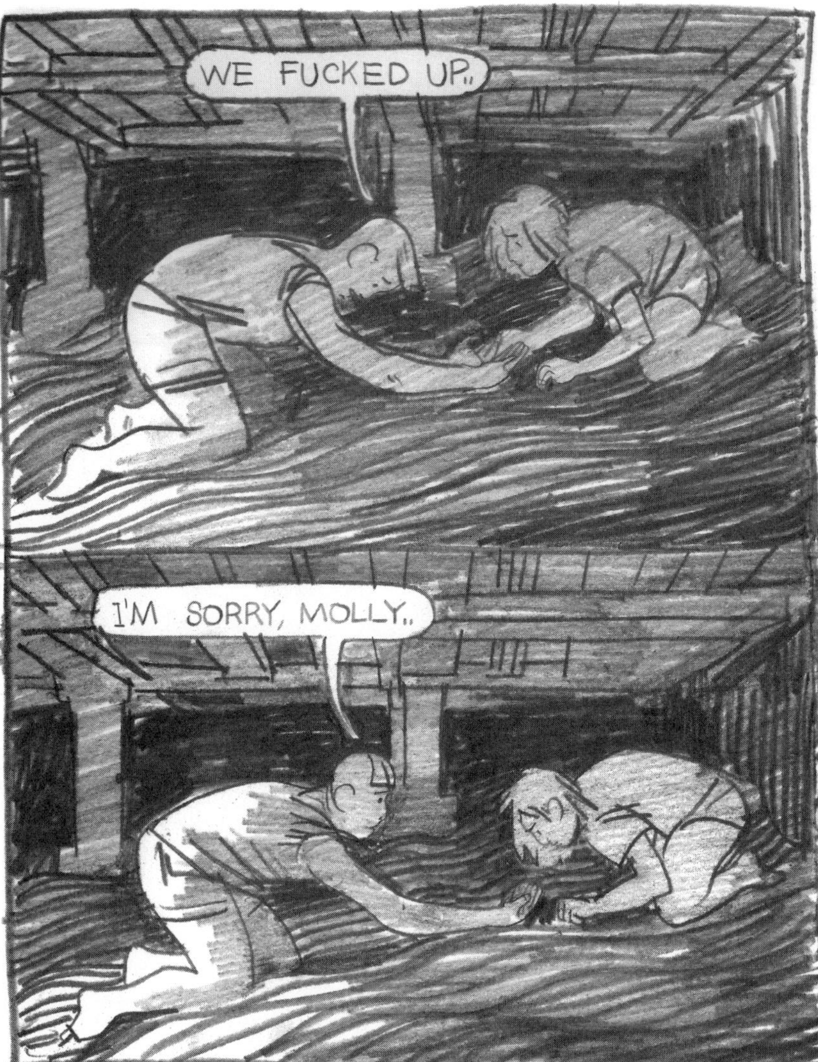
WE FUCKED UP..
I'M SORRY, MOLLY..

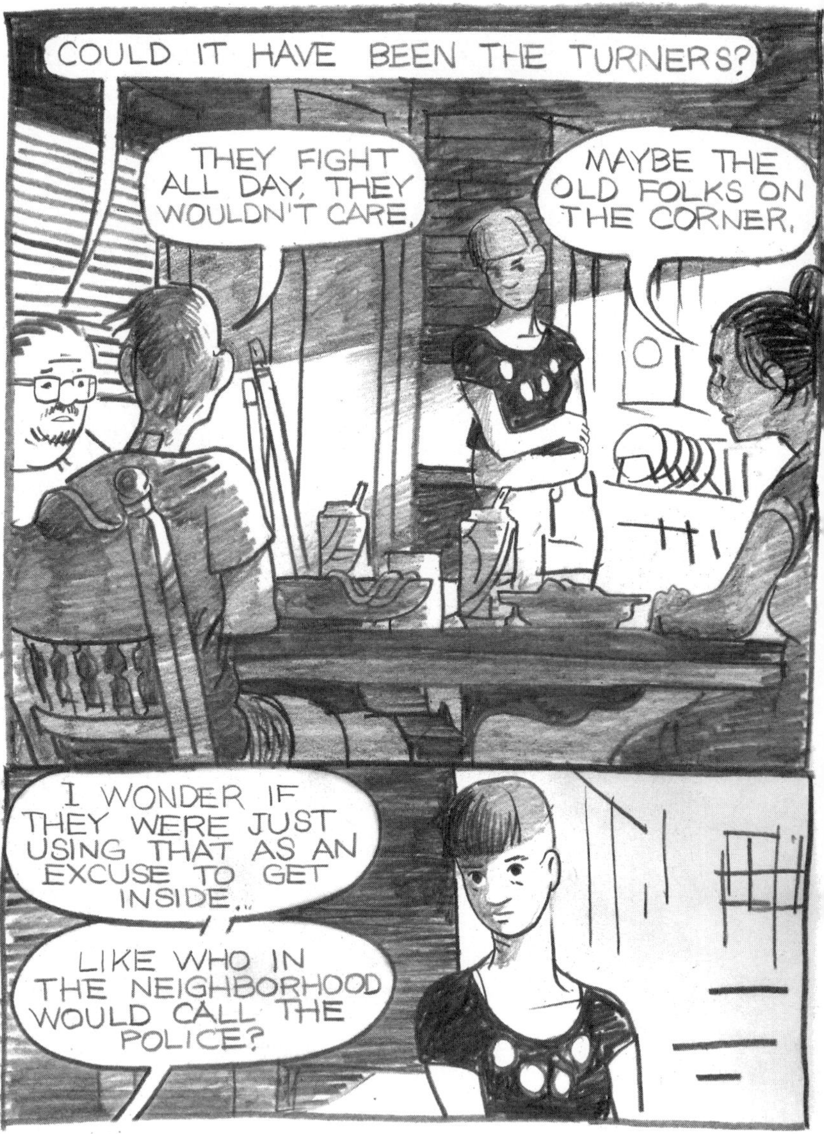
COULD IT HAVE BEEN THE TURNERS?
THEY FIGHT ALL DAY, THEY WOULDN'T CARE.
MAYBE THE OLD FOLKS ON THE CORNER.
I WONDER IF THEY WERE JUST USING THAT AS AN EXCUSE TO GET INSIDE..."
LIKE WHO IN THE NEIGHBORHOOD WOULD CALL THE POLICE?

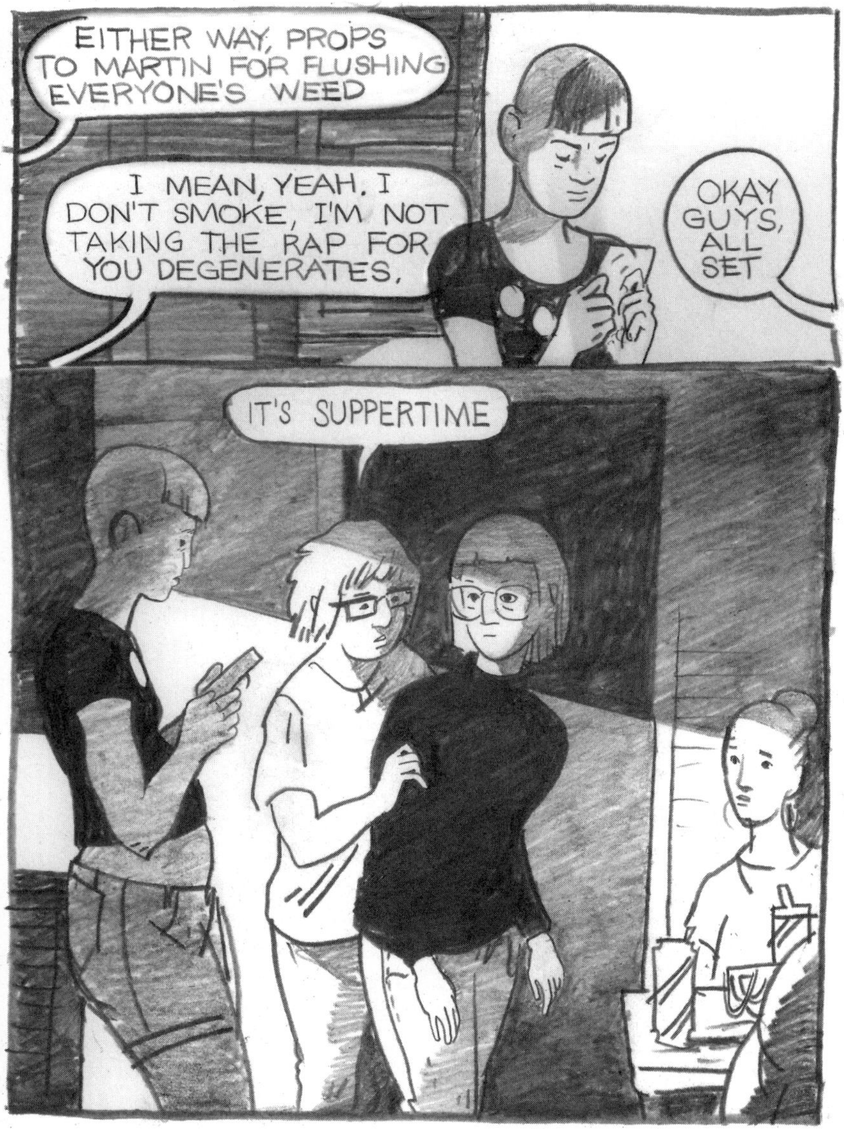
EITHER WAY, PROPS TO MARTIN FOR FLUSHING EVERYONE'S WEED
I MEAN, YEAH. I DON'T SMOKE, I'M NOT TAKING THE RAP FOR YOU DEGENERATES.
OKAY GUYS, ALL SET
IT'S SUPPERTIME

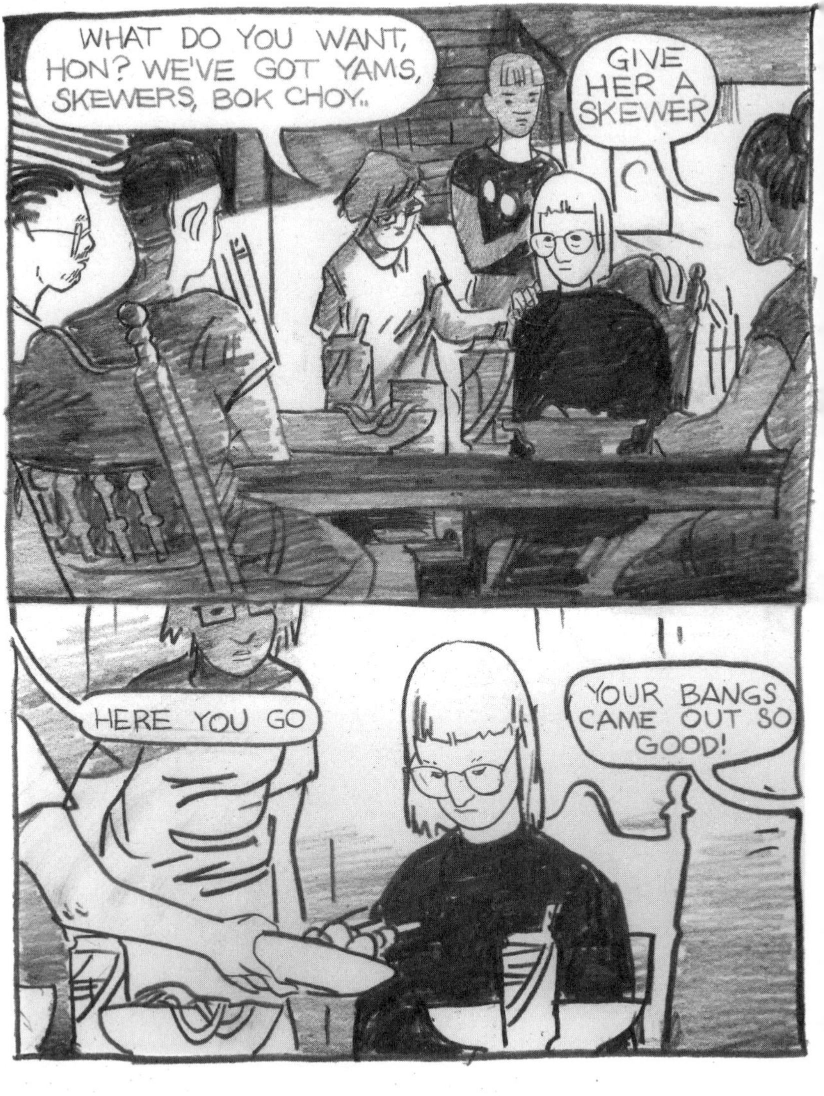
WHAT DO YOU WANT, HON? WE'VE GOT YAMS, SKEWERS, BOK CHOY..
GIVE HER A SKEWER
HERE YOU GO
YOUR BANGS CAME OUT SO GOOD!

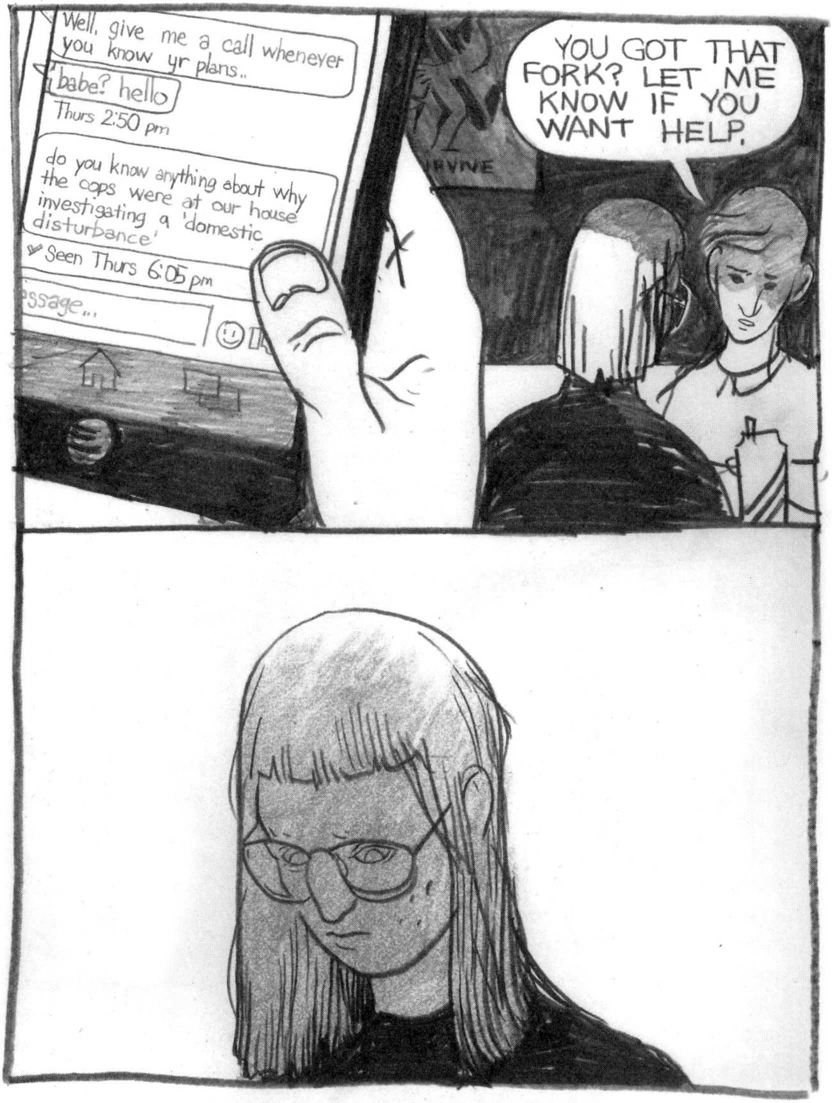
Well, give me a call whenever you know yr plans..
babe? hello
Thurs 2:50 pm
do you know anything about why the cops were at our house investigating a 'domestic disturbance'
Seen Thurs 6:05 pm
IRVINE
YOU GOT THAT FORK? LET ME KNOW IF YOU WANT HELP.

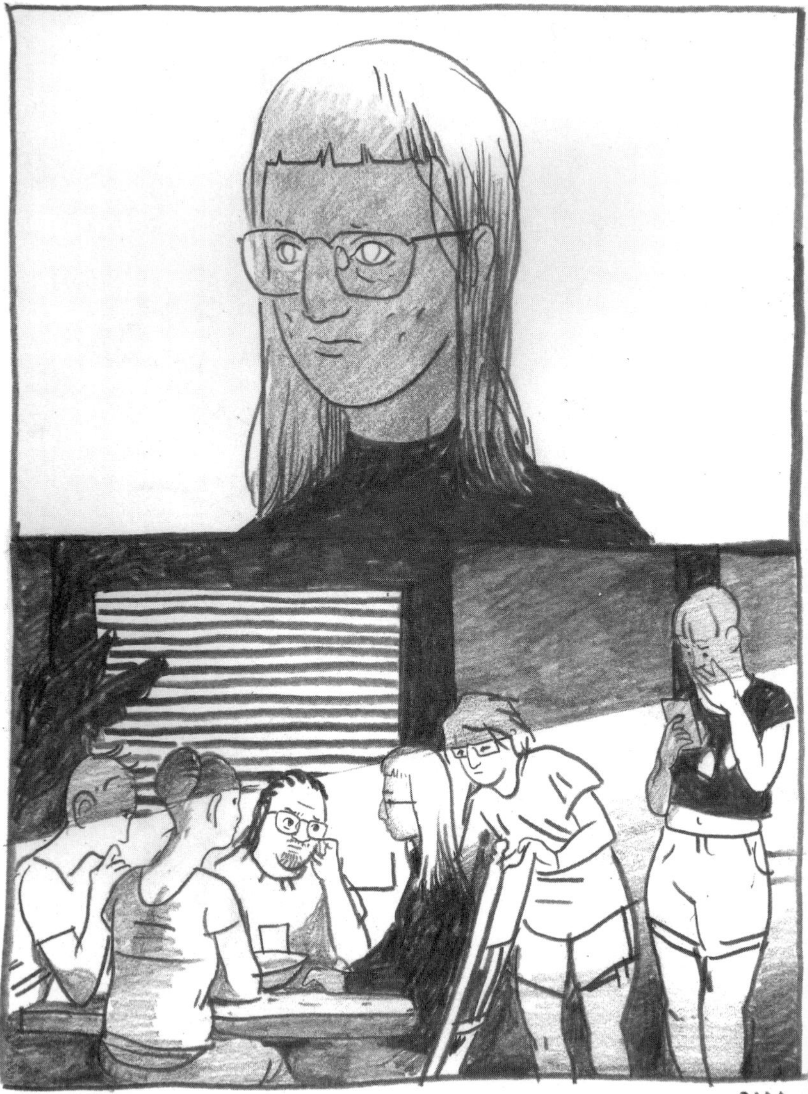

SAM

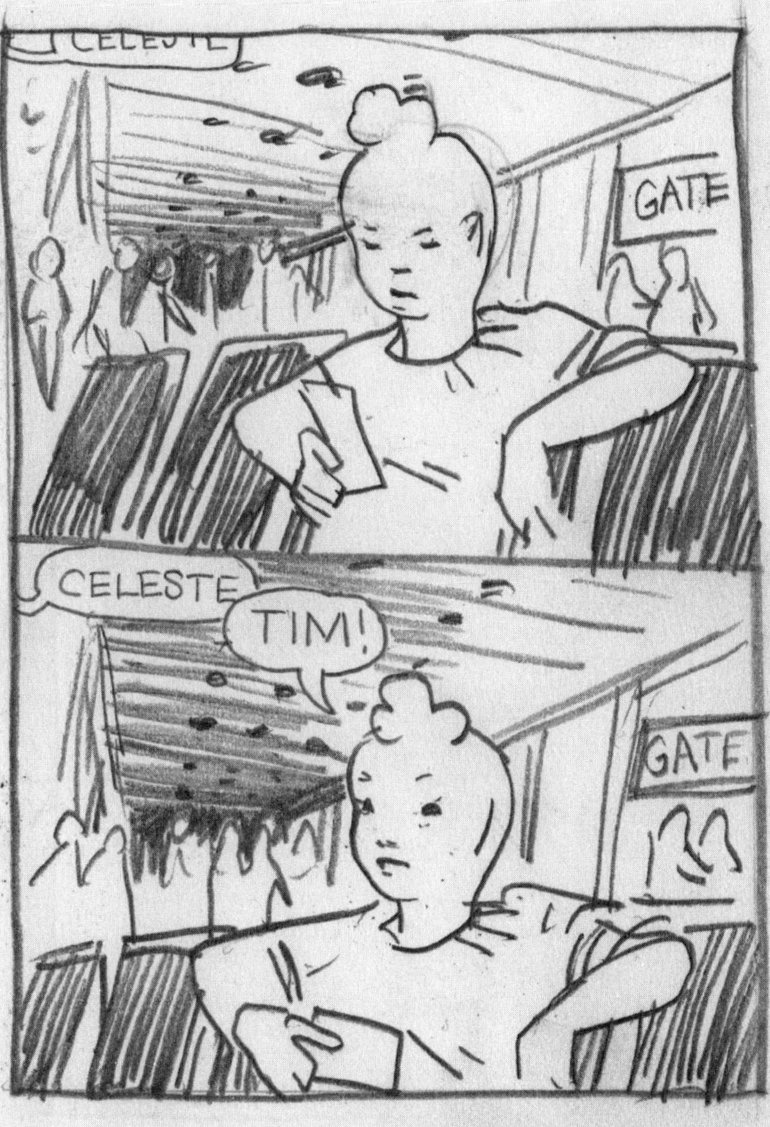
GATE
CELESTE
TIM!
GATE

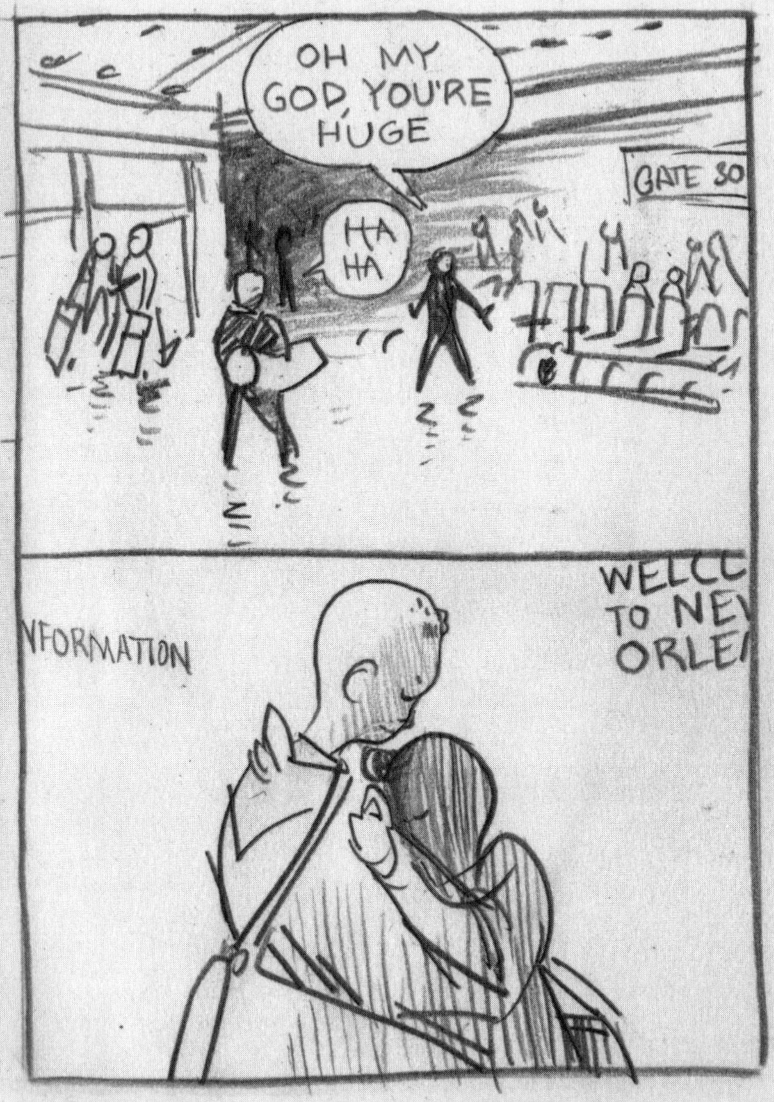
OH MY GOD, YOU'RE HUGE
HA HA
GATE 50
NFORMATION
WELC
TO NEV
ORLE

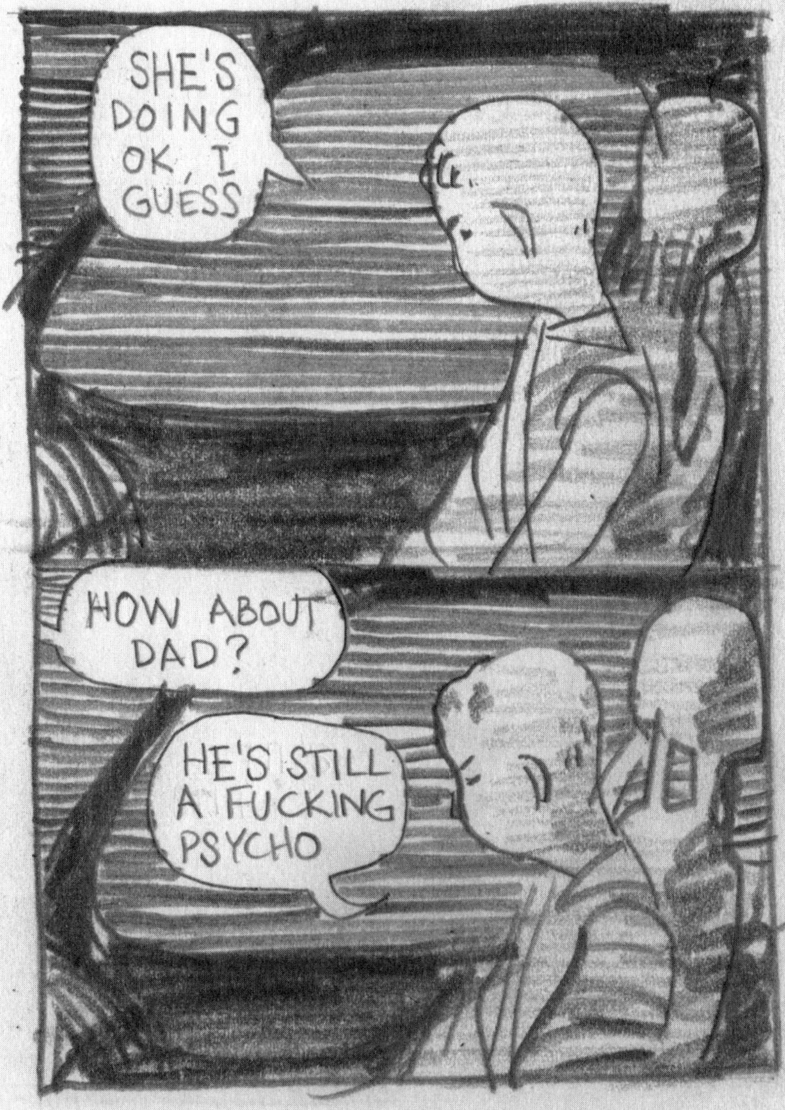
SHE'S DOING OK, I GUESS
HOW ABOUT DAD?
HE'S STILL A FUCKING PSYCHO

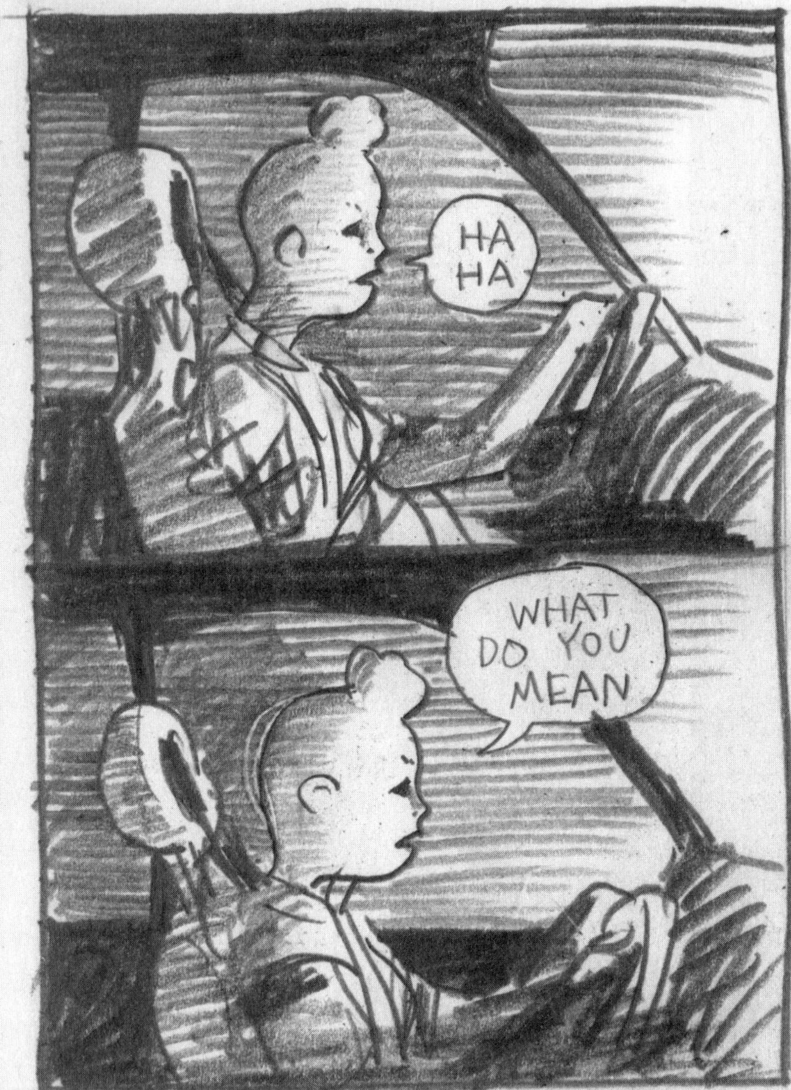
HA HA
WHAT DO YOU MEAN

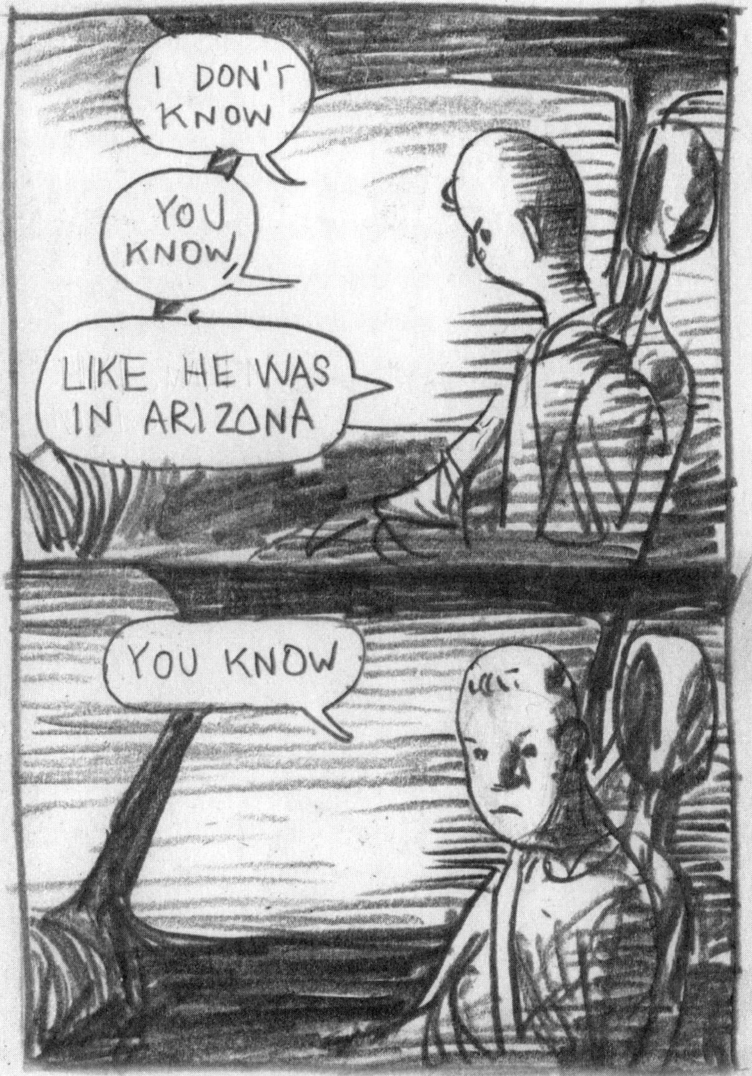
I DON'T KNOW
YOU KNOW,
LIKE HE WAS IN ARIZONA
YOU KNOW

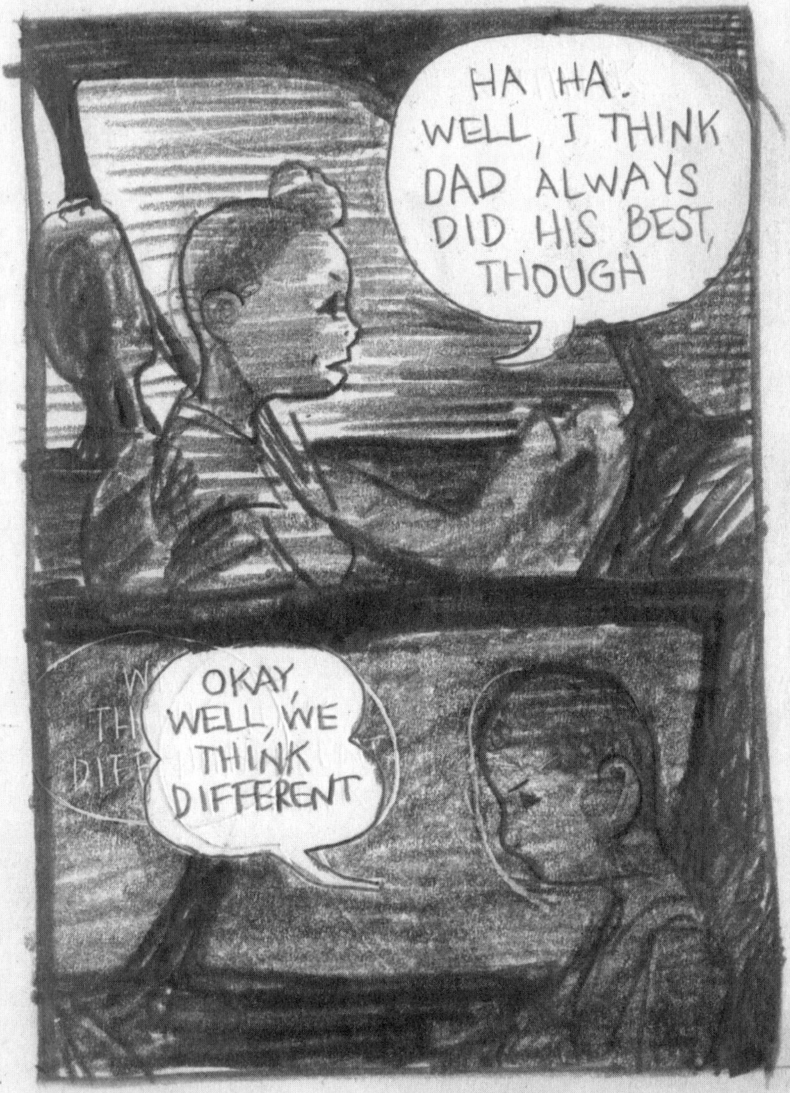
HA HA. WELL, I THINK DAD ALWAYS DID HIS BEST, THOUGH
OKAY, WELL, WE THINK DIFFERENT

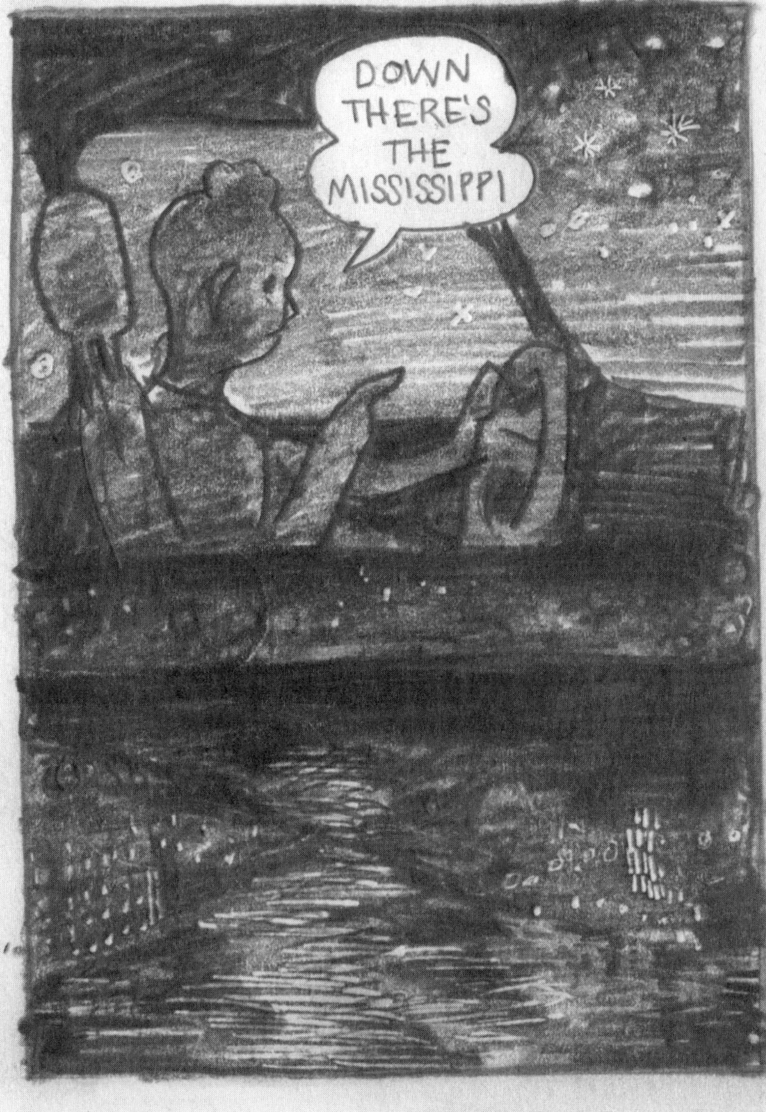
DOWN THERE'S THE MISSISSIPPI

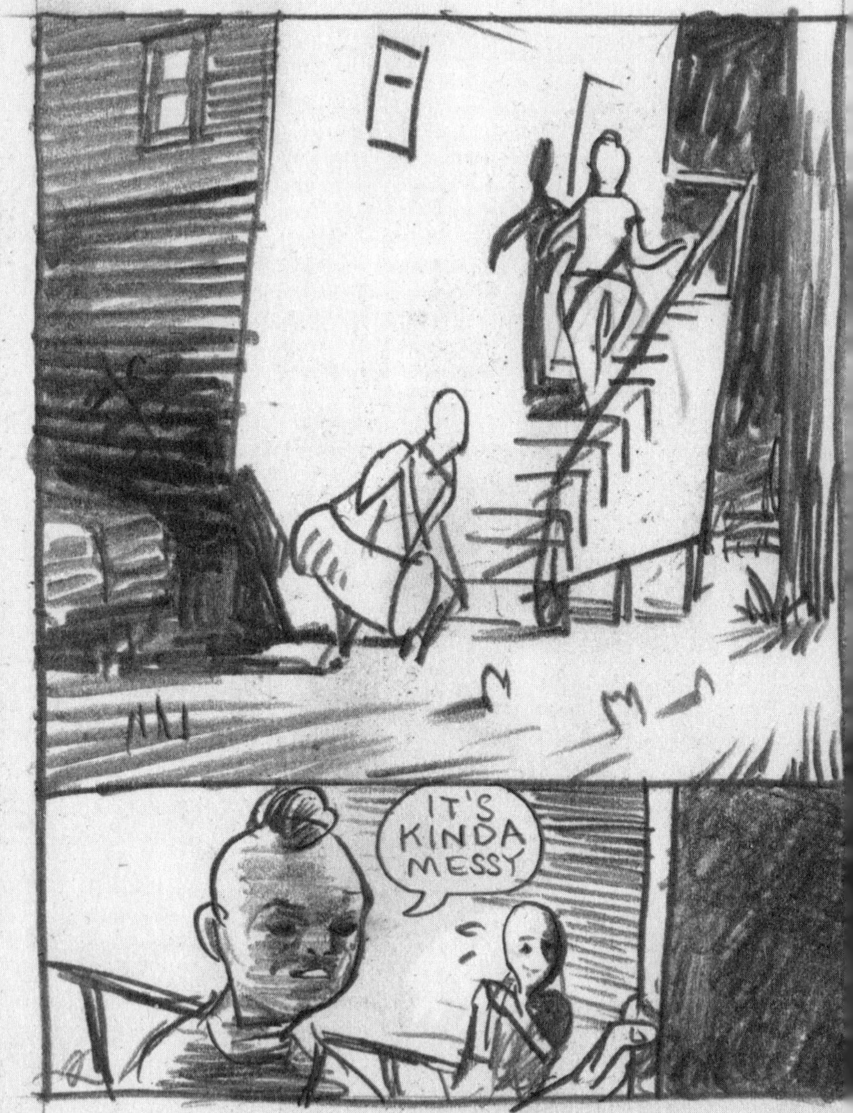
IT'S KINDA MESSY

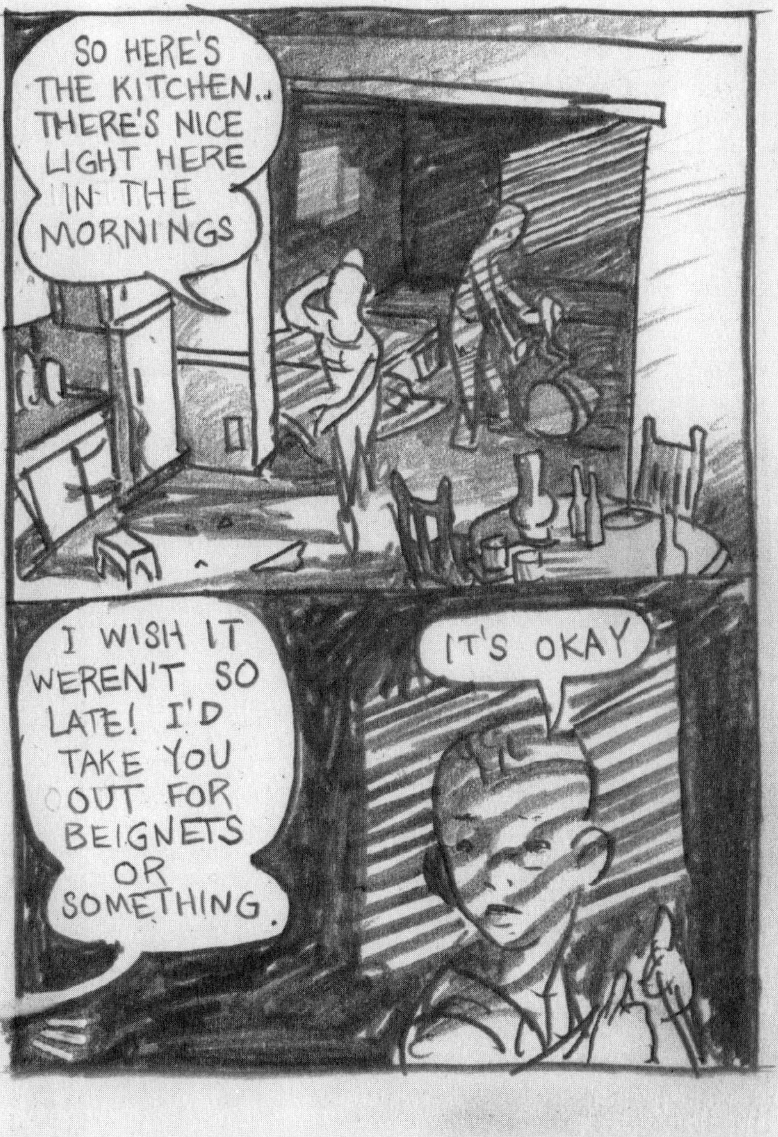
SO HERE'S THE KITCHEN.. THERE'S NICE LIGHT HERE IN THE MORNINGS
I WISH IT WEREN'T SO LATE! I'D TAKE YOU OUT FOR BEIGNETS OR SOMETHING.
IT'S OKAY

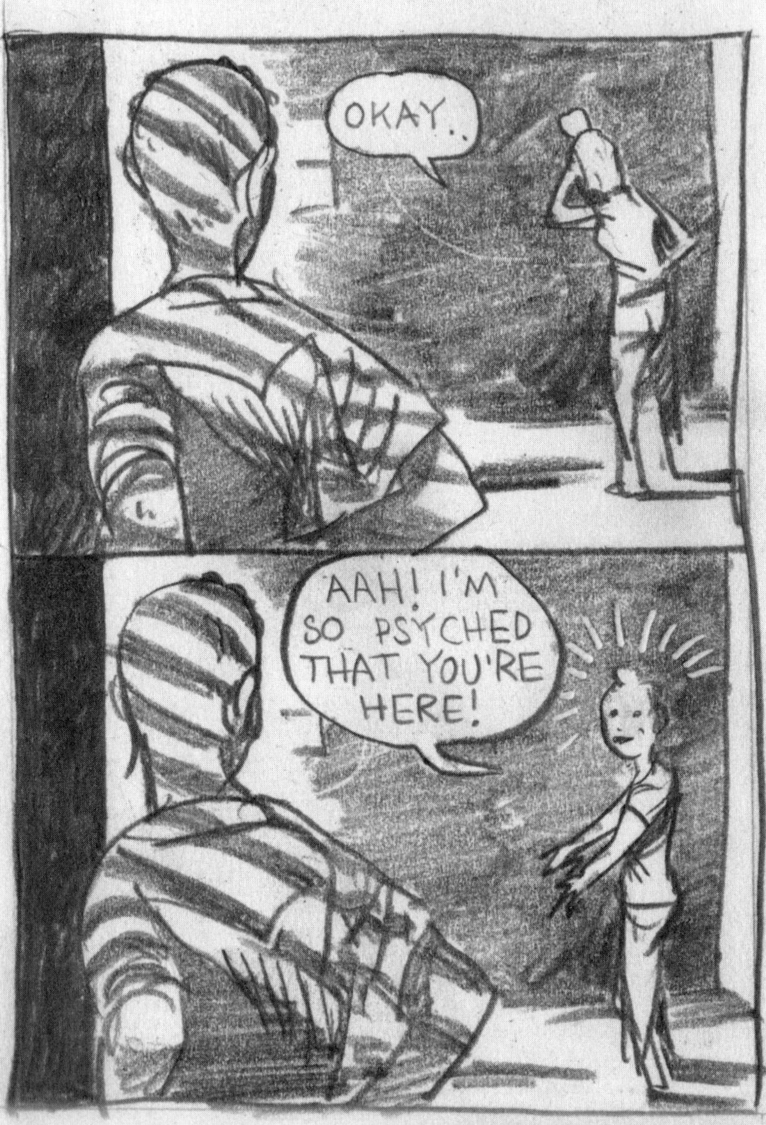
OKAY..
AAH! I'M SO PSYCHED THAT YOU'RE HERE!

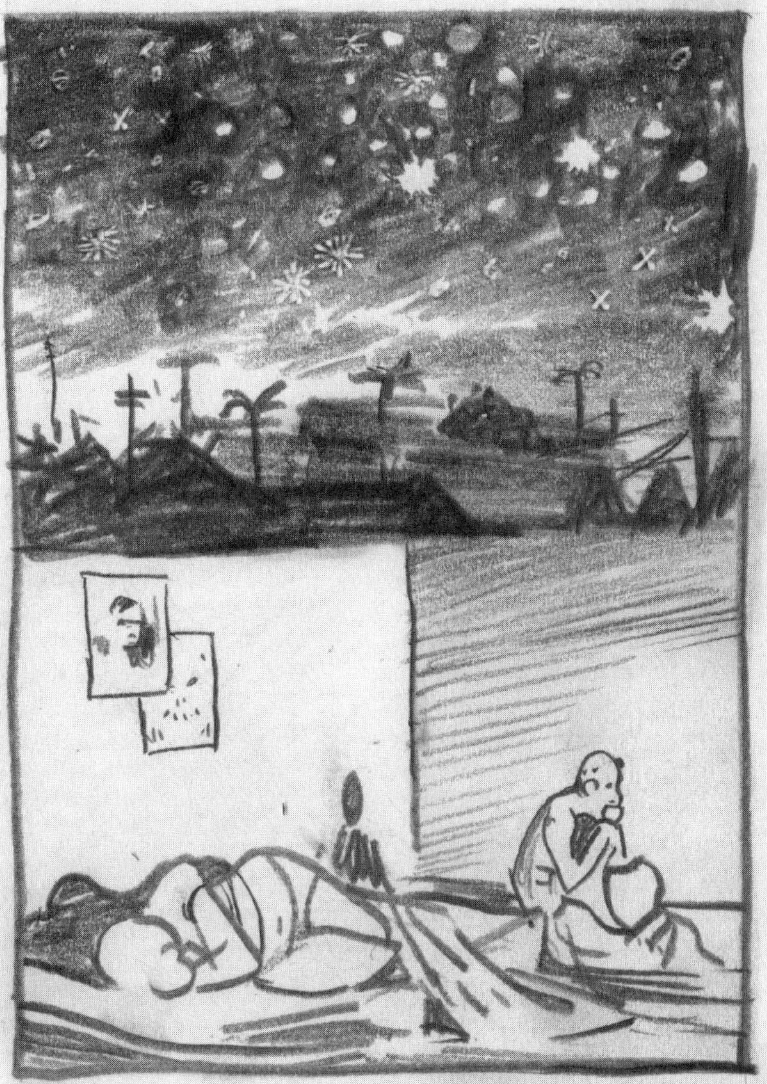

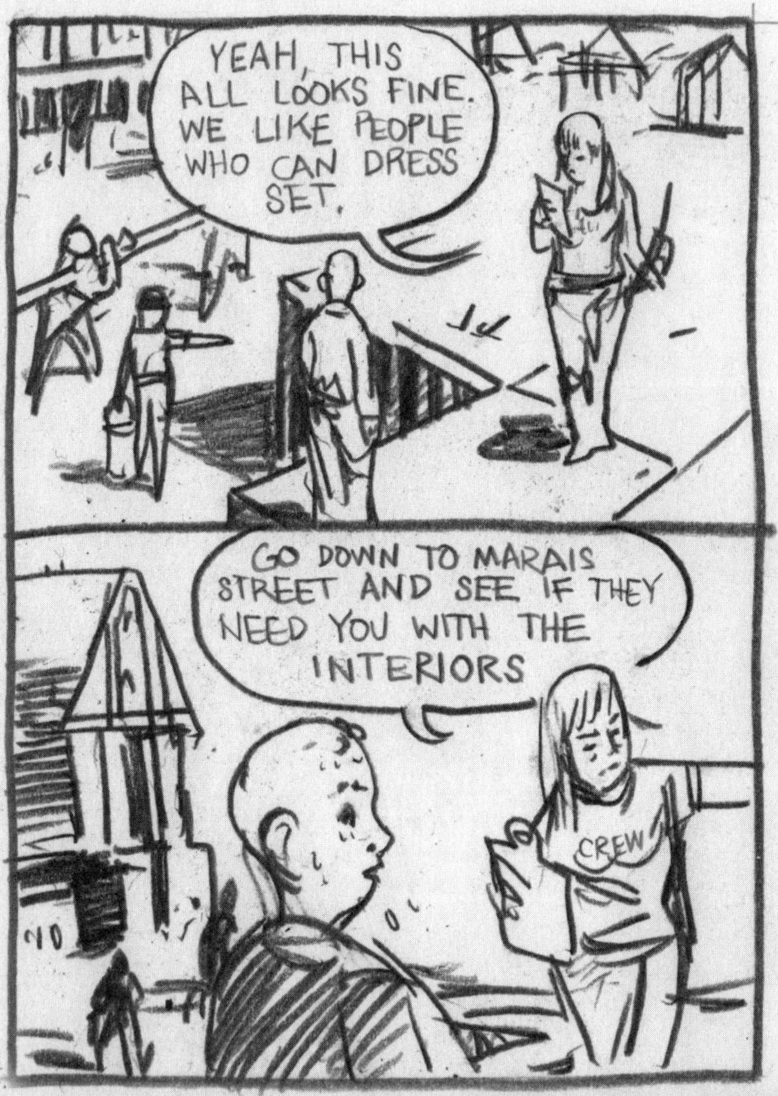
YEAH, THIS ALL LOOKS FINE. WE LIKE PEOPLE WHO CAN DRESS SET.
GO DOWN TO MARAIS STREET AND SEE IF THEY NEED YOU WITH THE INTERIORS
CREW

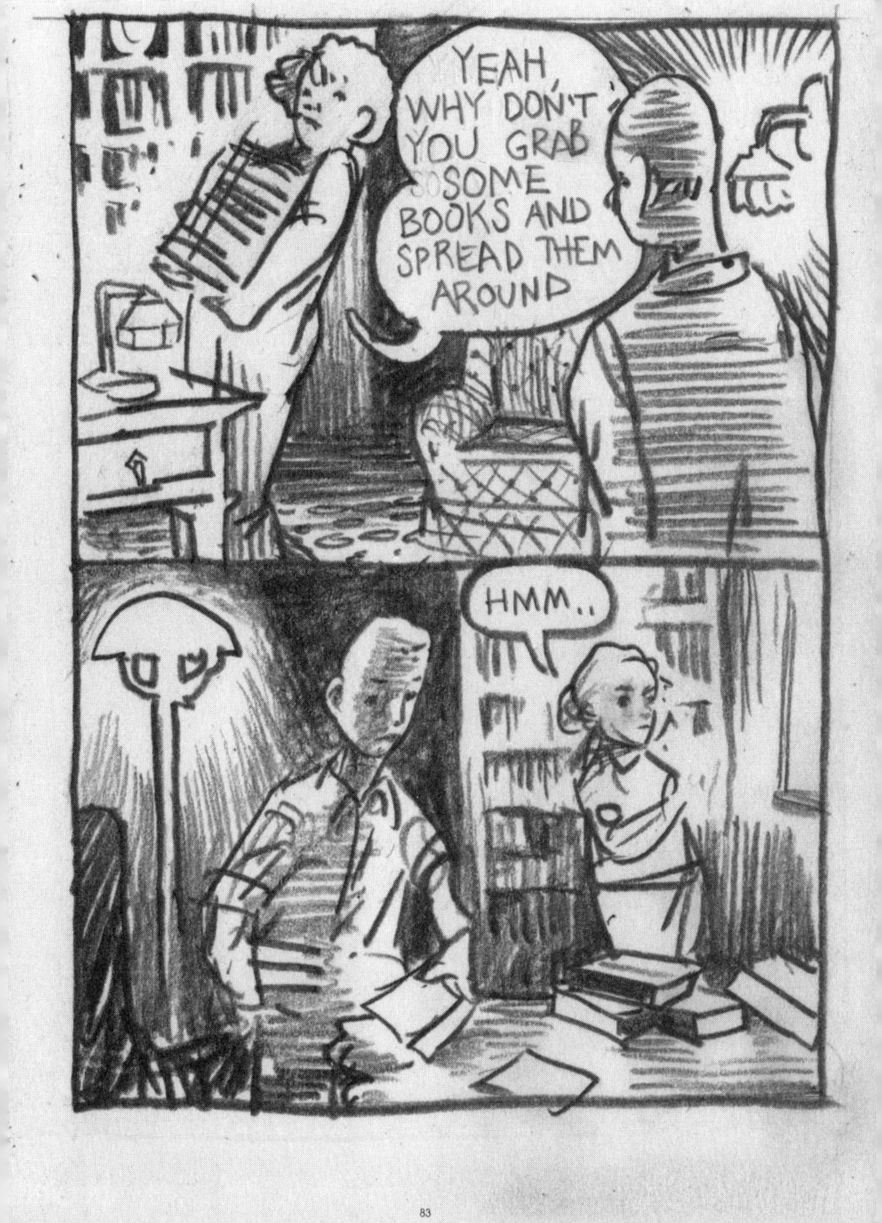
YEAH, WHY DON'T YOU GRAB SOME BOOKS AND SPREAD THEM AROUND
HMM..

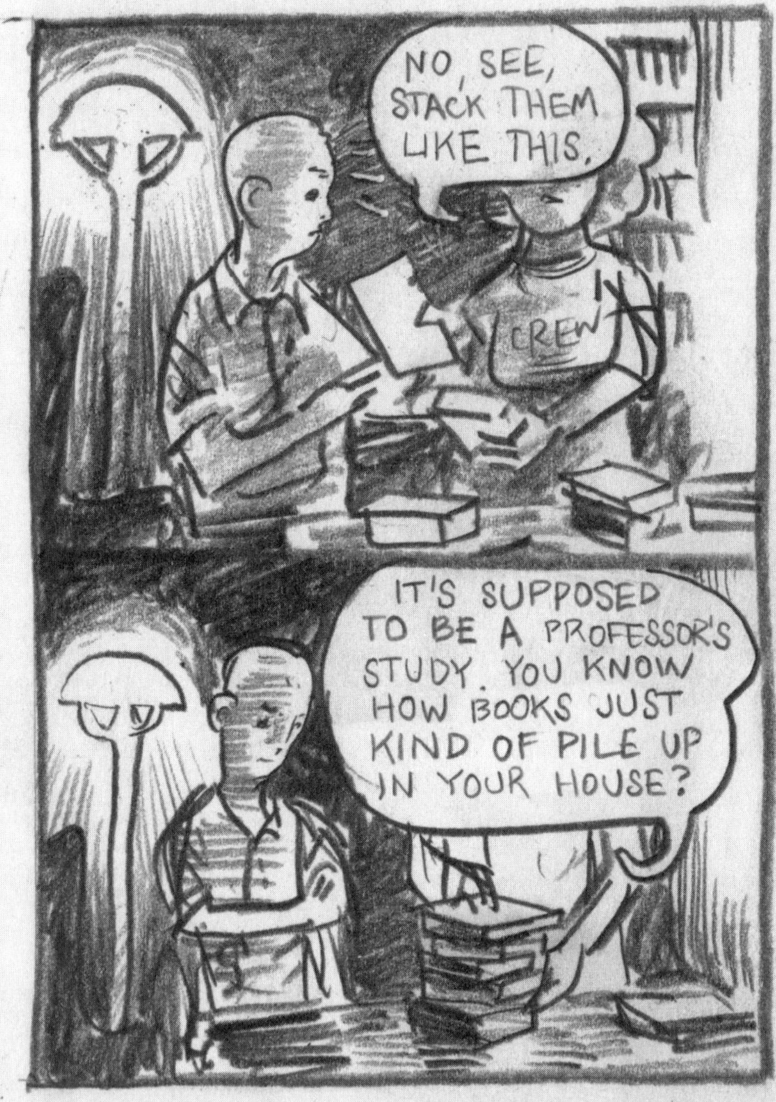
NO, SEE, STACK THEM LIKE THIS.
CREW
IT'S SUPPOSED TO BE A PROFESSOR'S STUDY. YOU KNOW HOW BOOKS JUST KIND OF PILE UP IN YOUR HOUSE?

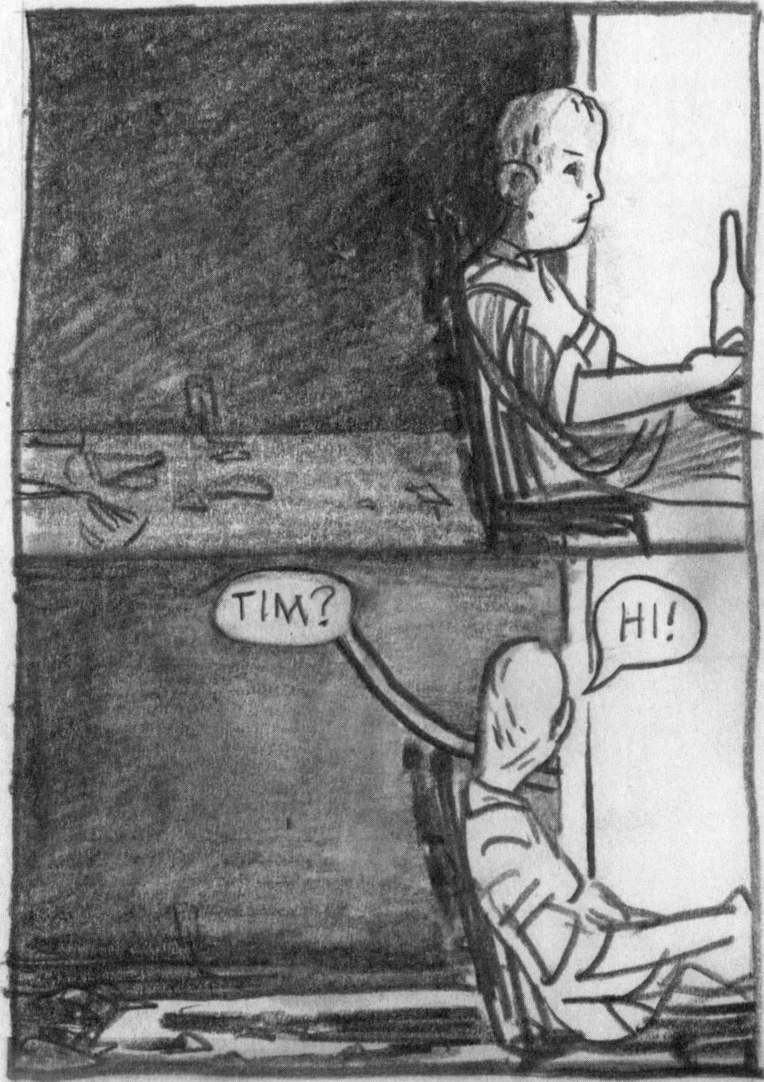
TIM?
HI!

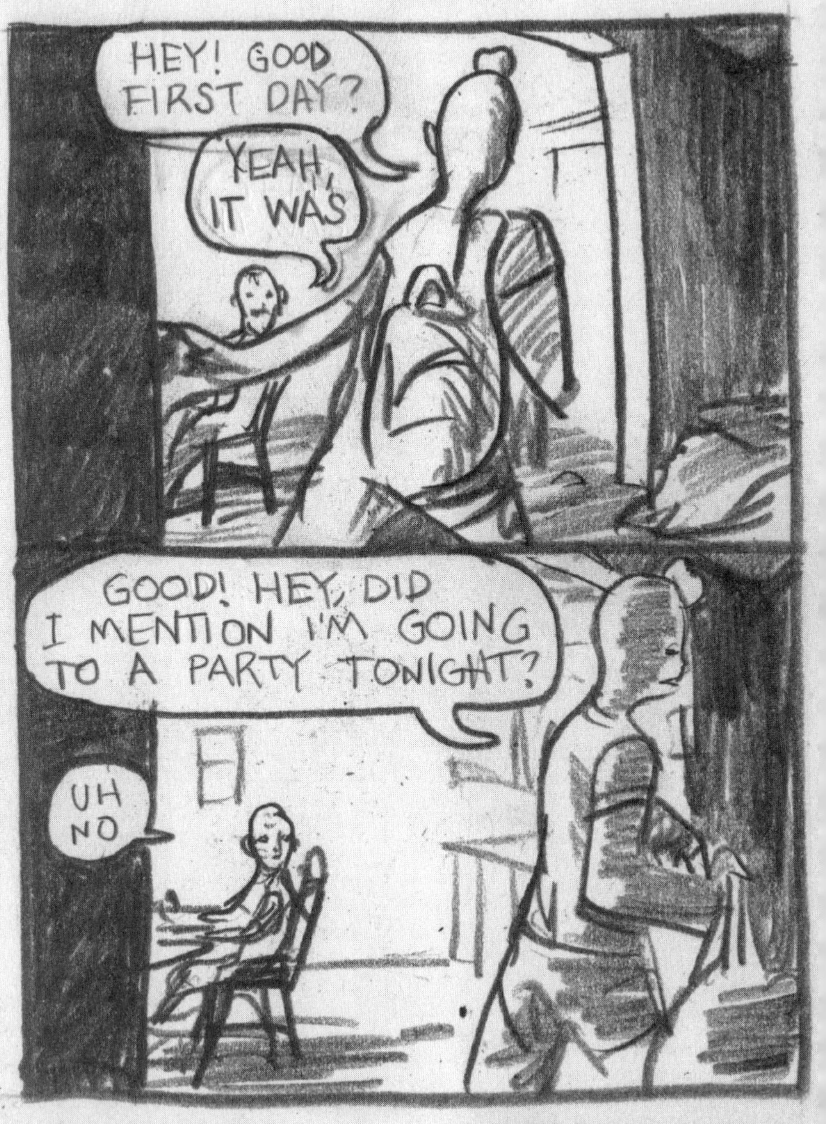
HEY! GOOD FIRST DAY?
YEAH, IT WAS
GOOD! HEY, DID I MENTION I'M GOING TO A PARTY TONIGHT?
UH NO

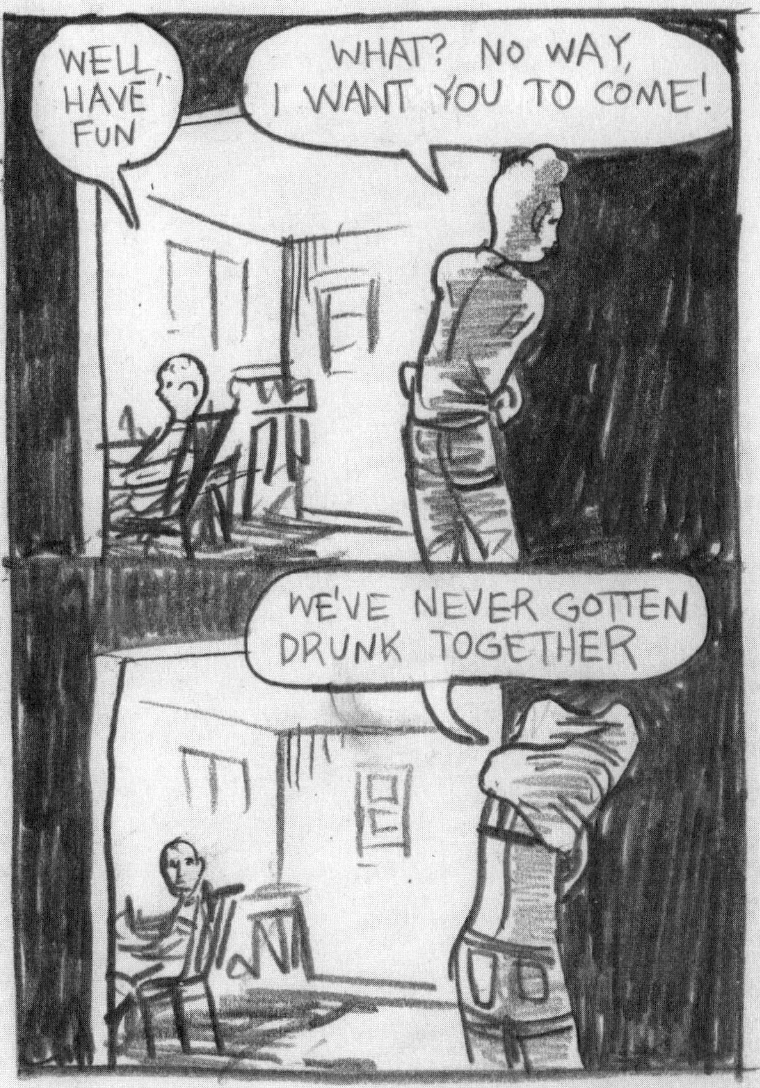
WELL, HAVE FUN
WHAT? NO WAY, I WANT YOU TO COME!
WE'VE NEVER GOTTEN DRUNK TOGETHER

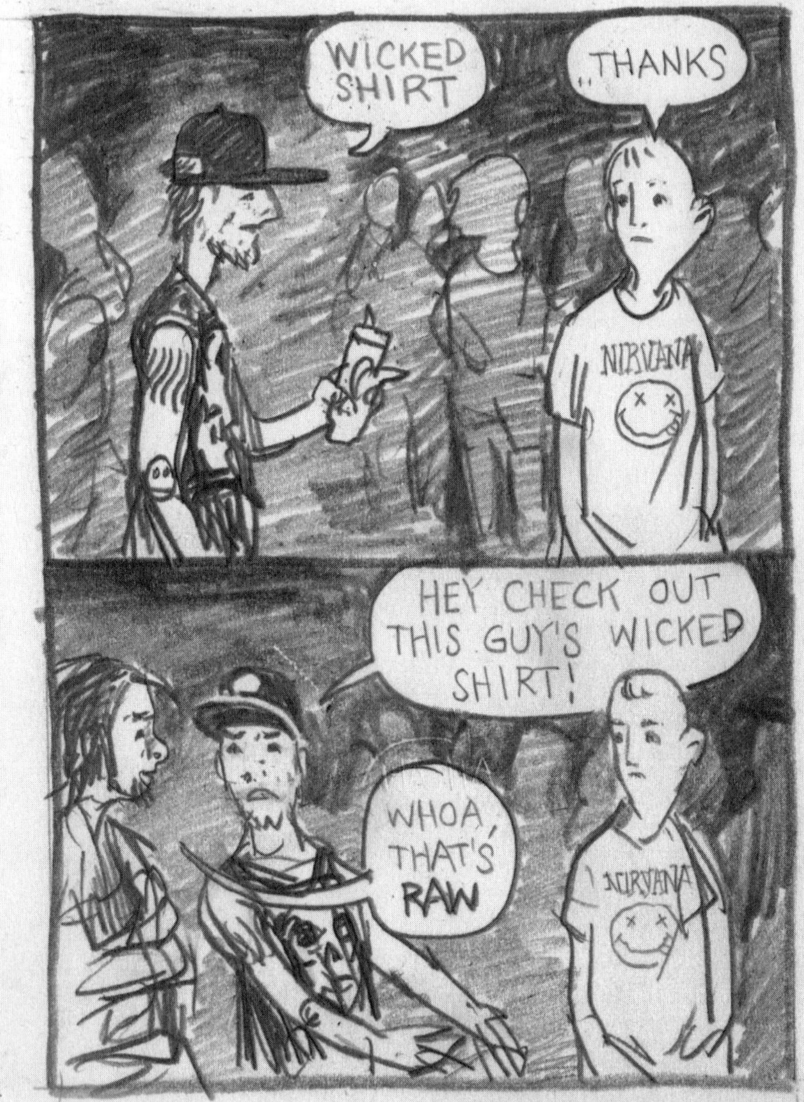
WICKED SHIRT
..THANKS
NIRVANA
HEY CHECK OUT THIS GUY'S WICKED SHIRT!
WHOA, THAT'S RAW
NIRVANA

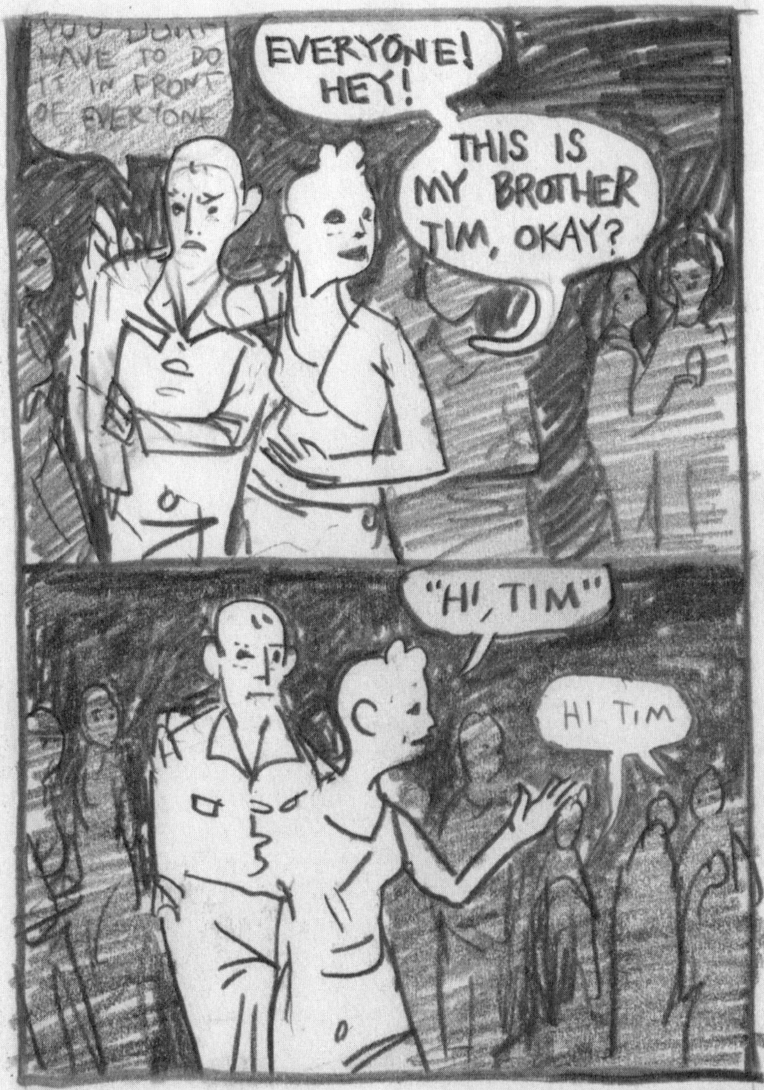
HAVE TO DO IT IN FRONT OF EVERYONE
EVERYONE! HEY!
THIS IS MY BROTHER TIM, OKAY?
"HI, TIM"
HI TIM

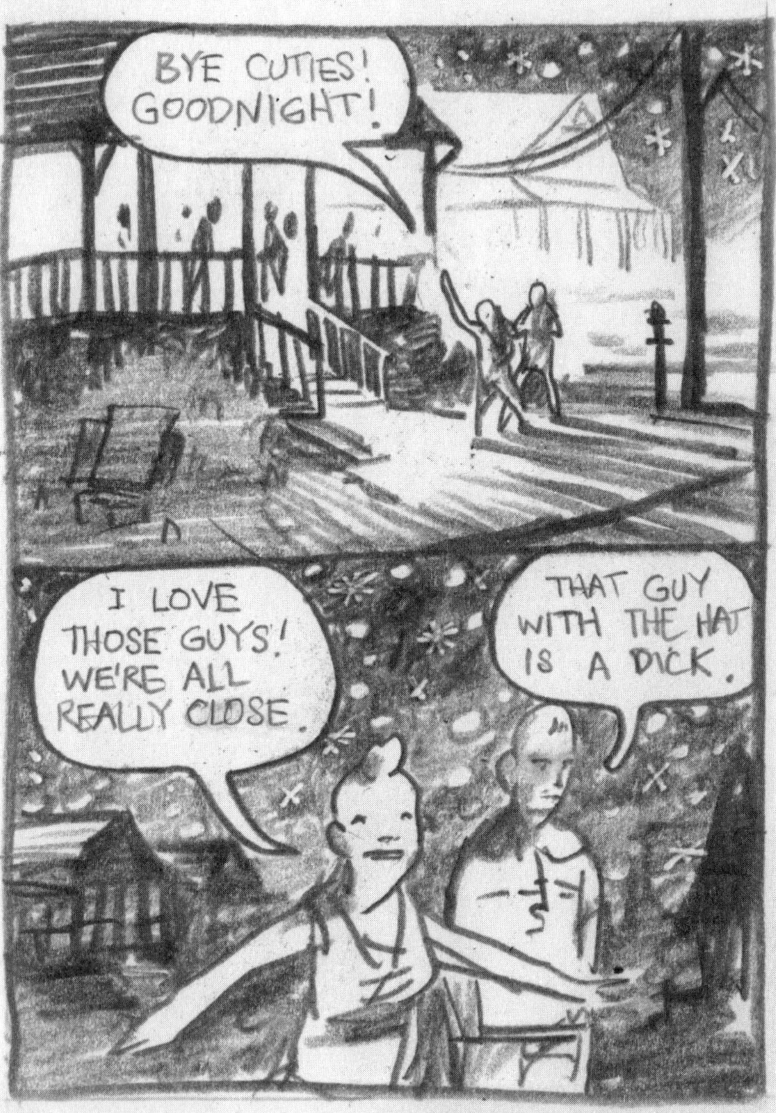
BYE CUTIES! GOODNIGHT!
I LOVE THOSE GUYS! WE'RE ALL REALLY CLOSE.
THAT GUY WITH THE HAT IS A DICK.

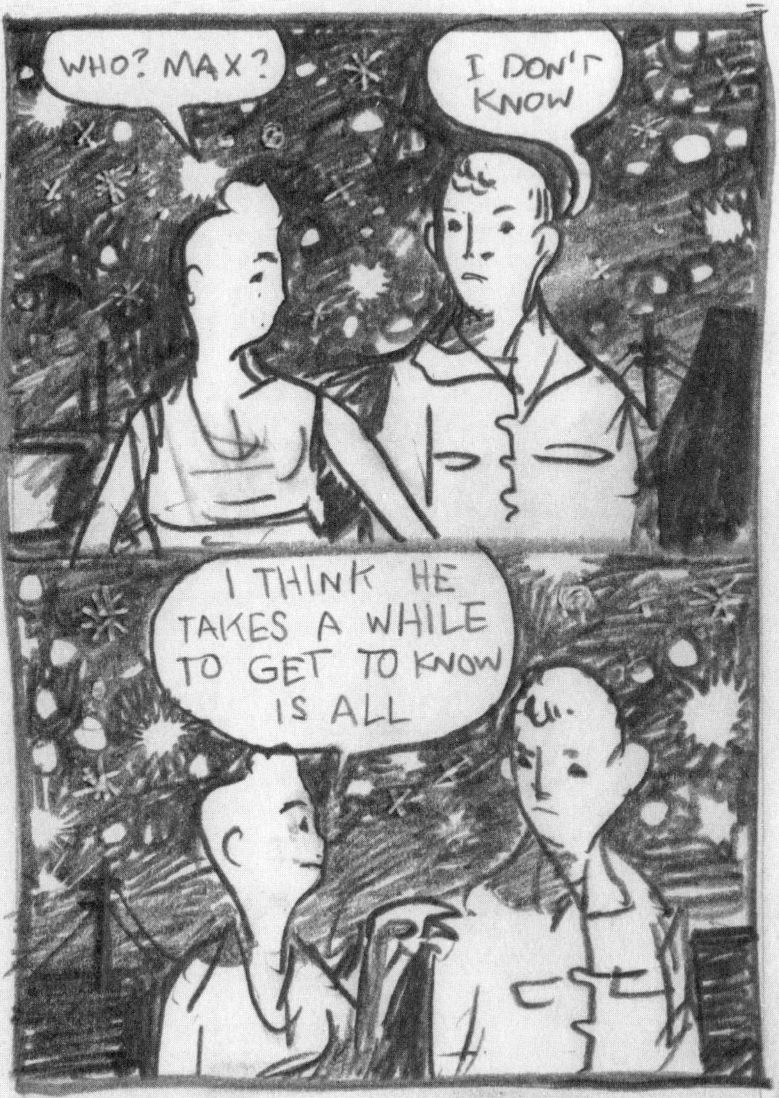
WHO? MAX?
I DON'T KNOW
I THINK HE TAKES A WHILE TO GET TO KNOW IS ALL

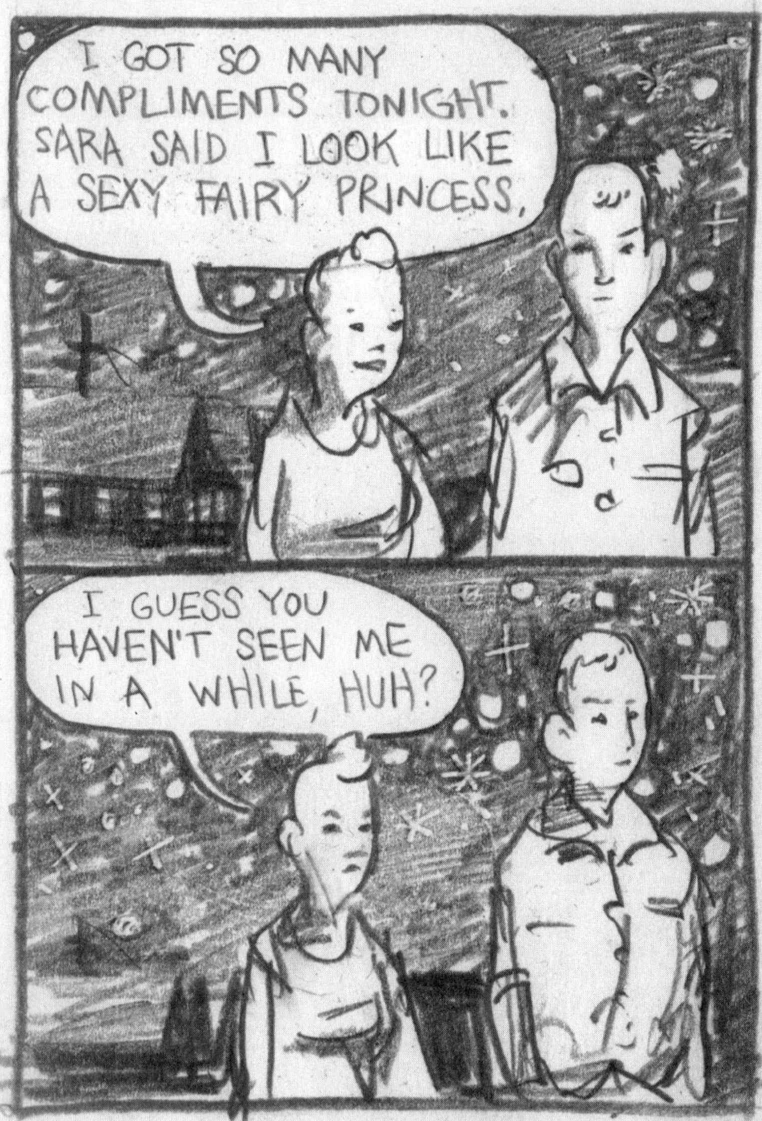
I GOT SO MANY COMPLIMENTS TONIGHT. SARA SAID I LOOK LIKE A SEXY FAIRY PRINCESS.
I GUESS YOU HAVEN'T SEEN ME IN A WHILE, HUH?

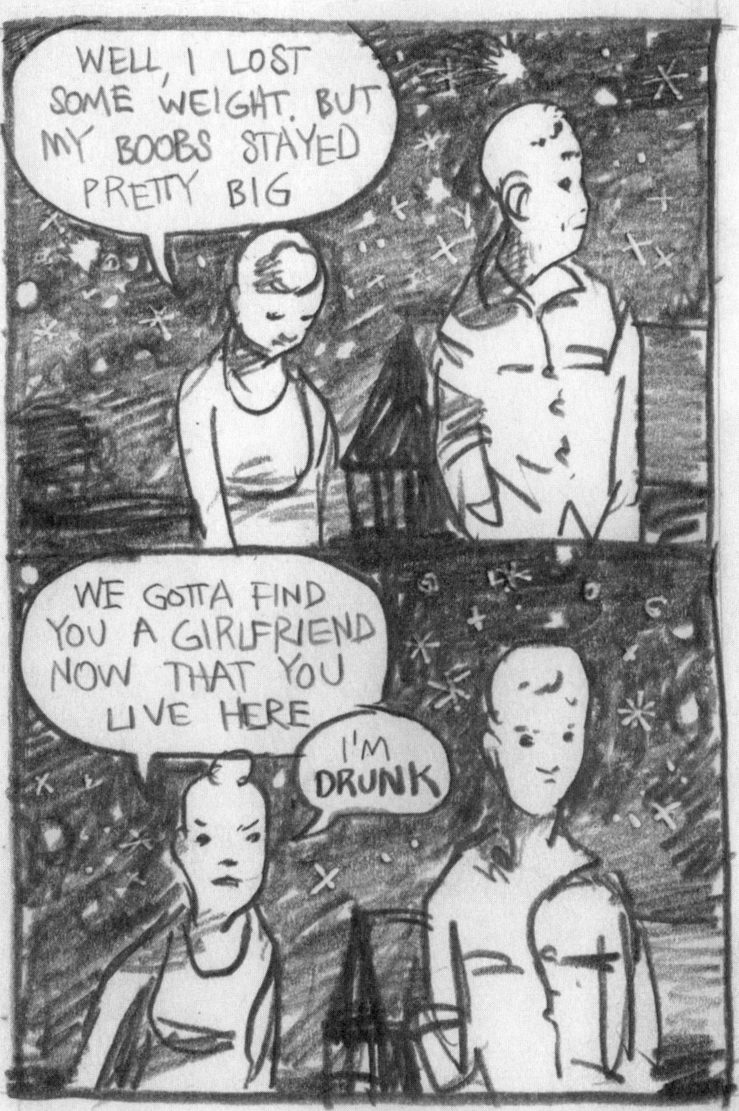
WELL, I LOST SOME WEIGHT. BUT MY BOOBS STAYED PRETTY BIG
WE GOTTA FIND YOU A GIRLFRIEND NOW THAT YOU LIVE HERE
I'M DRUNK

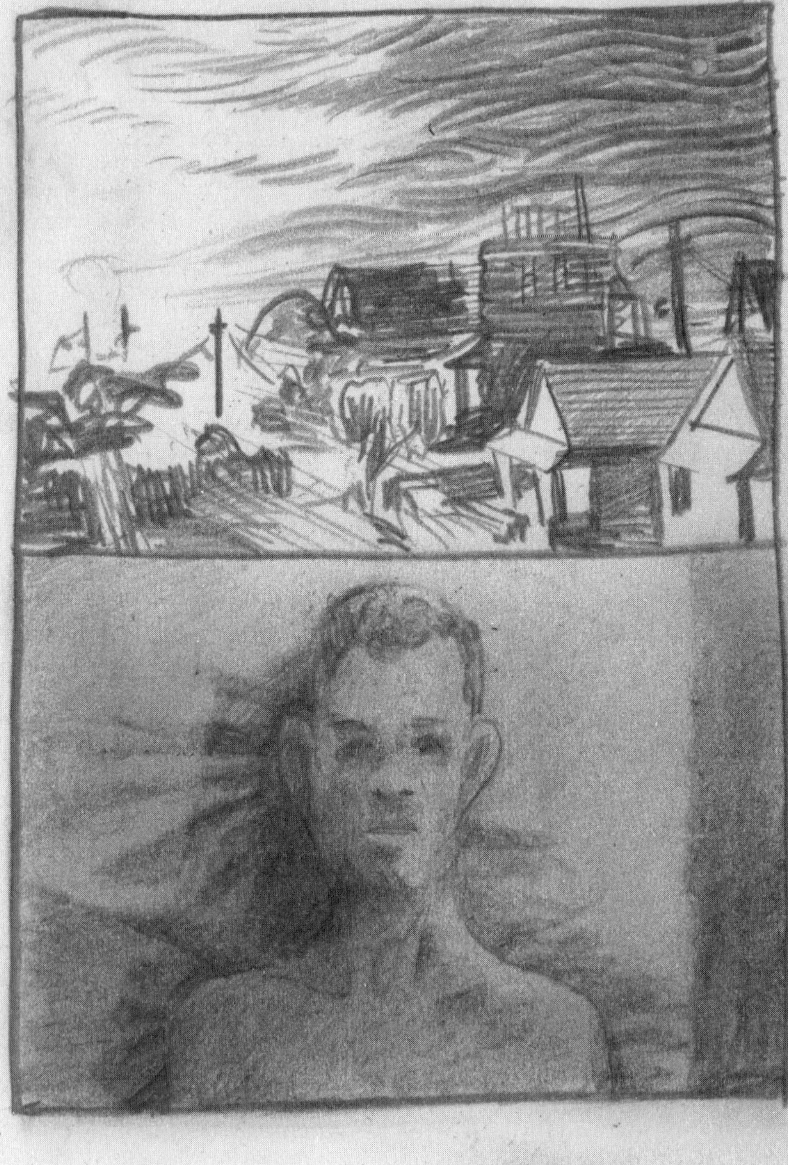

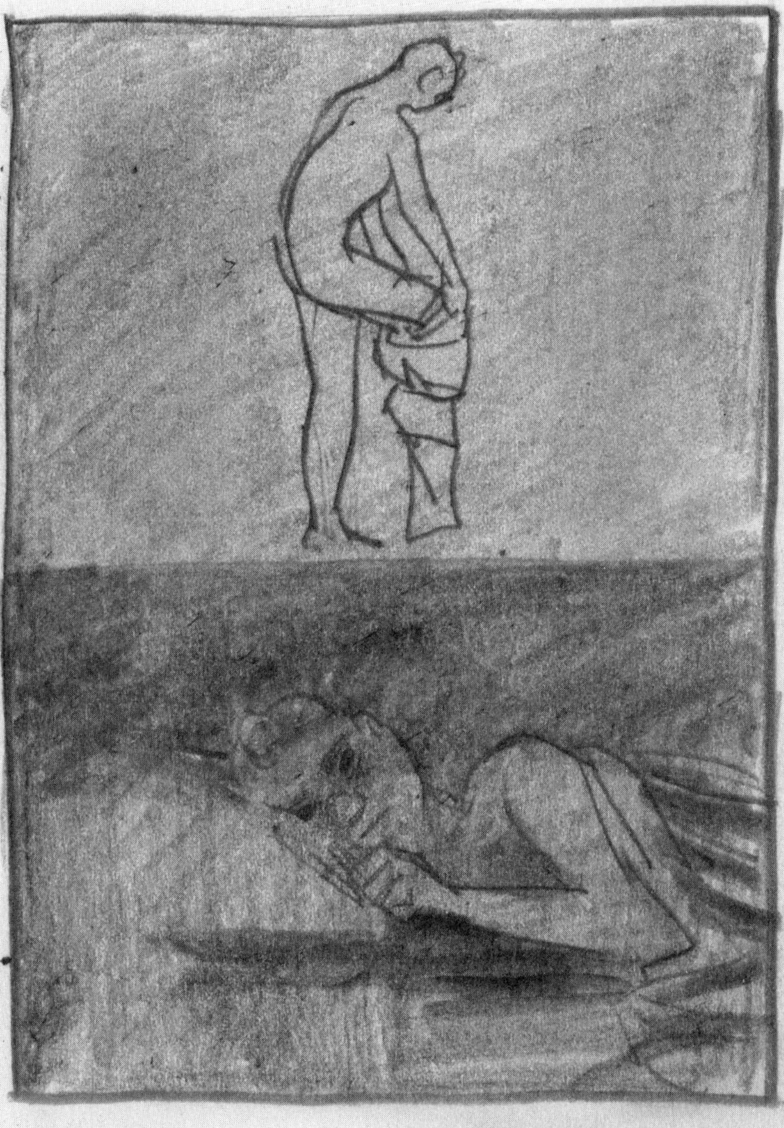

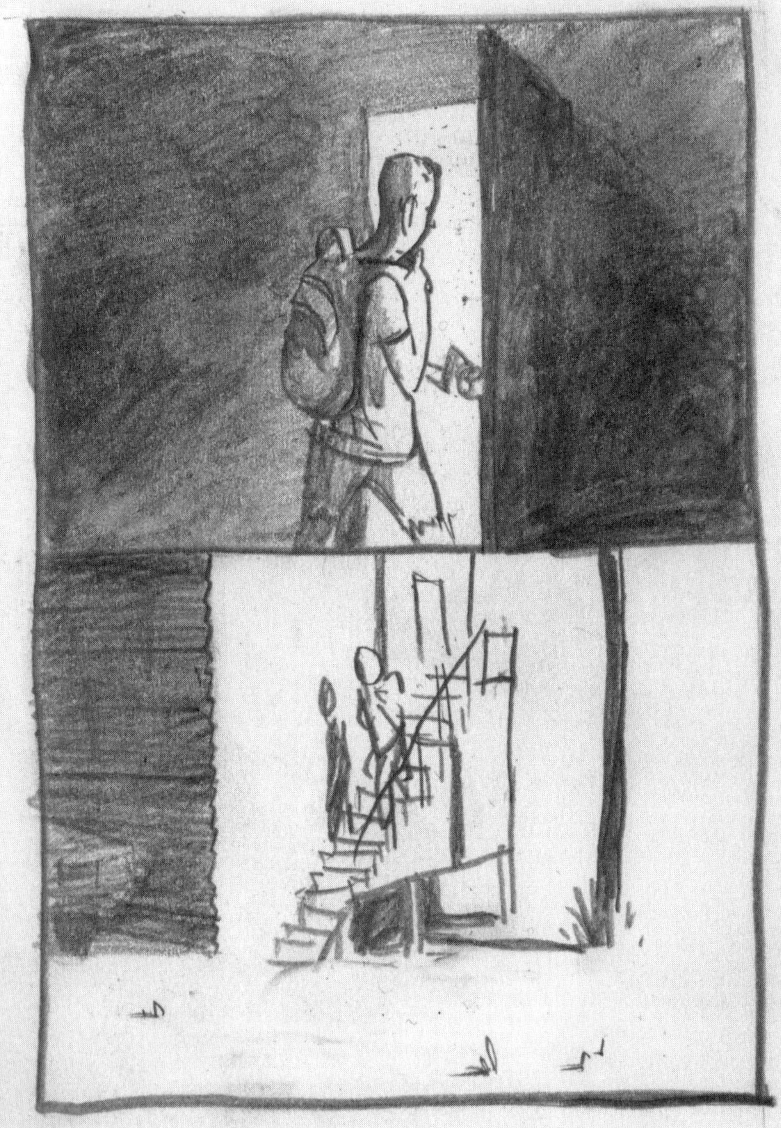

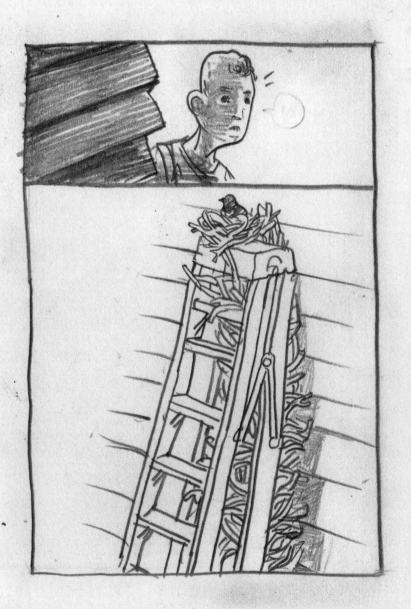

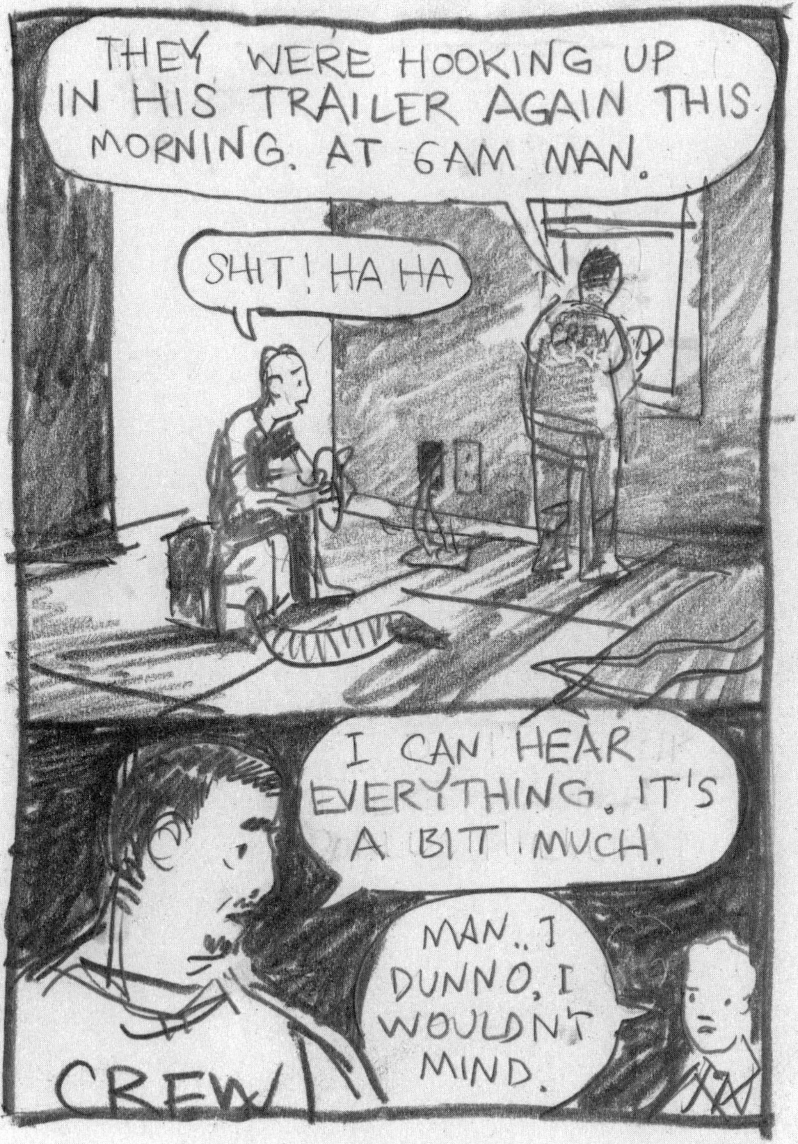
THEY WERE HOOKING UP IN HIS TRAILER AGAIN THIS MORNING. AT 6AM MAN.
SHIT! HA HA
I CAN HEAR EVERYTHING. IT'S A BIT MUCH.
MAN.. I DUNNO, I WOULDN'T MIND.
CREW

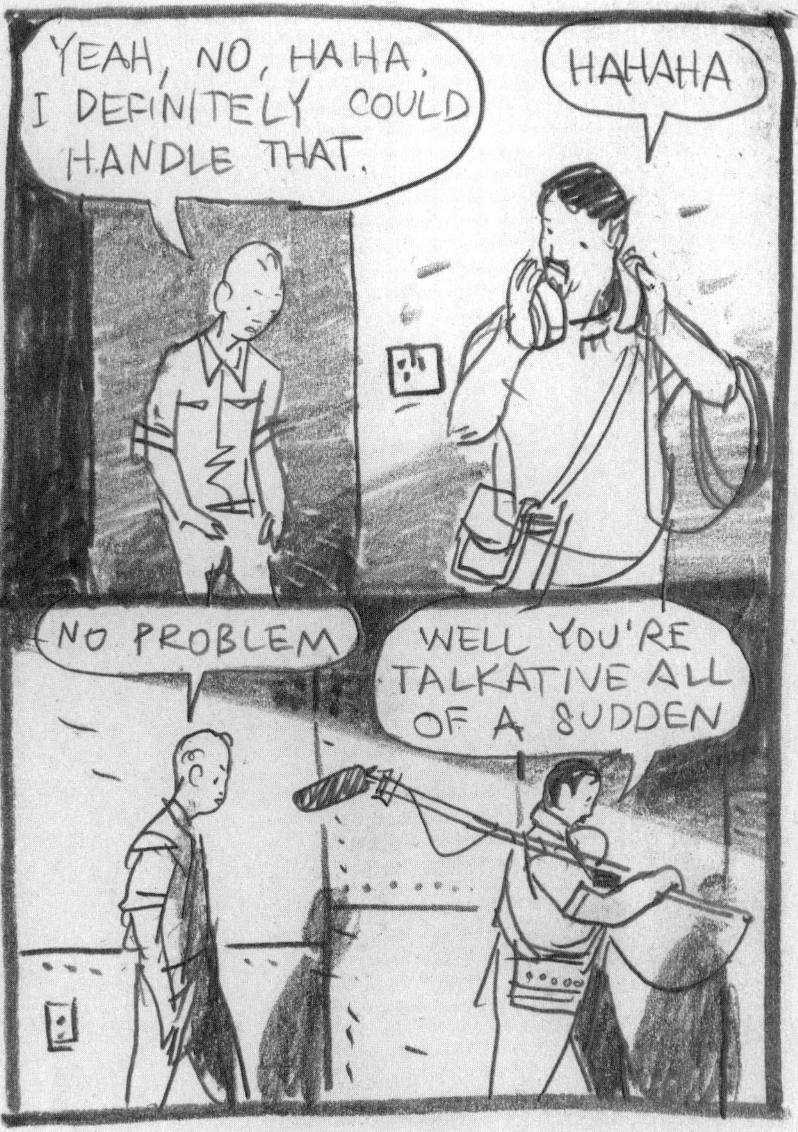
YEAH, NO, HAHA, I DEFINITELY COULD HANDLE THAT.
HAHAHA
NO PROBLEM
WELL YOU'RE TALKATIVE ALL OF A SUDDEN

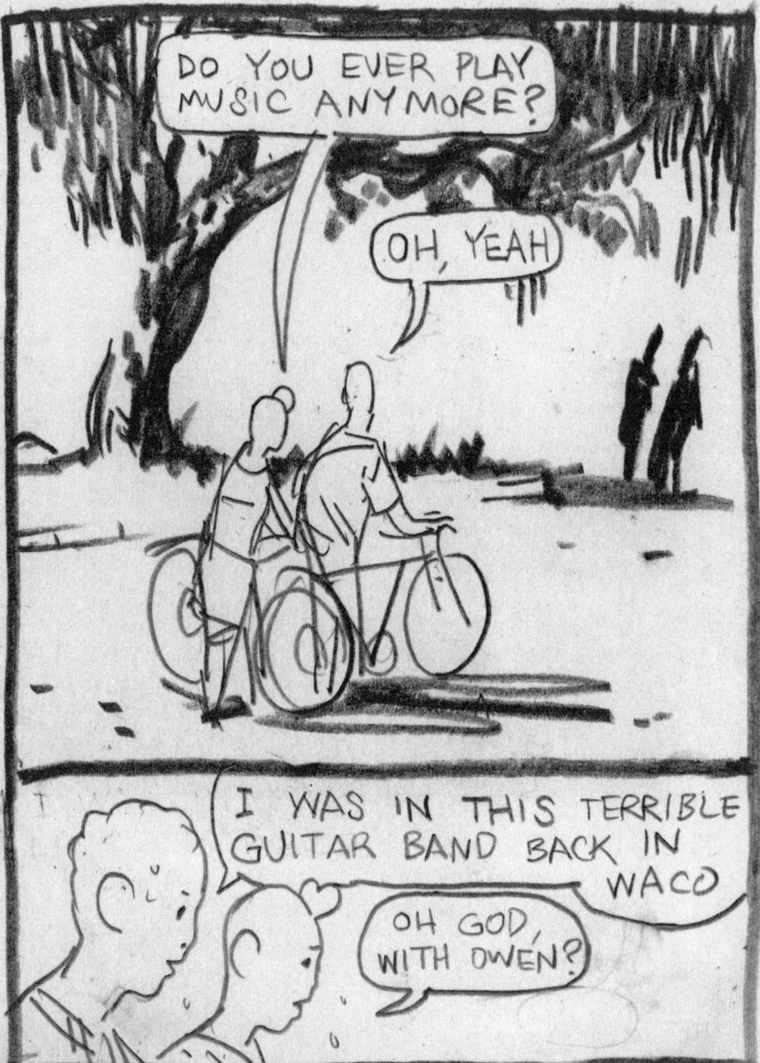
DO YOU EVER PLAY MUSIC ANYMORE?
OH, YEAH
I WAS IN THIS TERRIBLE GUITAR BAND BACK IN WACO
OH GOD, WITH OWEN?

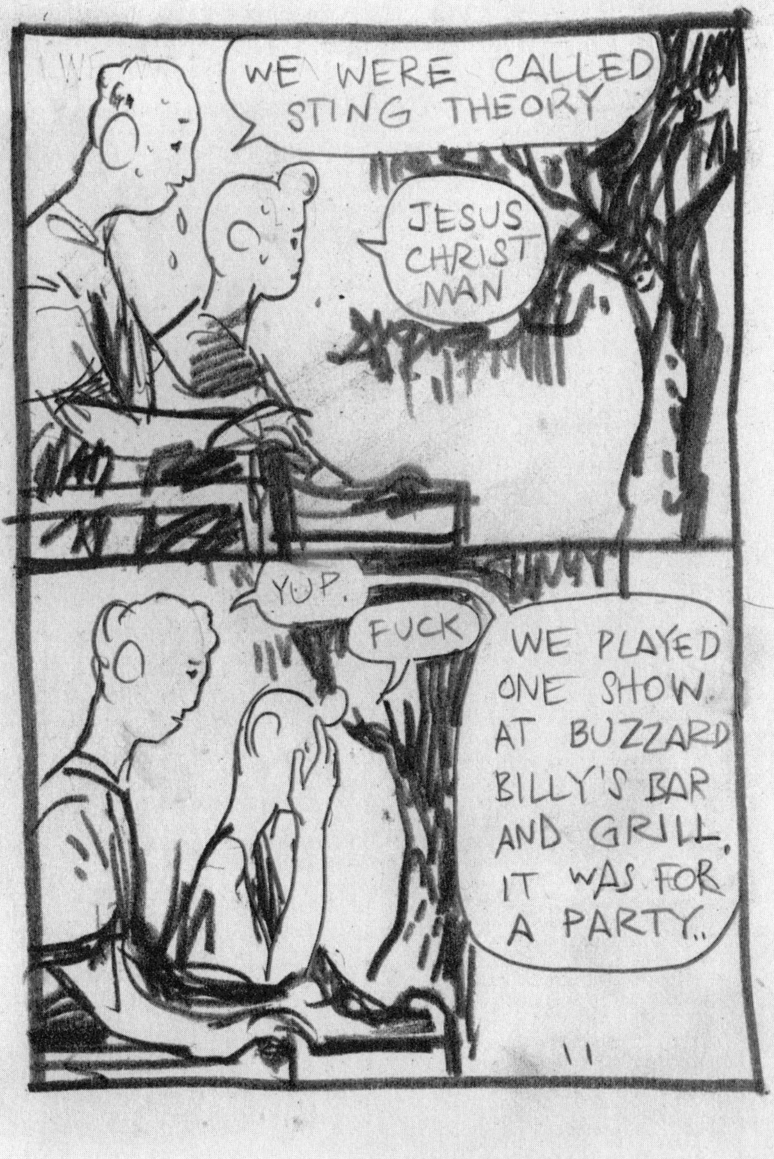
WE WERE CALLED STING THEORY
JESUS CHRIST MAN
YUP.
FUCK
WE PLAYED ONE SHOW. AT BUZZARD BILLY'S BAR AND GRILL. IT WAS FOR A PARTY..

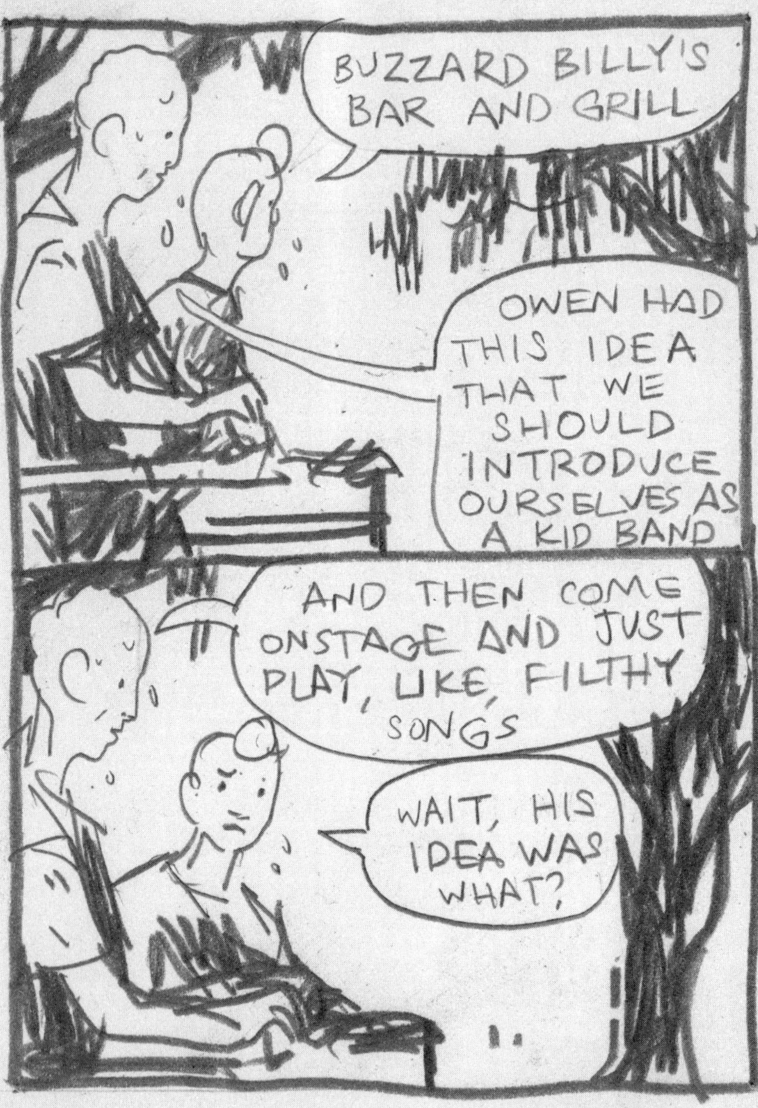
BUZZARD BILLY'S BAR AND GRILL
OWEN HAD THIS IDEA THAT WE SHOULD INTRODUCE OURSELVES AS A KID BAND
AND THEN COME ONSTAGE AND JUST PLAY, LIKE, FILTHY SONGS
WAIT, HIS IDEA WAS WHAT?

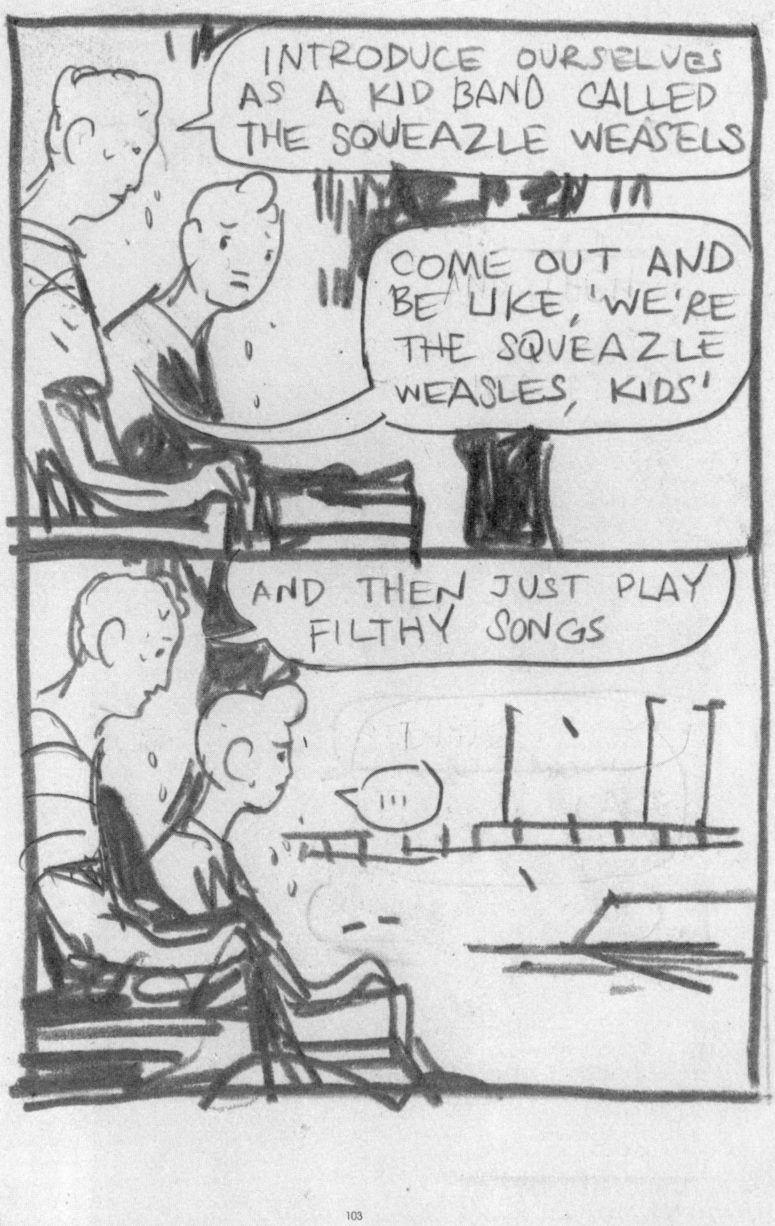
INTRODUCE OURSELVES AS A KID BAND CALLED THE SQUEAZLE WEASELS
COME OUT AND BE LIKE, 'WE'RE THE SQUEAZLE WEASLES, KIDS'
AND THEN JUST PLAY FILTHY SONGS

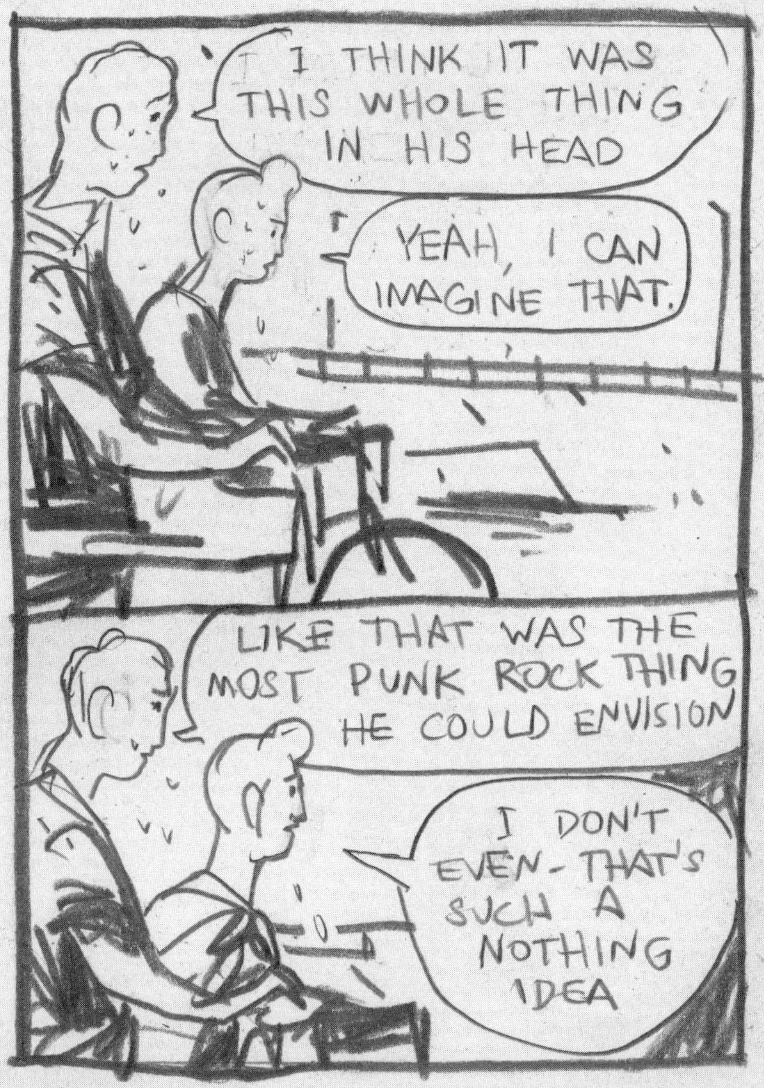
I THINK IT WAS THIS WHOLE THING IN HIS HEAD
YEAH, I CAN IMAGINE THAT.
LIKE THAT WAS THE MOST PUNK ROCK THING HE COULD ENVISION
I DON'T EVEN - THAT'S SUCH A NOTHING IDEA

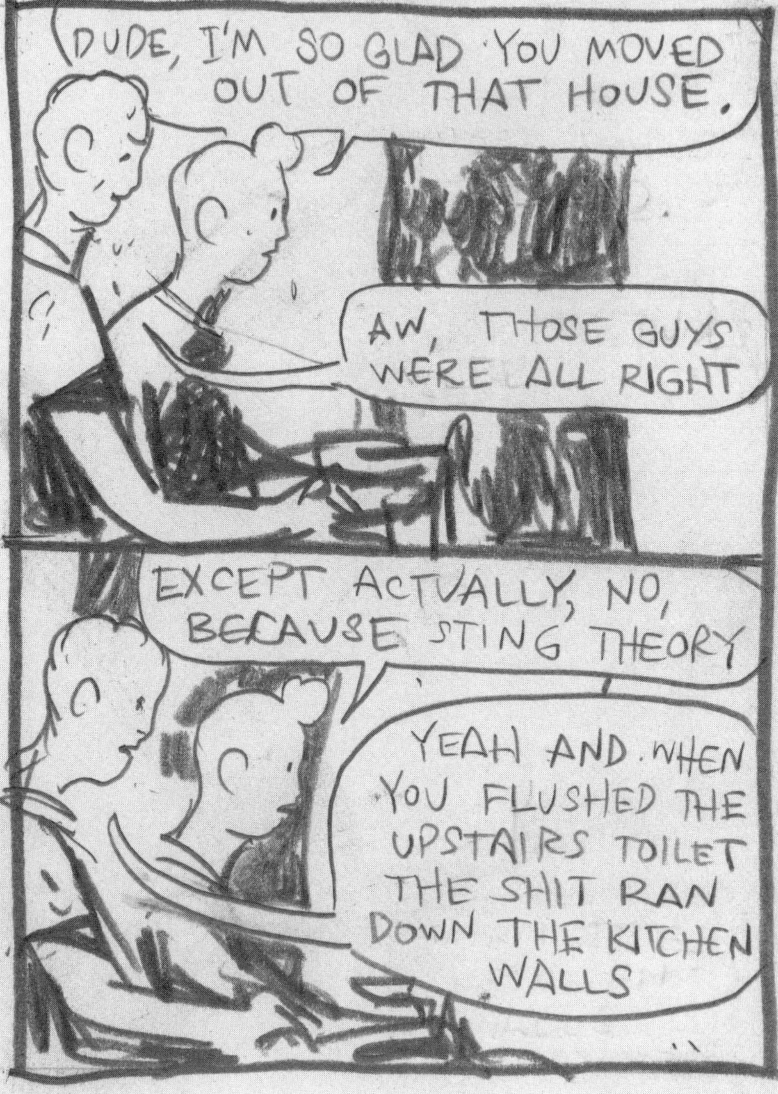
DUDE, I'M SO GLAD YOU MOVED OUT OF THAT HOUSE.
AW, THOSE GUYS WERE ALL RIGHT
EXCEPT ACTUALLY, NO, BECAUSE STING THEORY
YEAH AND WHEN YOU FLUSHED THE UPSTAIRS TOILET THE SHIT RAN DOWN THE KITCHEN WALLS

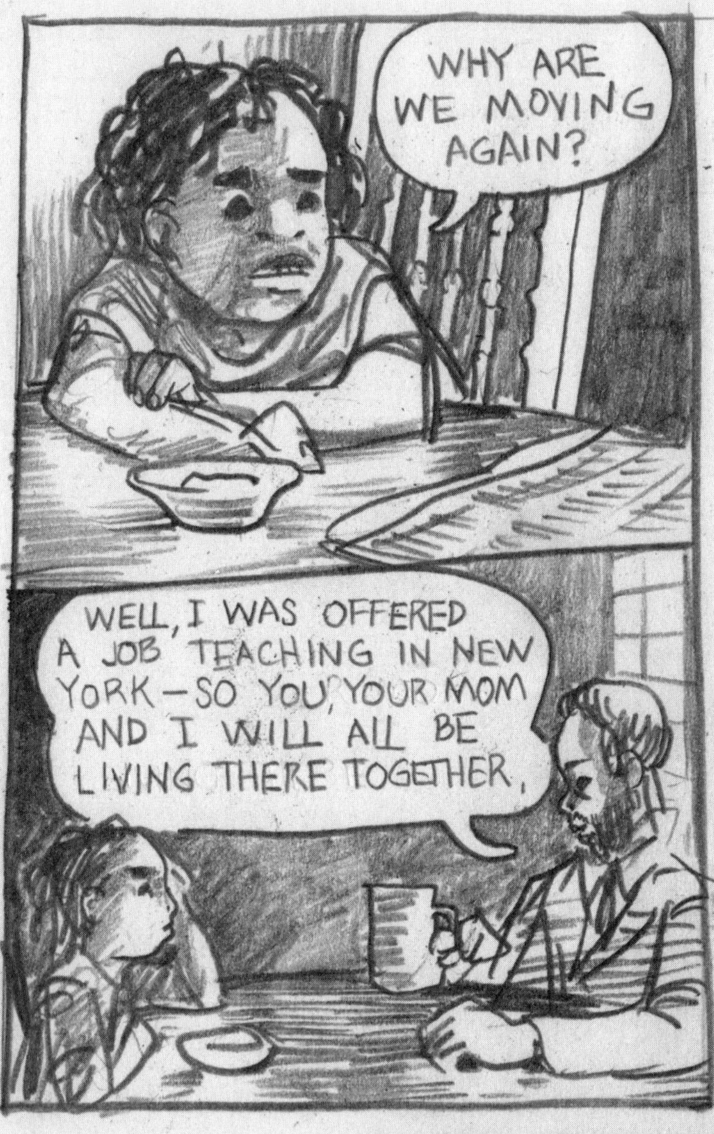
WHY ARE WE MOVING AGAIN?
WELL, I WAS OFFERED A JOB TEACHING IN NEW YORK—SO YOU, YOUR MOM AND I WILL ALL BE LIVING THERE TOGETHER.

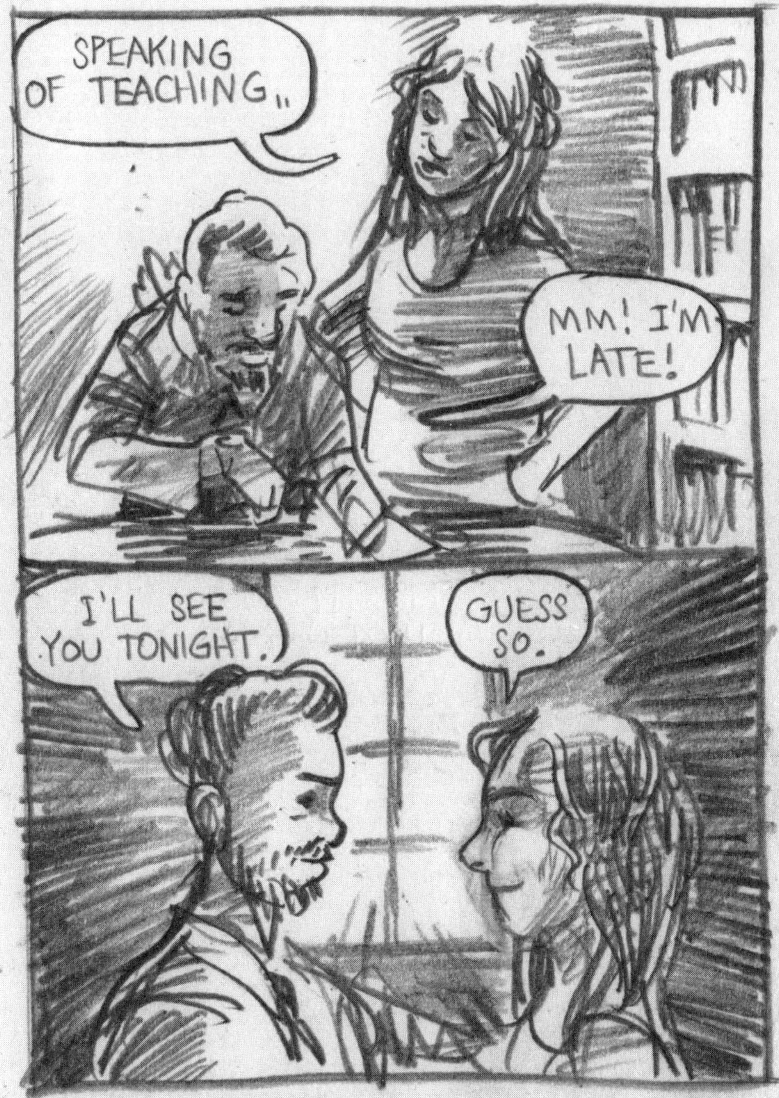
SPEAKING OF TEACHING..
MM! I'M LATE!
I'LL SEE YOU TONIGHT.
GUESS SO.

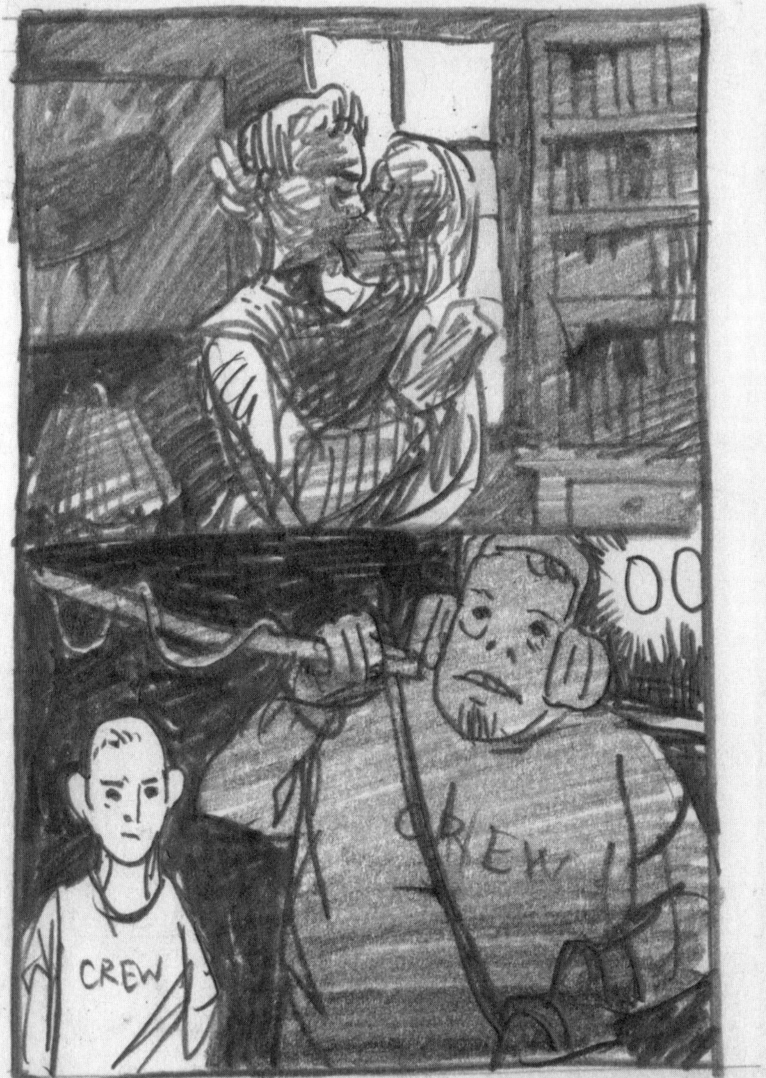
CREW
CREW

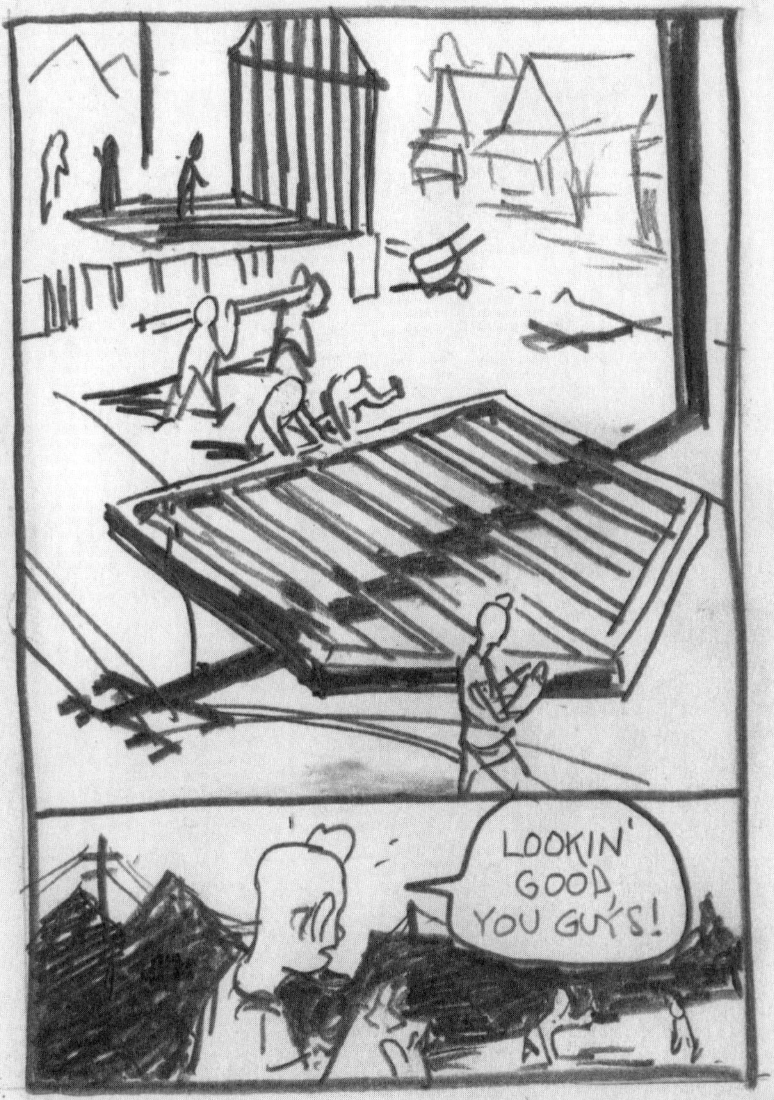
LOOKIN' GOOD, YOU GUYS!

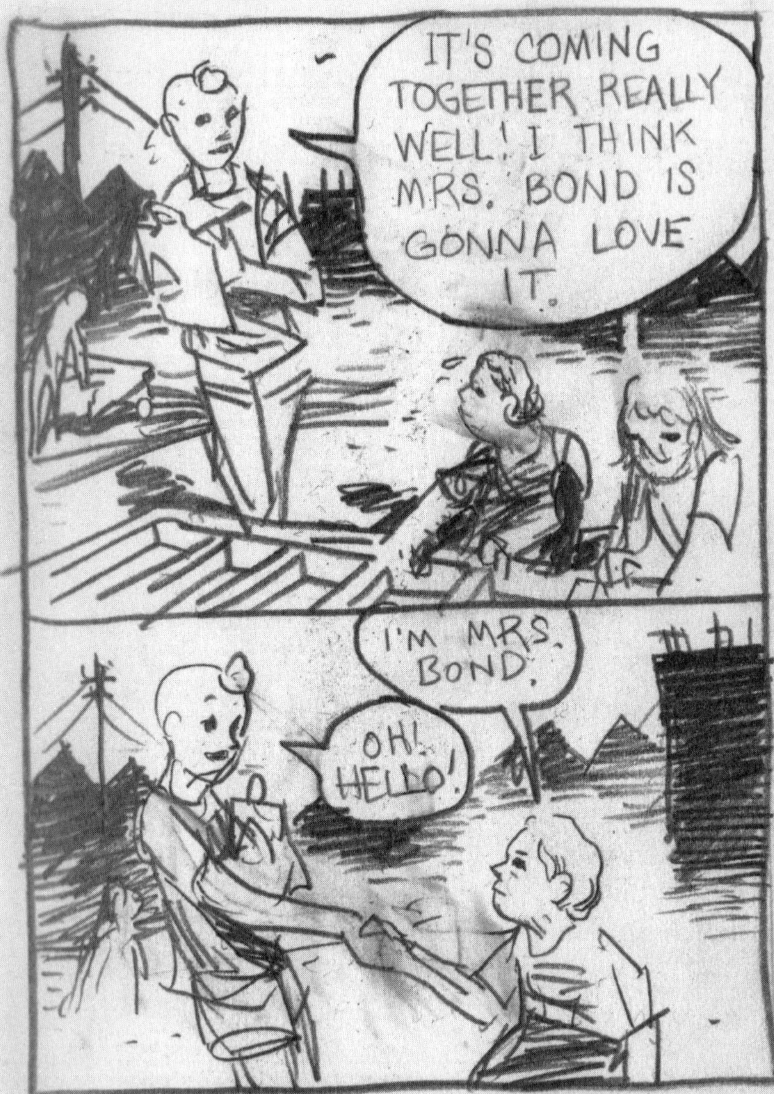
IT'S COMING TOGETHER REALLY WELL! I THINK MRS. BOND IS GONNA LOVE IT.
I'M MRS. BOND.
OH! HELLO!

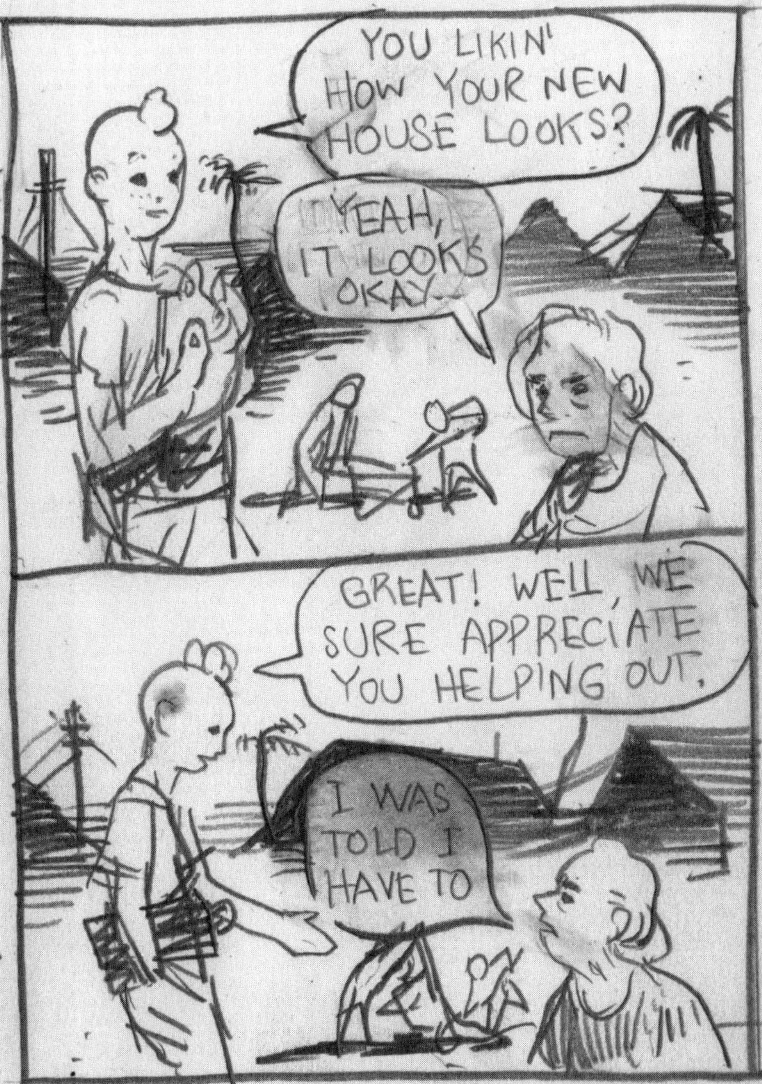
YOU LIKIN' HOW YOUR NEW HOUSE LOOKS?
YEAH, IT LOOKS OKAY.
GREAT! WELL, WE SURE APPRECIATE YOU HELPING OUT,
I WAS TOLD I HAVE TO

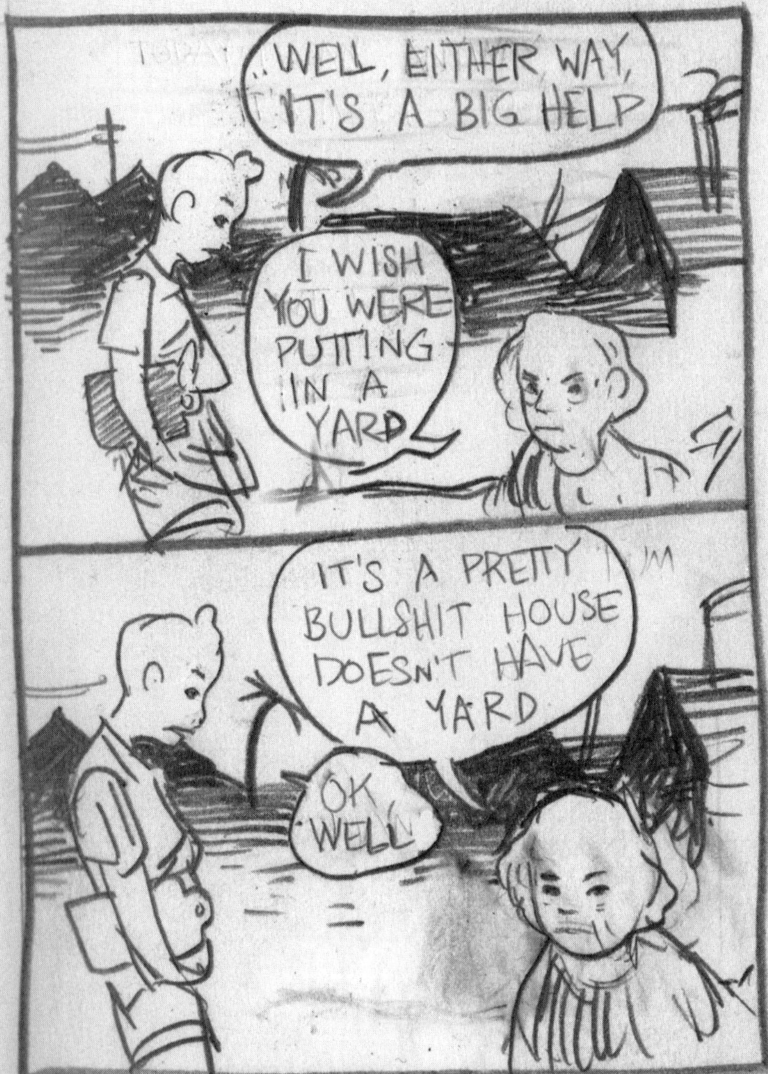
WELL, EITHER WAY, IT'S A BIG HELP
I WISH YOU WERE PUTTING IN A YARD
IT'S A PRETTY BULLSHIT HOUSE DOESN'T HAVE A YARD
OK WELL

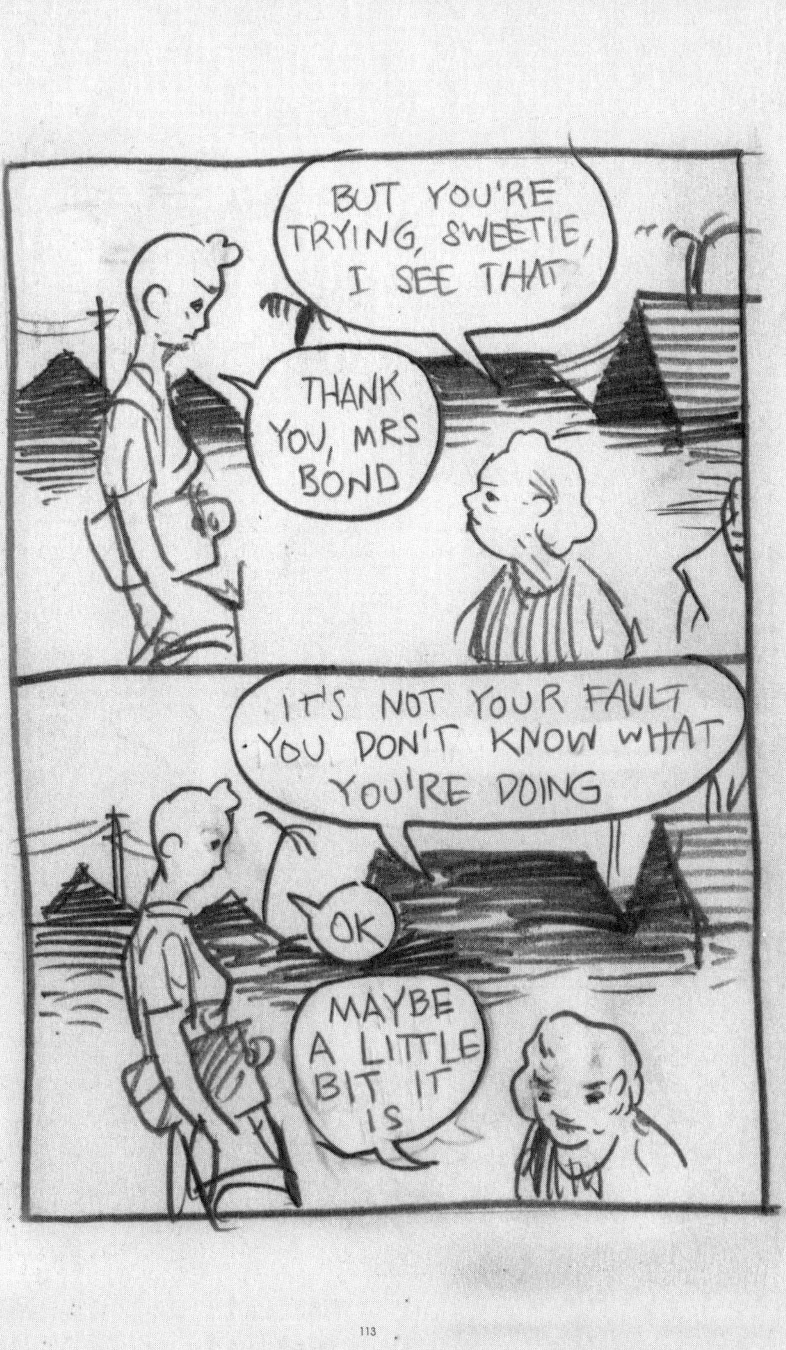
BUT YOU'RE TRYING, SWEETIE, I SEE THAT
THANK YOU, MRS BOND
IT'S NOT YOUR FAULT YOU DON'T KNOW WHAT YOU'RE DOING
OK
MAYBE A LITTLE BIT IT IS

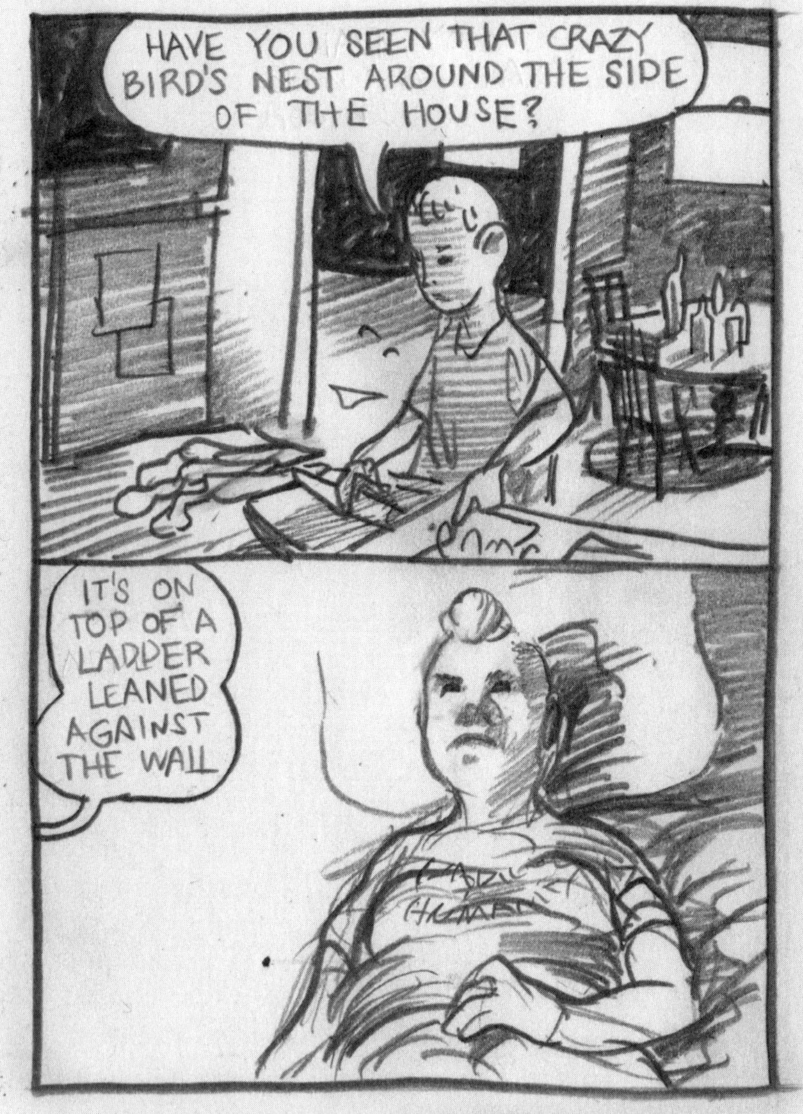
HAVE YOU SEEN THAT CRAZY BIRD'S NEST AROUND THE SIDE OF THE HOUSE?
IT'S ON TOP OF A LADDER LEANED AGAINST THE WALL

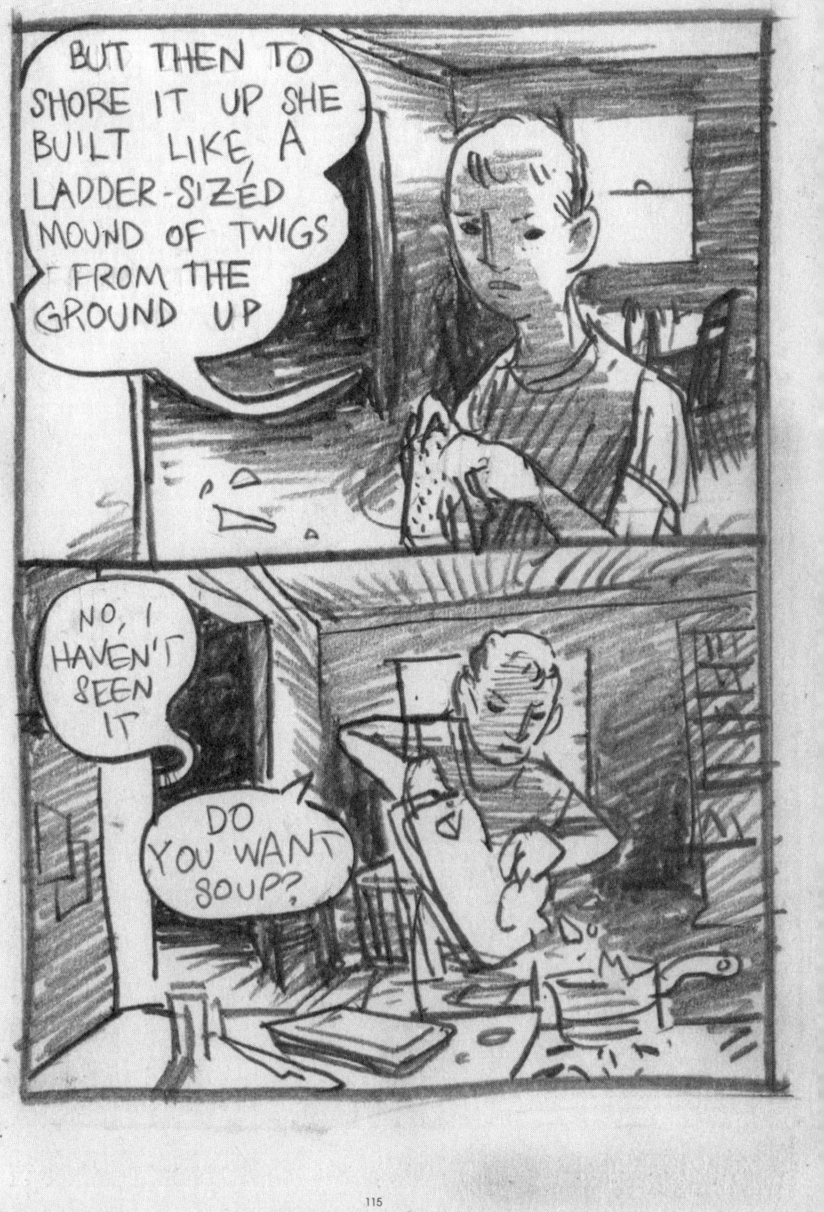
BUT THEN TO SHORE IT UP SHE BUILT LIKE, A LADDER-SIZED MOUND OF TWIGS FROM THE GROUND UP
NO, I HAVEN'T SEEN IT
DO YOU WANT SOUP?

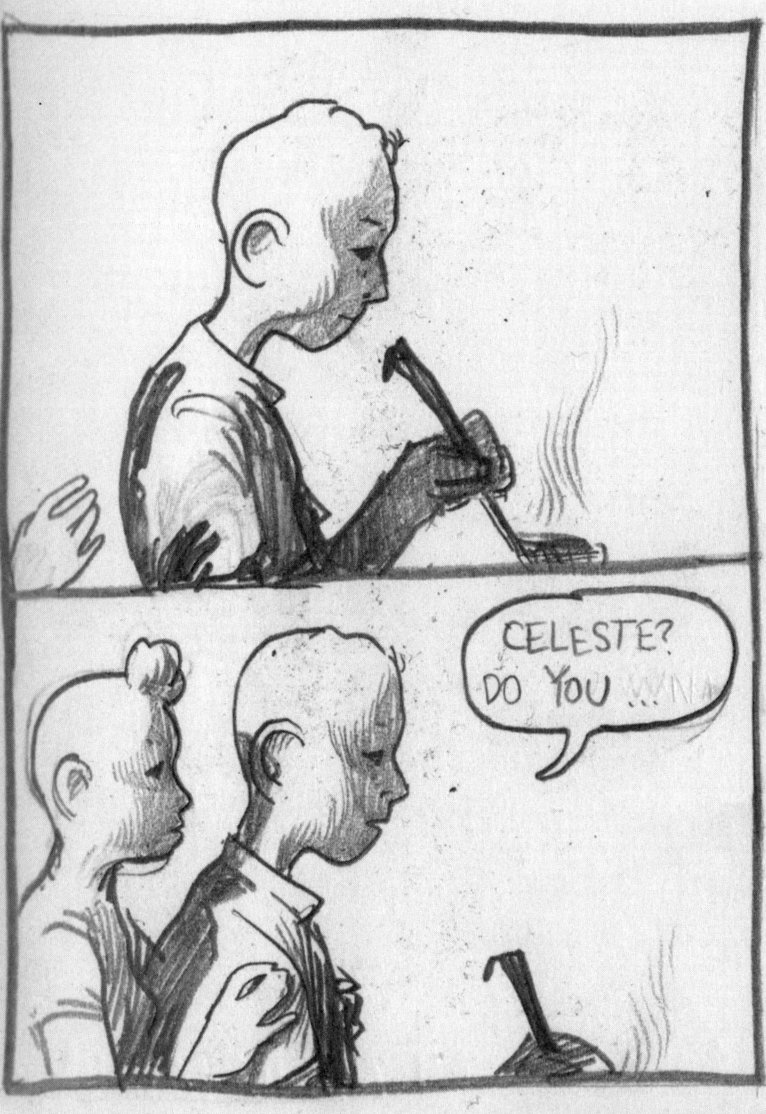
CELESTE?
DO YOU ...

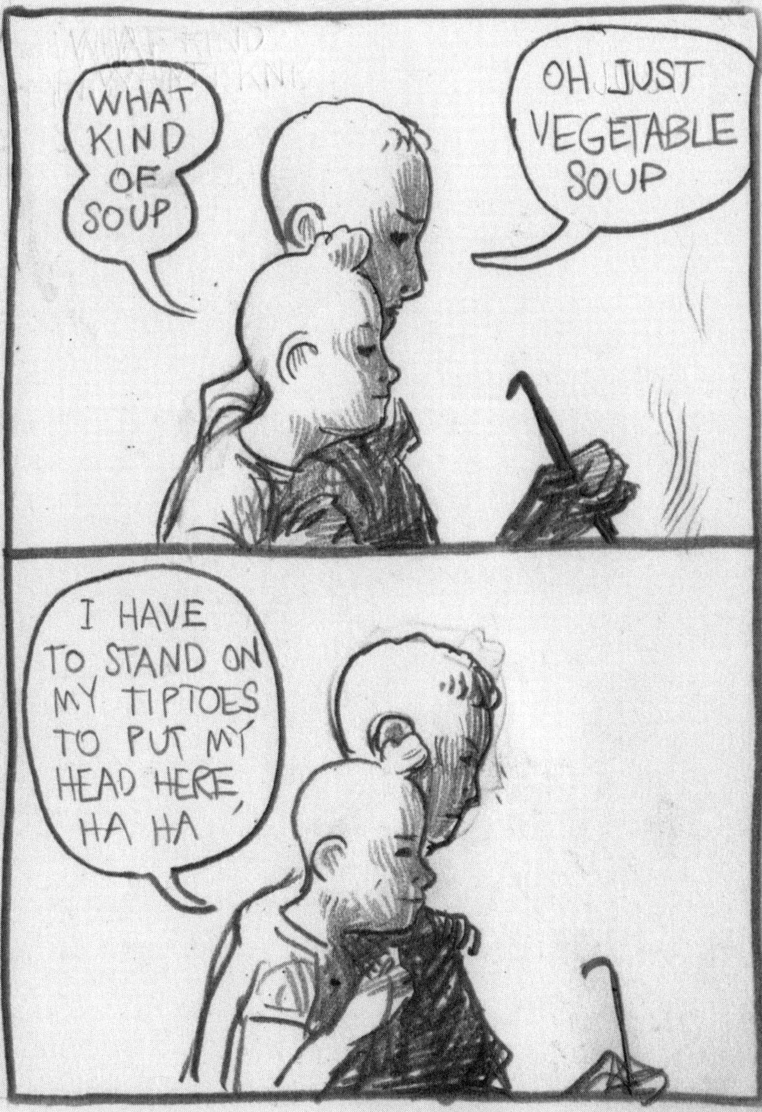
WHAT KIND OF SOUP
OH JUST VEGETABLE SOUP
I HAVE TO STAND ON MY TIPTOES TO PUT MY HEAD HERE, HA HA

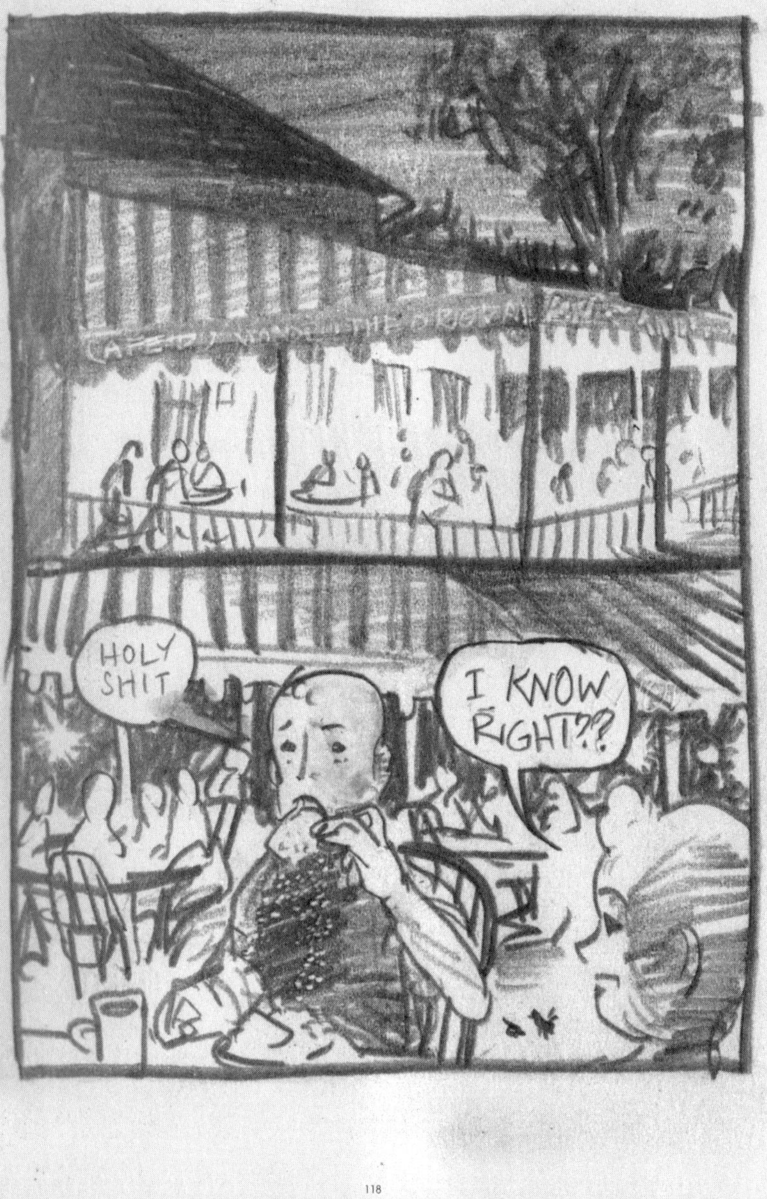
HOLY SHIT
I KNOW RIGHT??

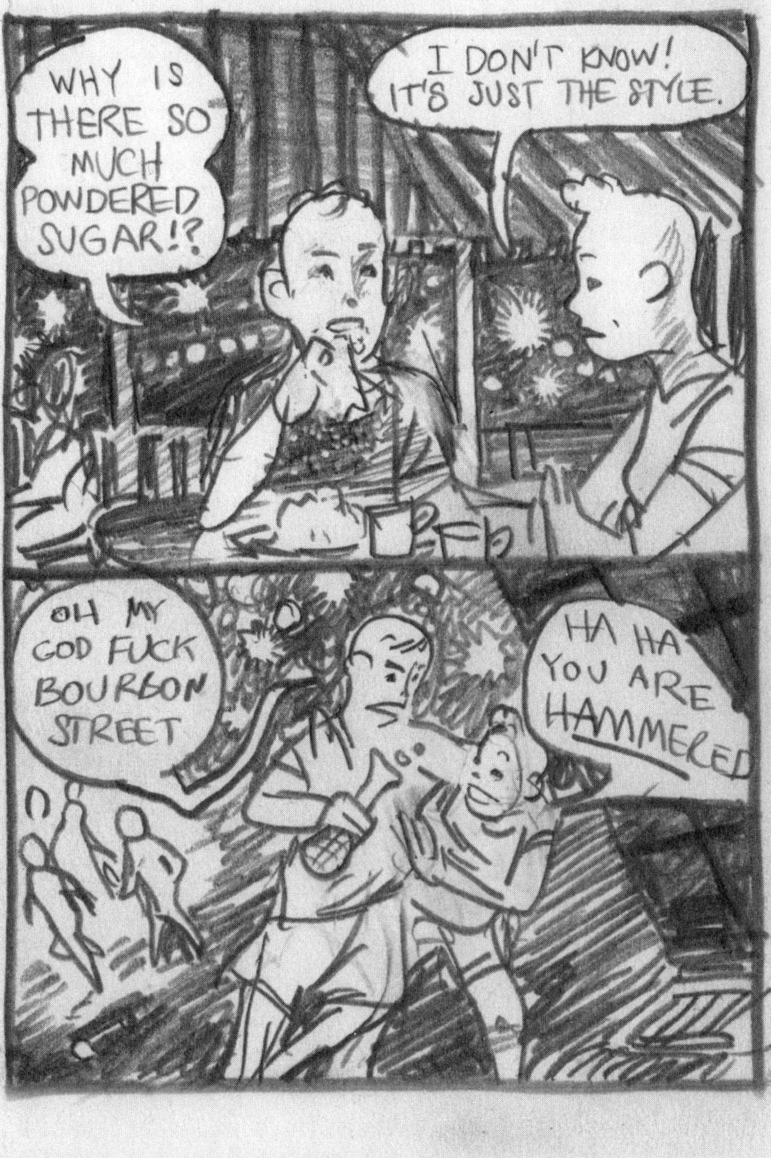
WHY IS THERE SO MUCH POWDERED SUGAR!?
I DON'T KNOW! IT'S JUST THE STYLE.
OH MY GOD FUCK BOURBON STREET
HA HA YOU ARE HAMMERED

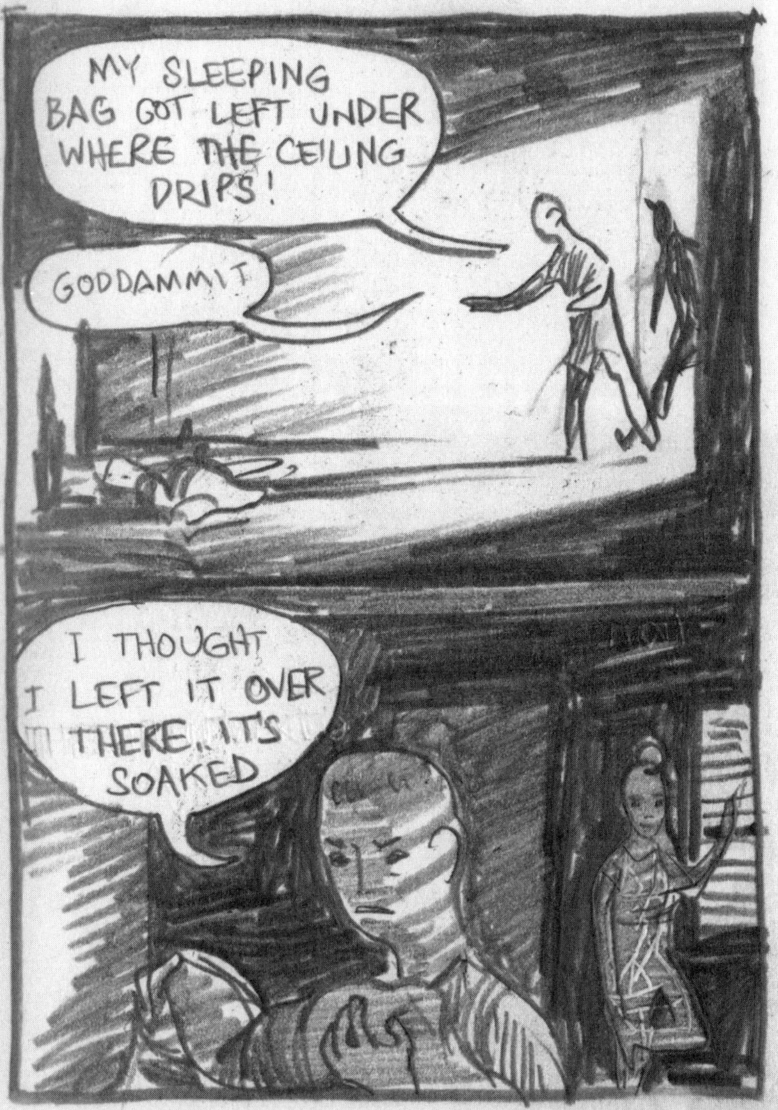
MY SLEEPING BAG GOT LEFT UNDER WHERE THE CEILING DRIPS!
GODDAMMIT
I THOUGHT I LEFT IT OVER THERE. IT'S SOAKED

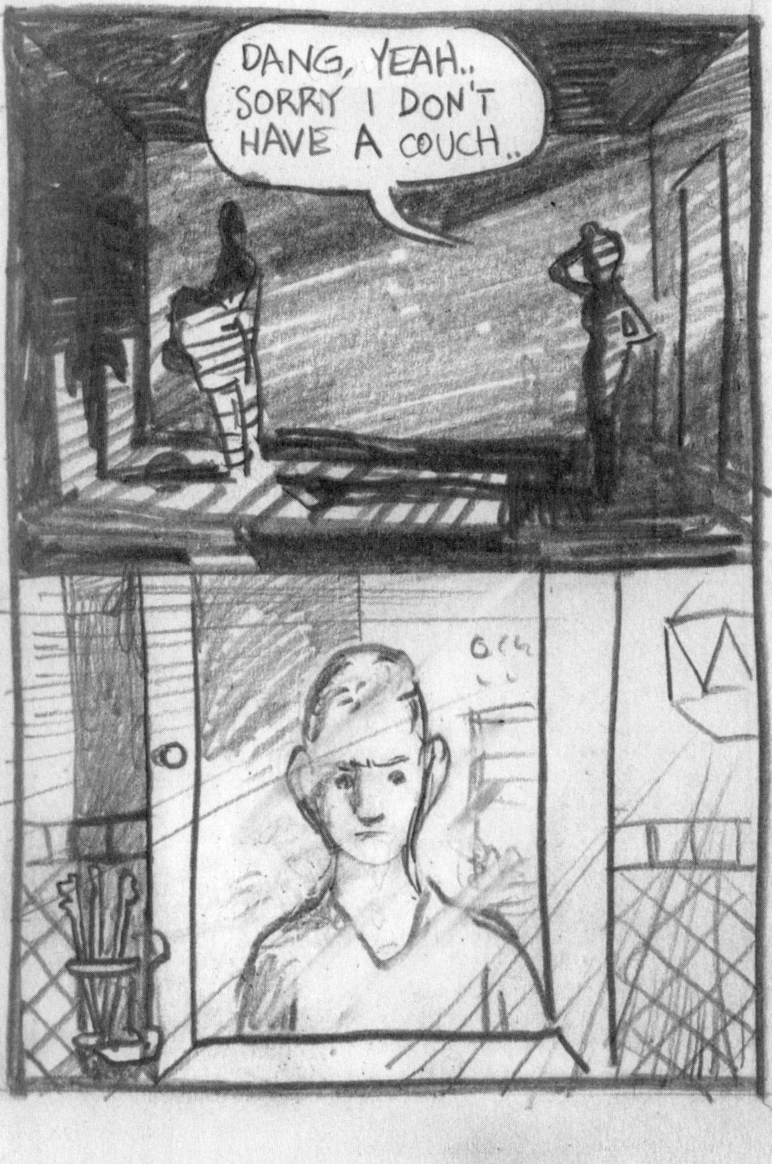
DANG, YEAH.. SORRY I DON'T HAVE A COUCH..

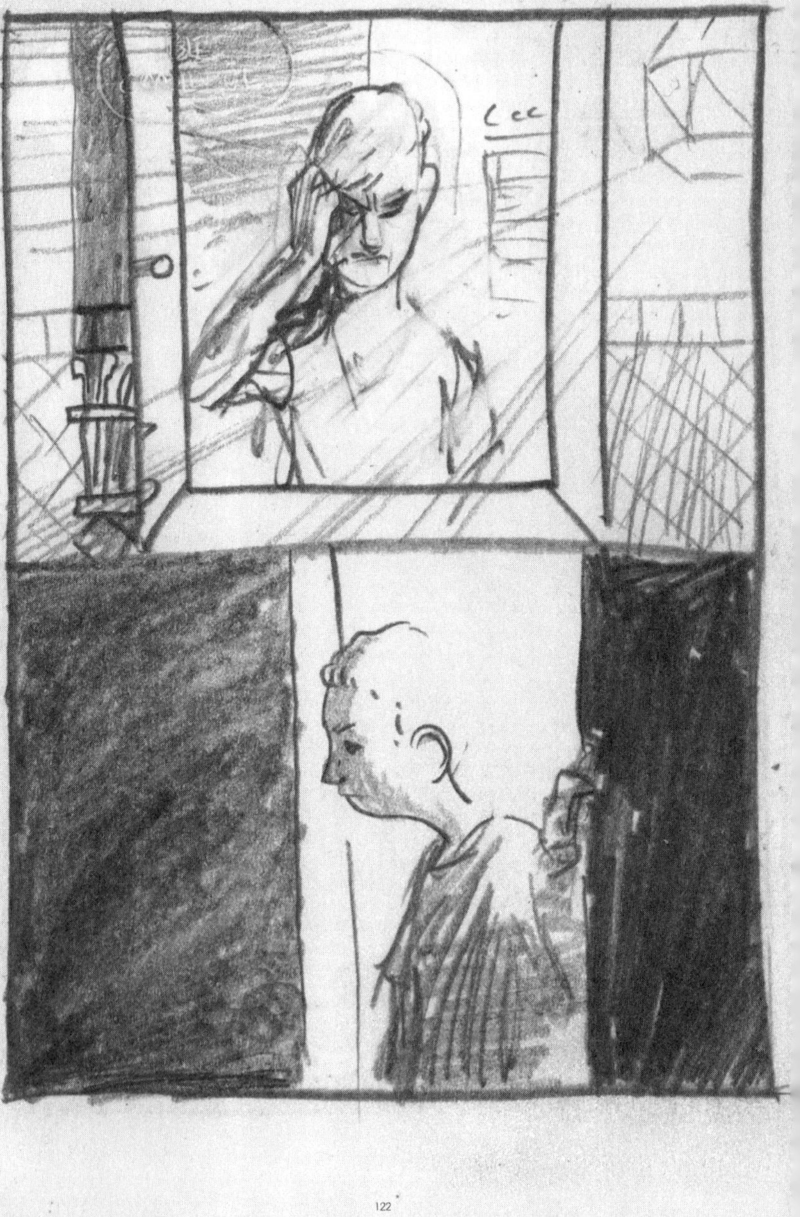

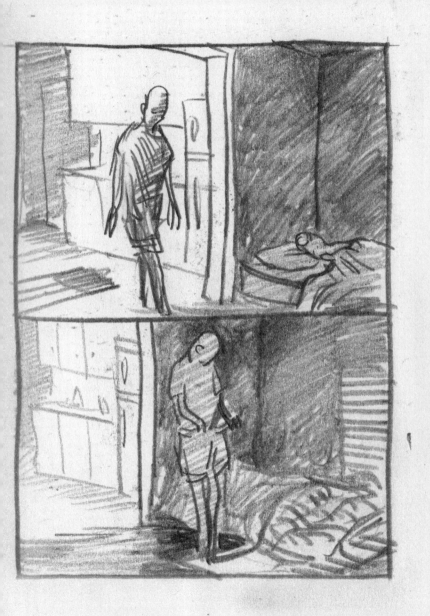

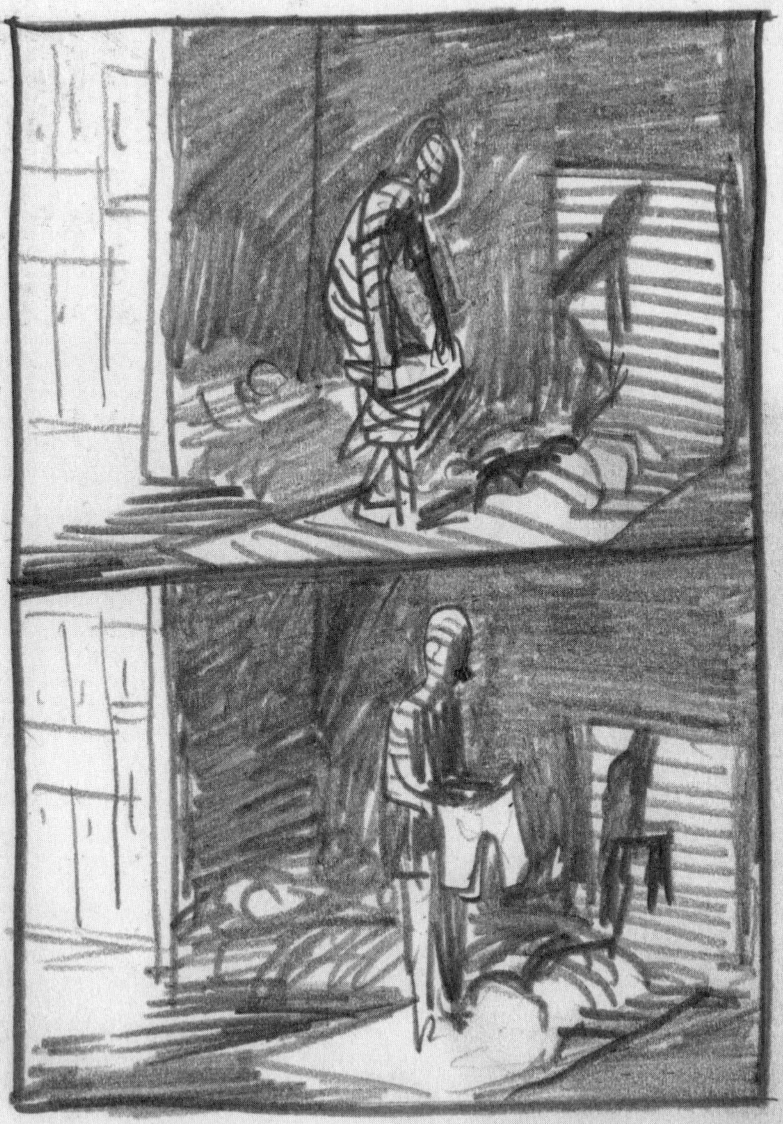

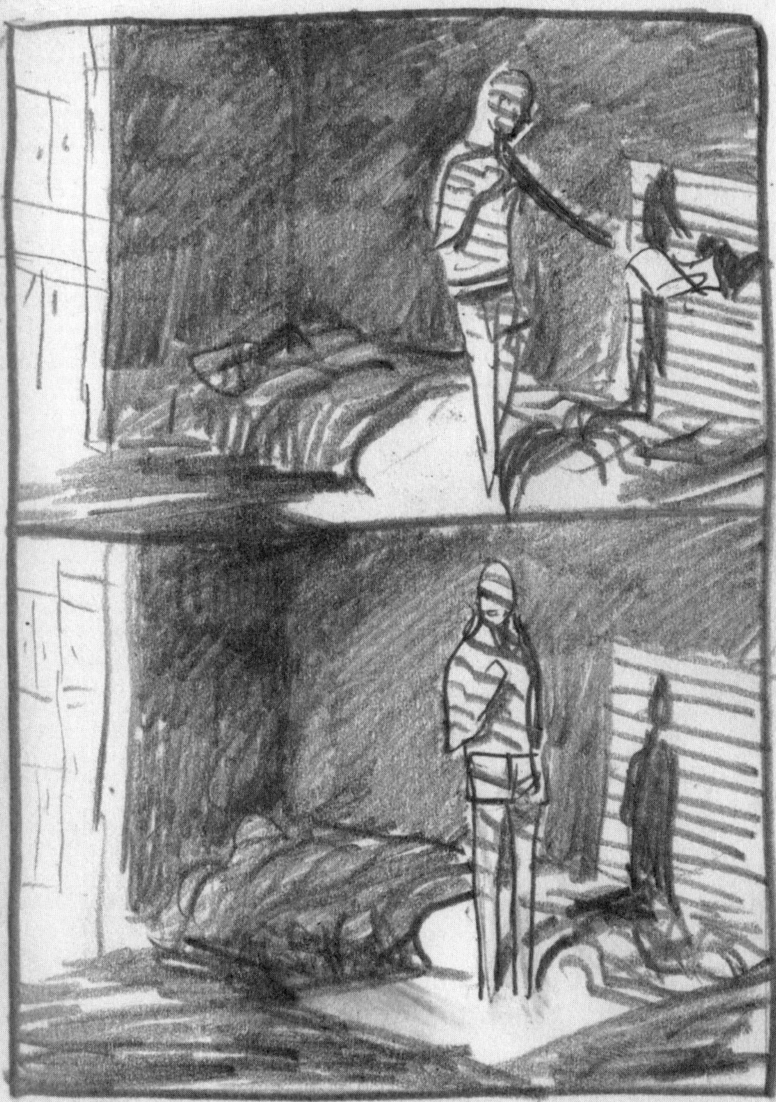

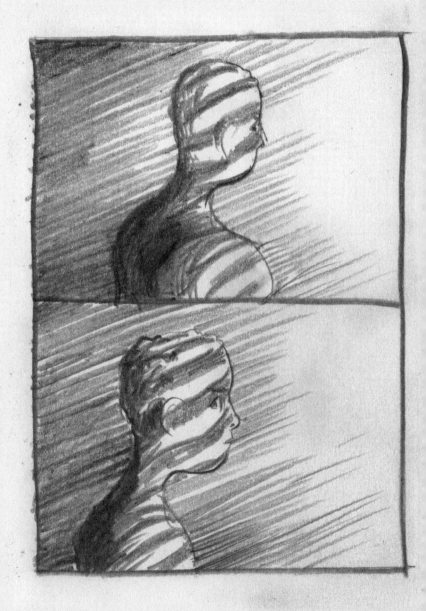

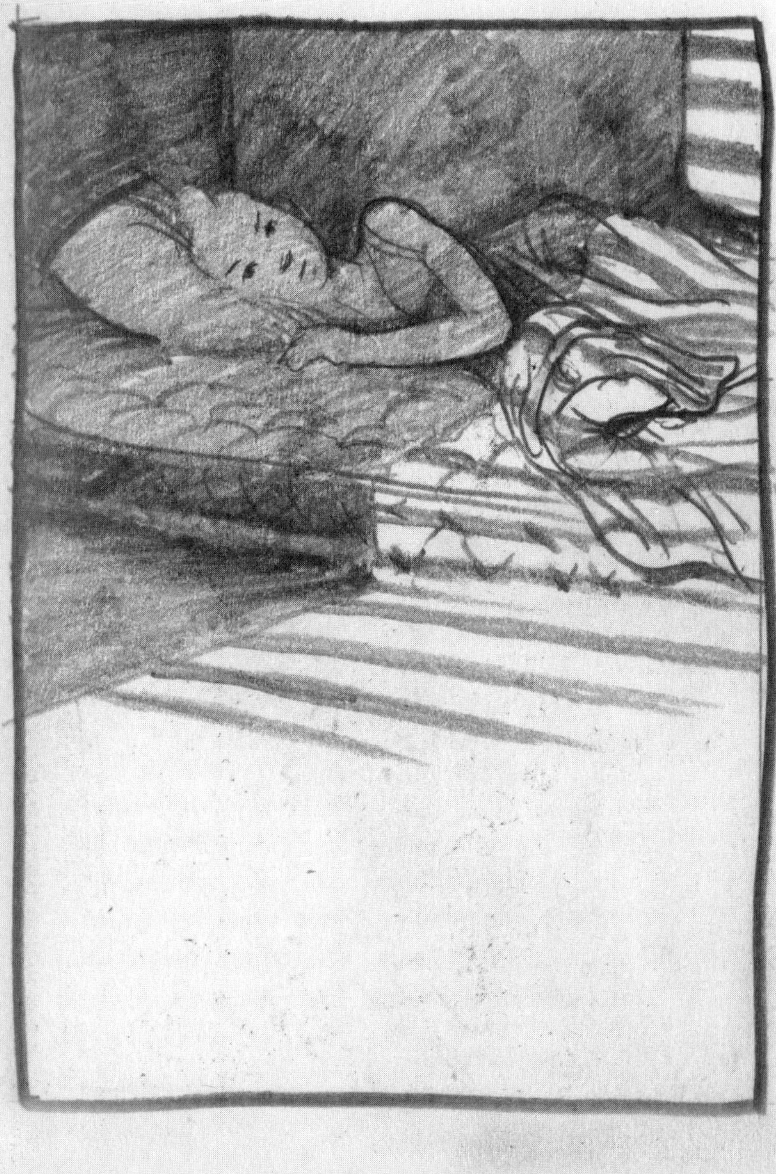

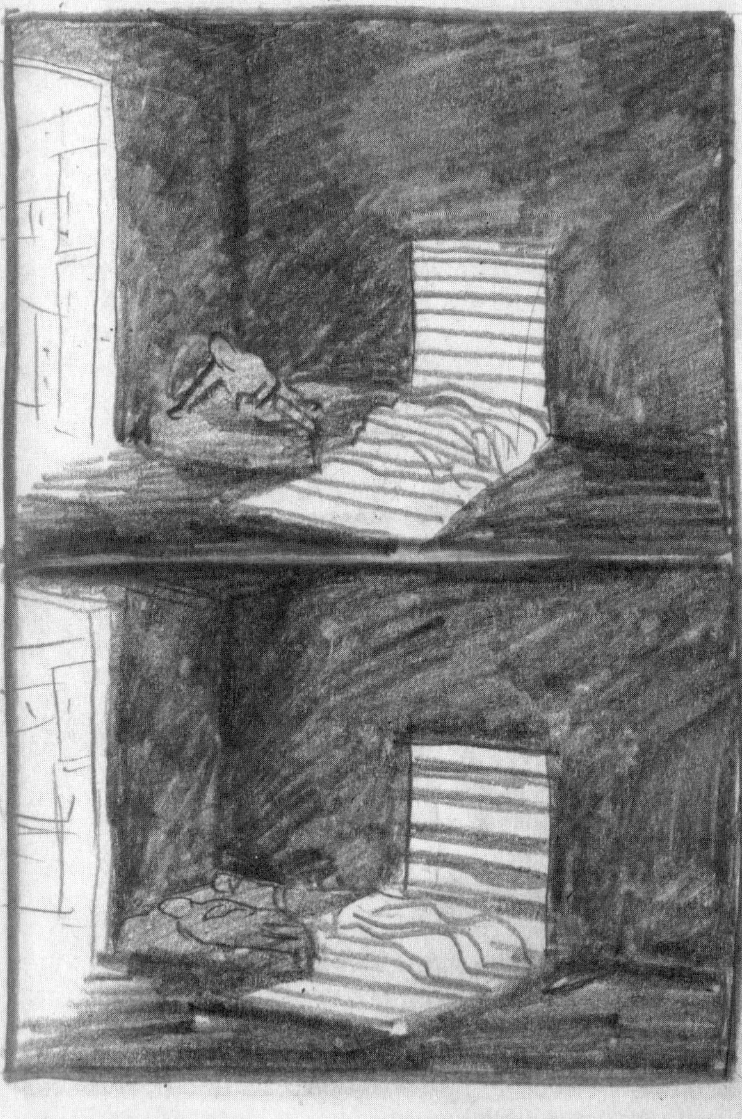

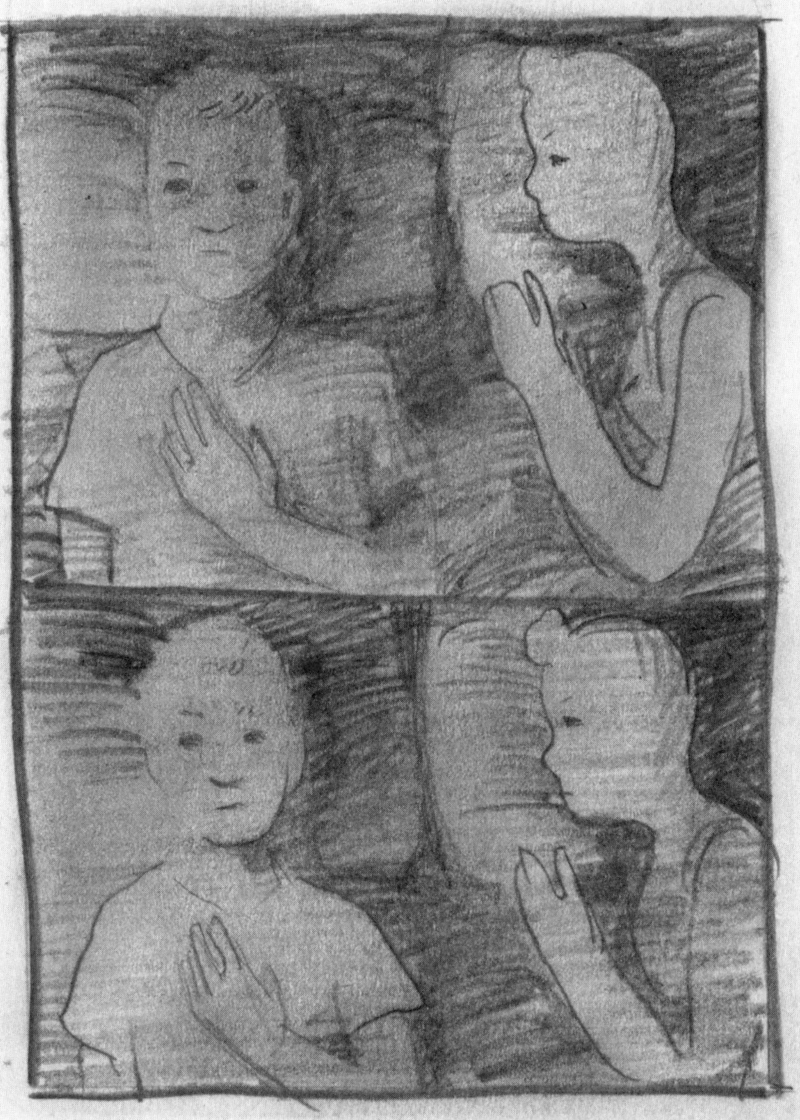

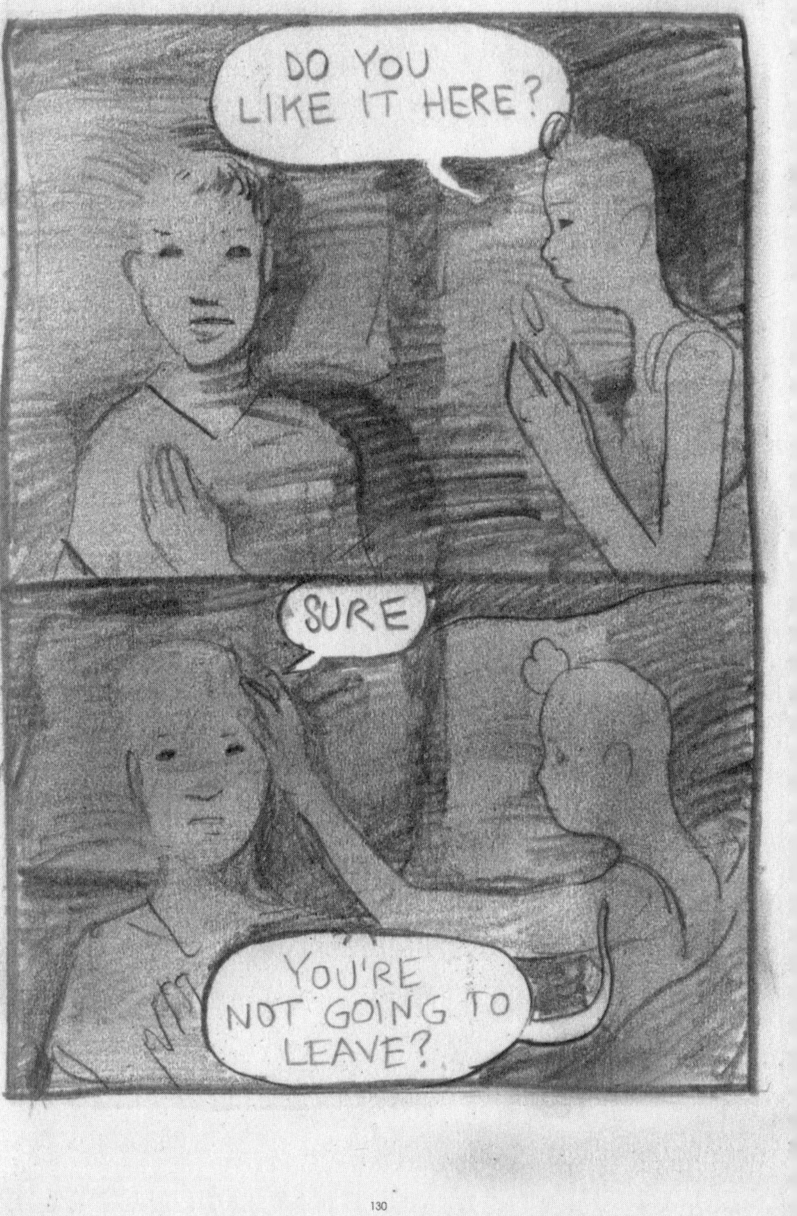
DO YOU LIKE IT HERE?
SURE
YOU'RE NOT GOING TO LEAVE?

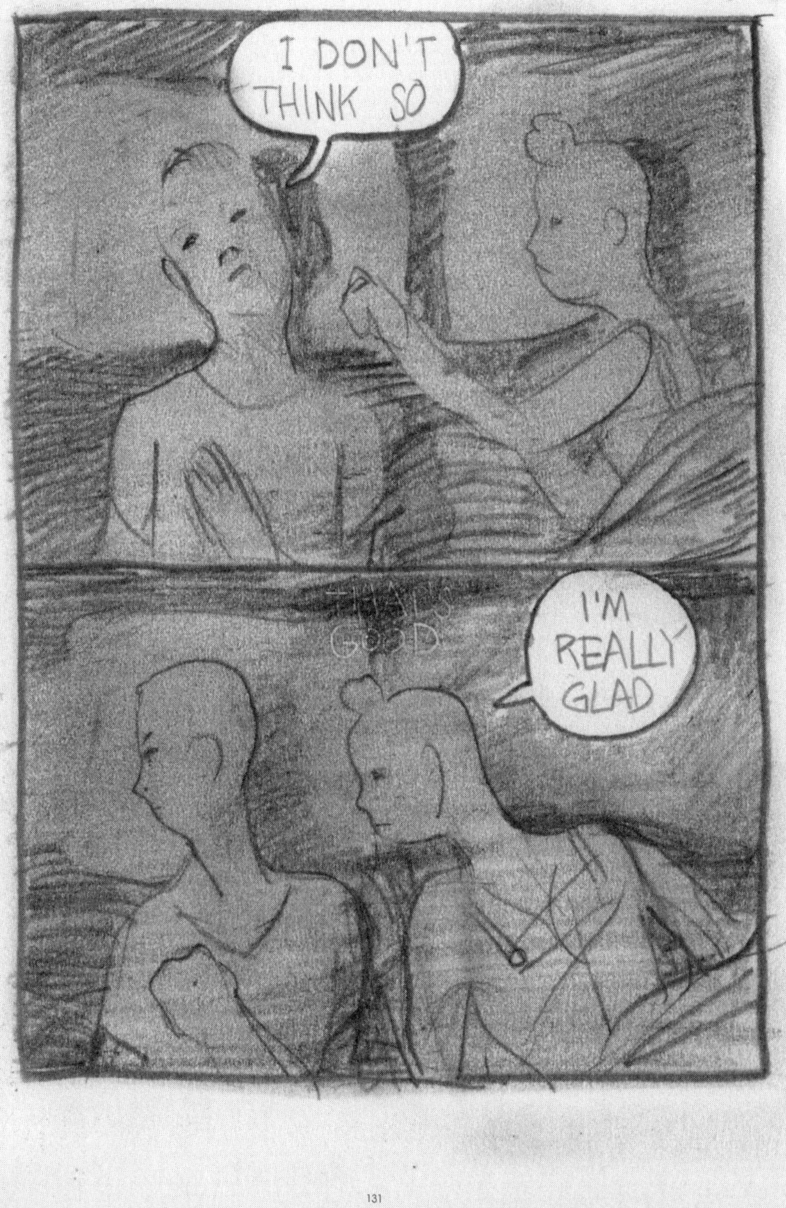
I DON'T THINK SO
THAT'S GOOD
I'M REALLY GLAD

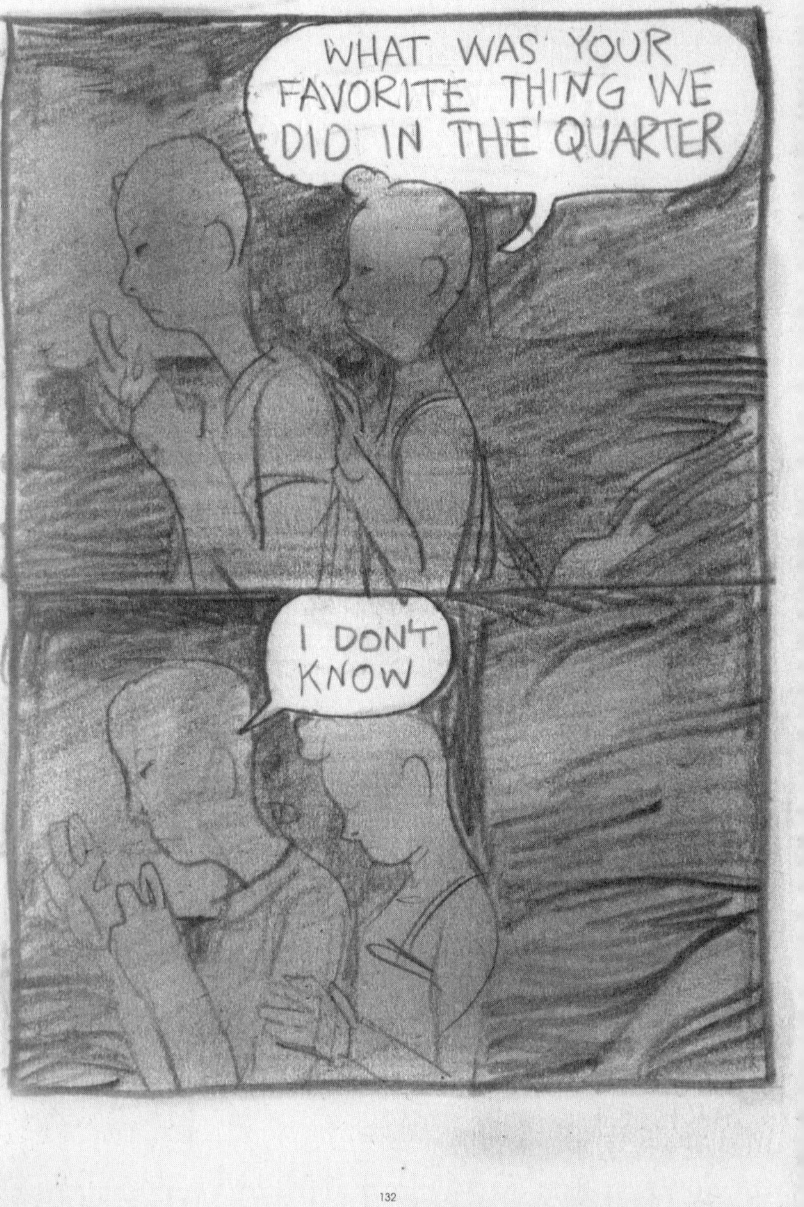
WHAT WAS YOUR FAVORITE THING WE DID IN THE QUARTER
I DON'T KNOW

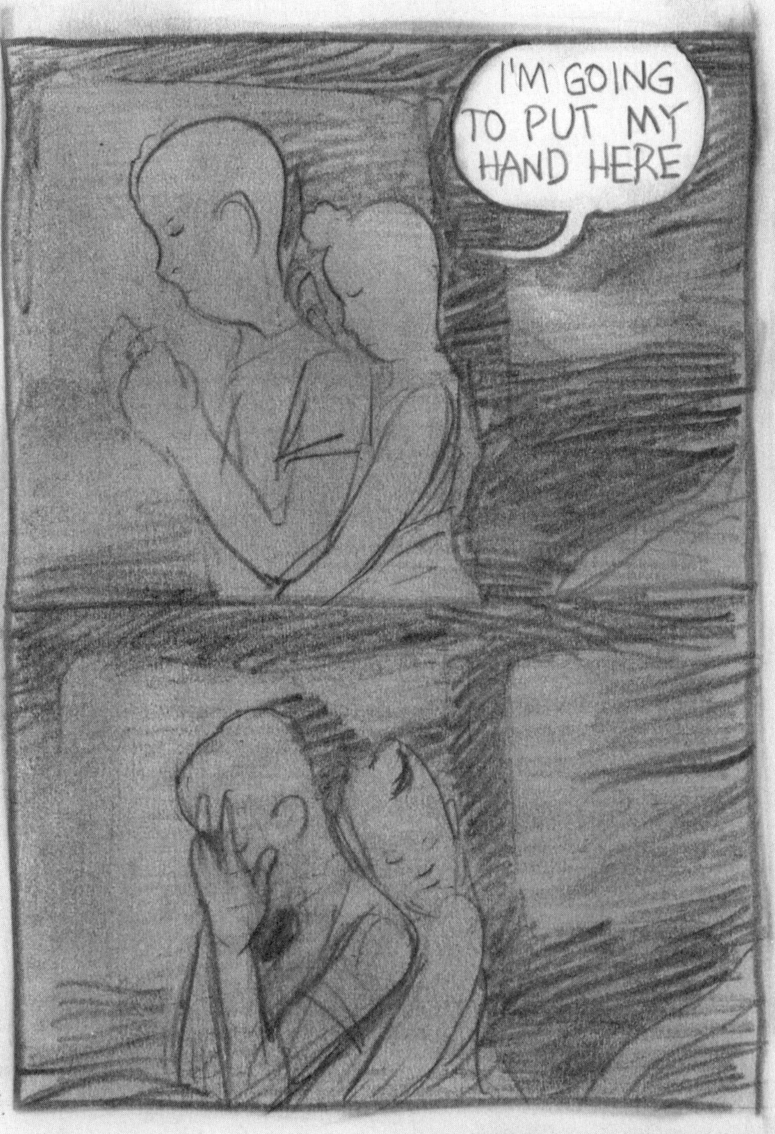
I'M GOING TO PUT MY HAND HERE

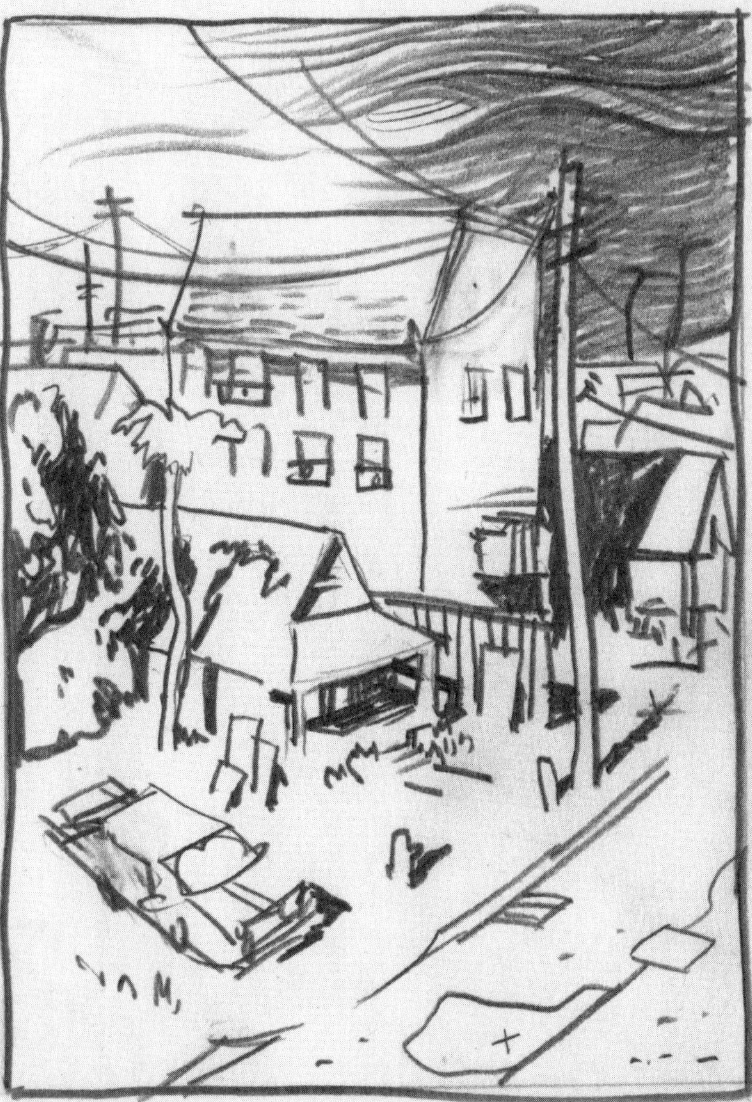

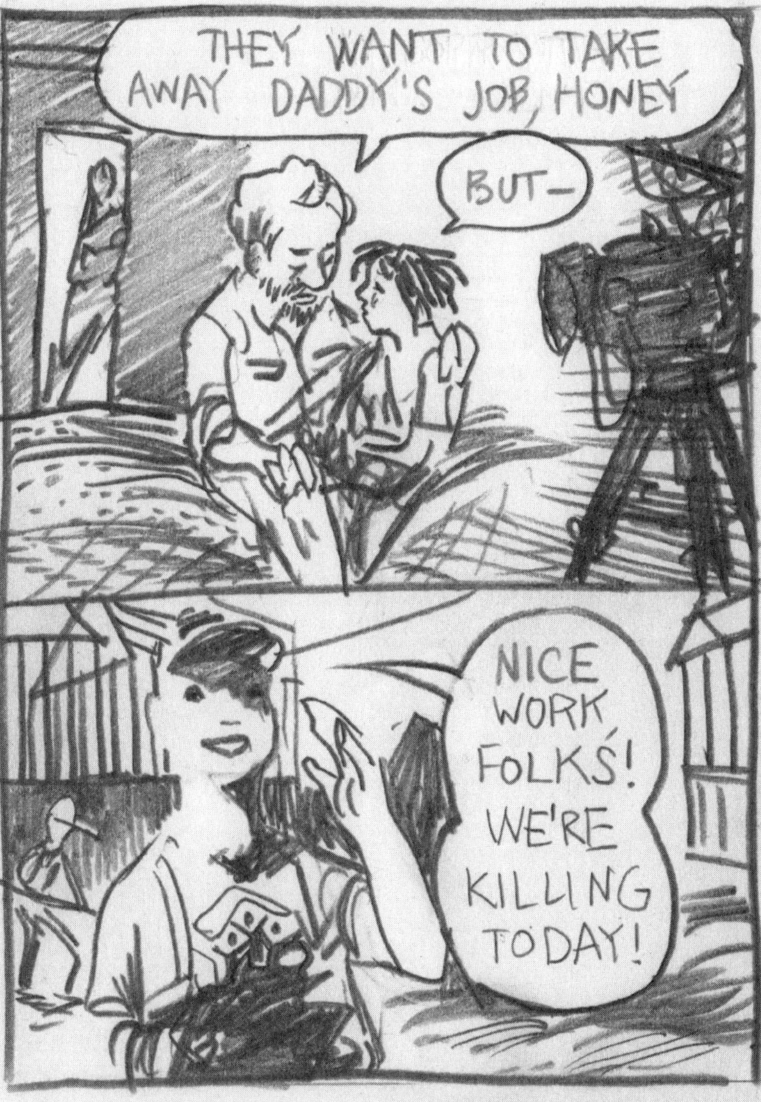
THEY WANT TO TAKE AWAY DADDY'S JOB, HONEY
BUT–
NICE WORK FOLKS! WE'RE KILLING TODAY!

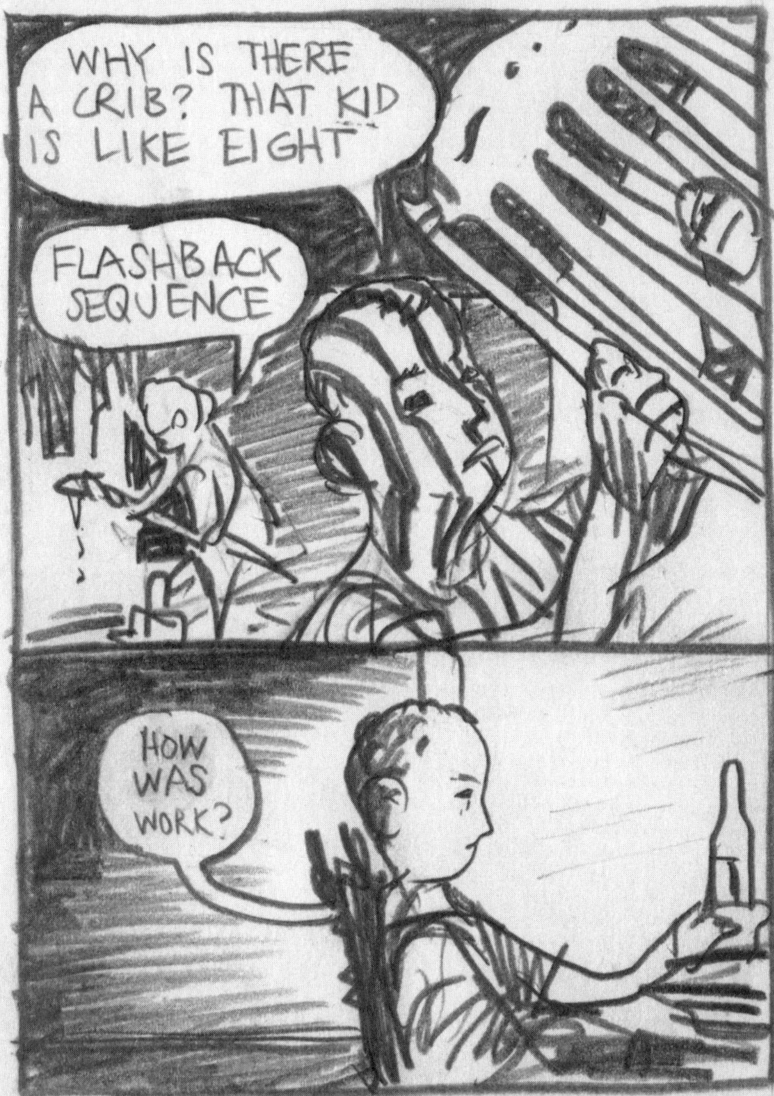
WHY IS THERE A CRIB? THAT KID IS LIKE EIGHT
FLASHBACK SEQUENCE
HOW WAS WORK?

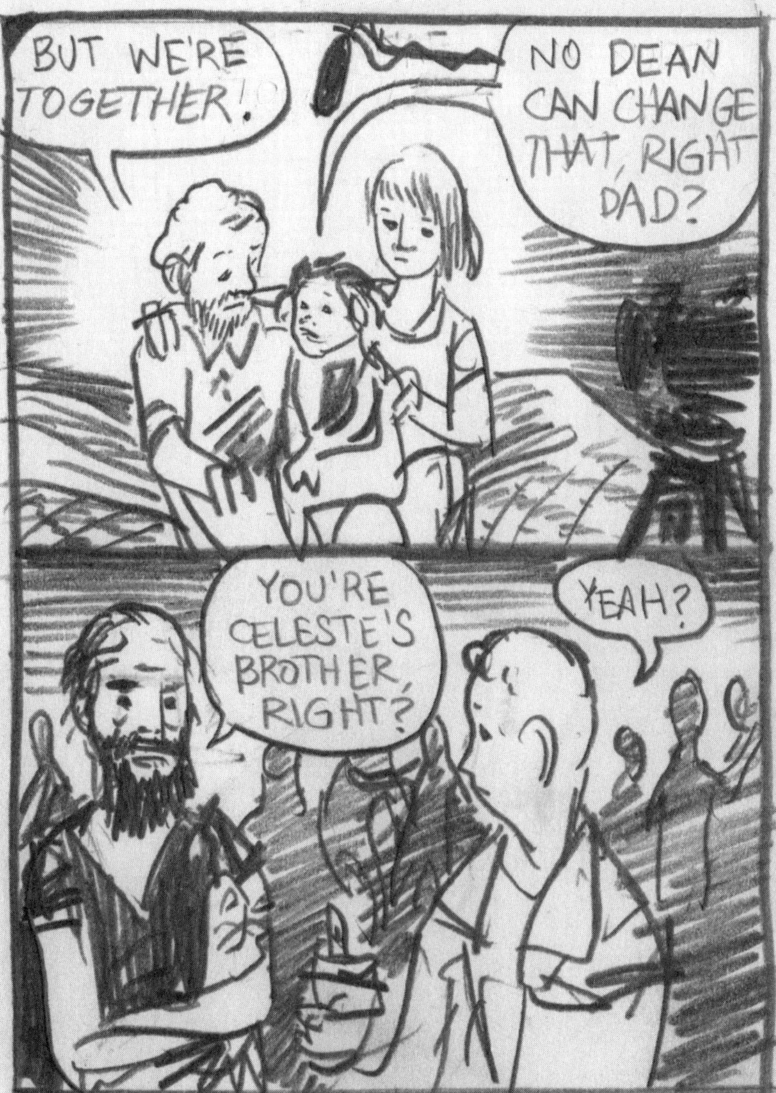
BUT WE'RE TOGETHER!
NO DEAN CAN CHANGE THAT, RIGHT DAD?
YOU'RE CELESTE'S BROTHER, RIGHT?
YEAH?

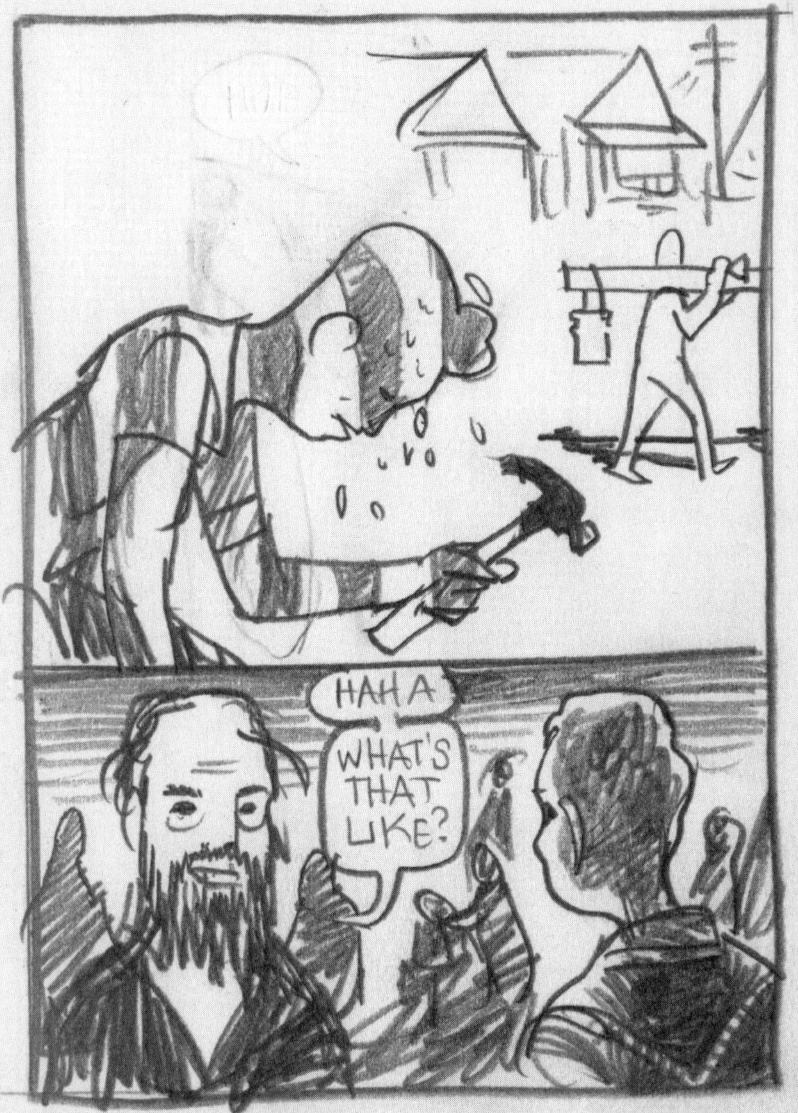
HAHA
WHAT'S THAT LIKE?

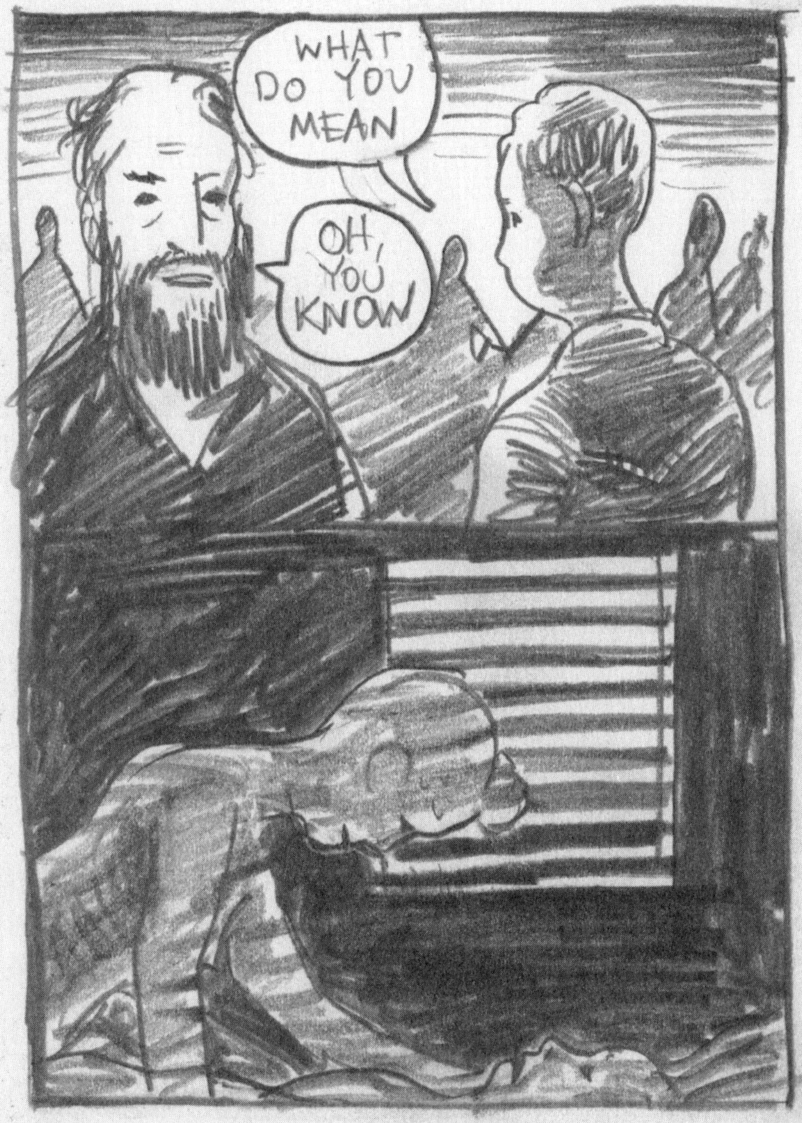
WHAT DO YOU MEAN
OH, YOU KNOW

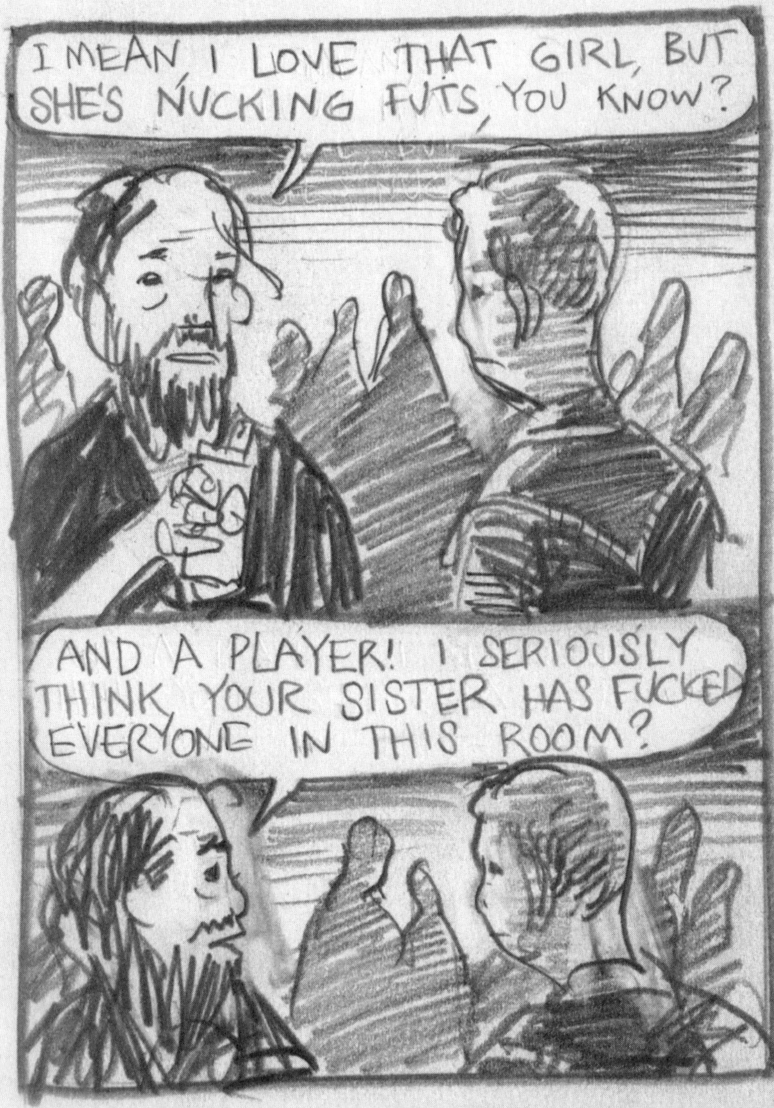
I MEAN I LOVE THAT GIRL, BUT SHE'S NUCKING FUTS, YOU KNOW?
AND A PLAYER! I SERIOUSLY THINK YOUR SISTER HAS FUCKED EVERYONE IN THIS ROOM?

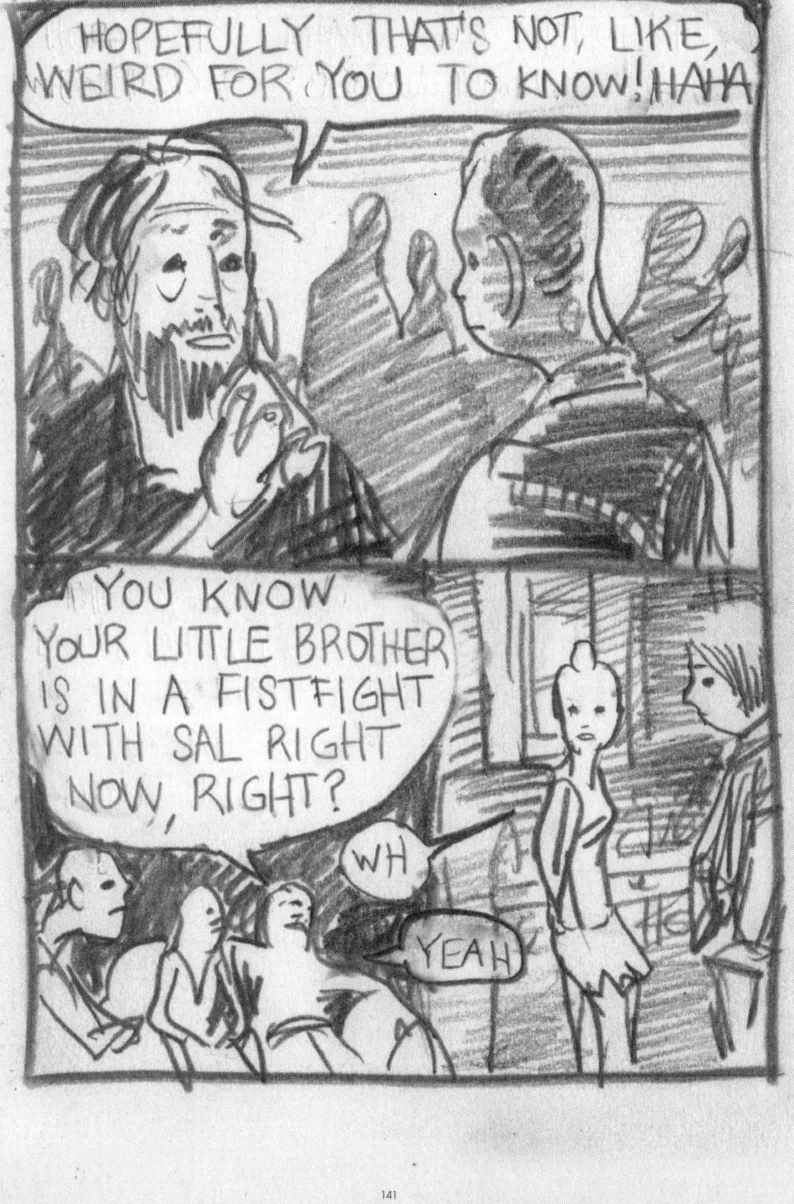
HOPEFULLY THAT'S NOT, LIKE, WEIRD FOR YOU TO KNOW! HAHA
YOU KNOW YOUR LITTLE BROTHER IS IN A FISTFIGHT WITH SAL RIGHT NOW, RIGHT?
WH
YEAH

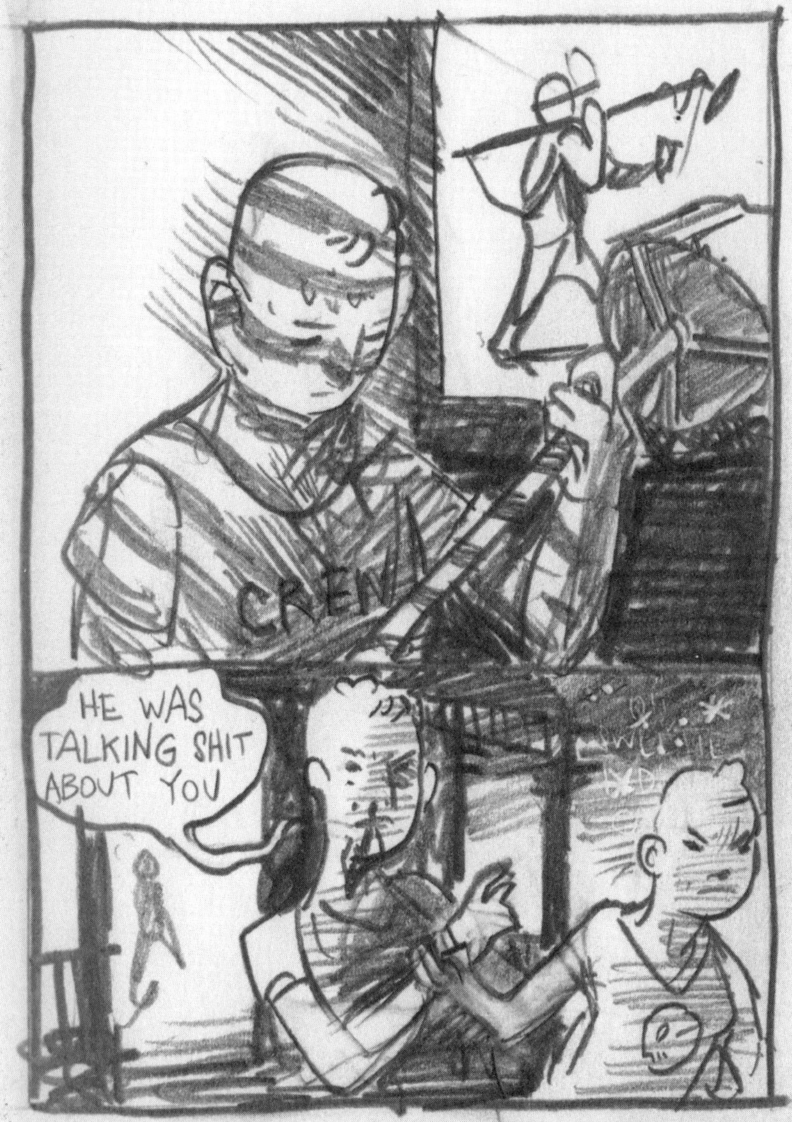
CREW
HE WAS TALKING SHIT ABOUT YOU

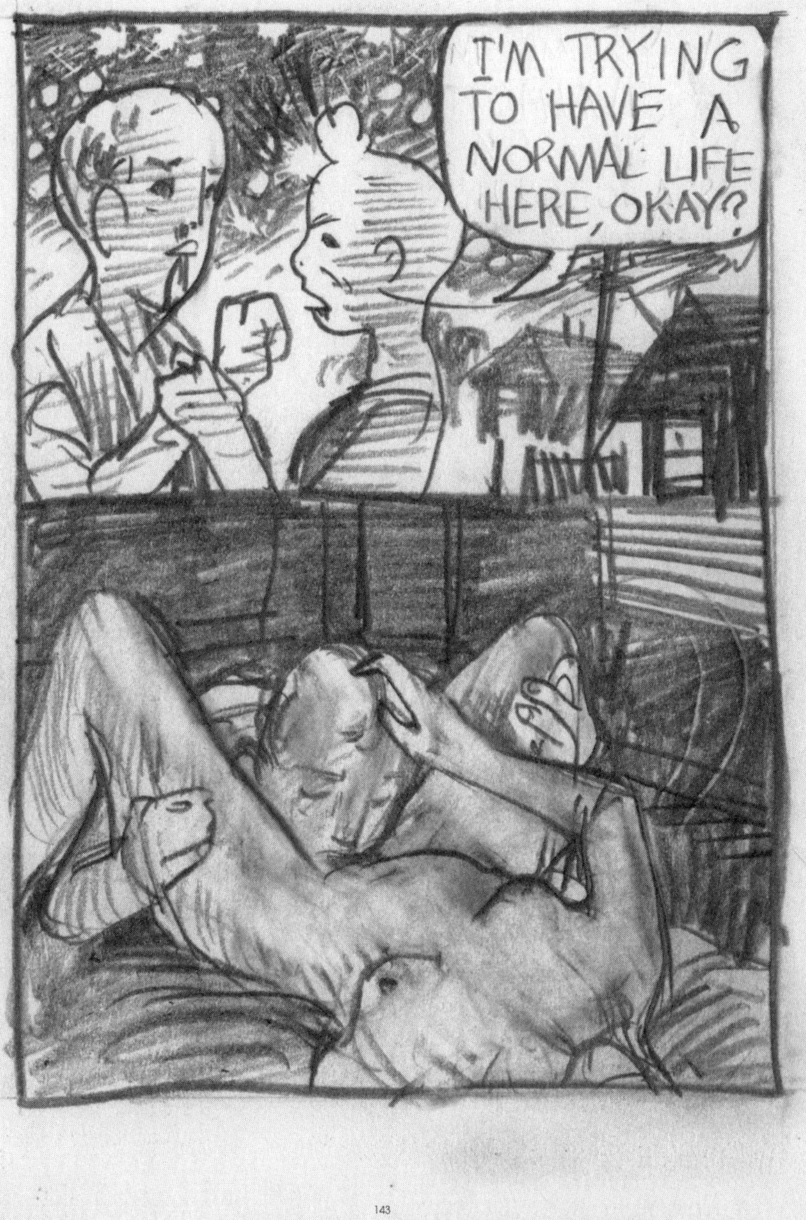
I'M TRYING TO HAVE A NORMAL LIFE HERE, OKAY?

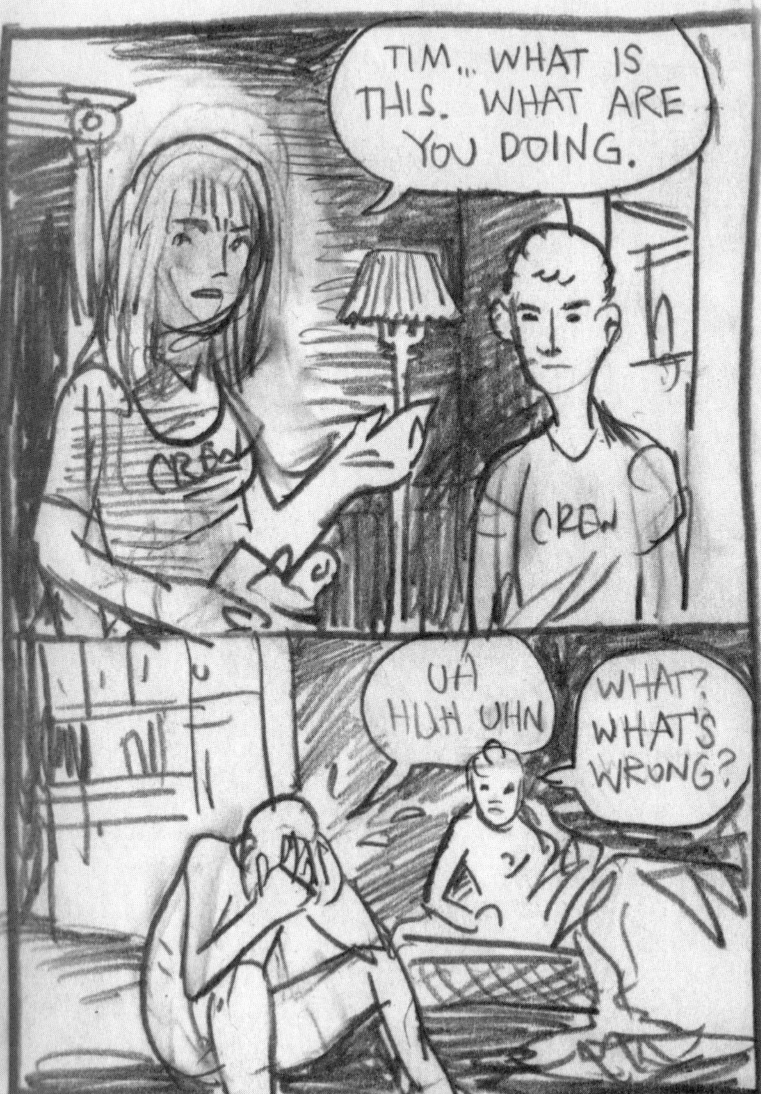
TIM... WHAT IS THIS. WHAT ARE YOU DOING.
CREW
UH HUH UHN
WHAT? WHAT'S WRONG?

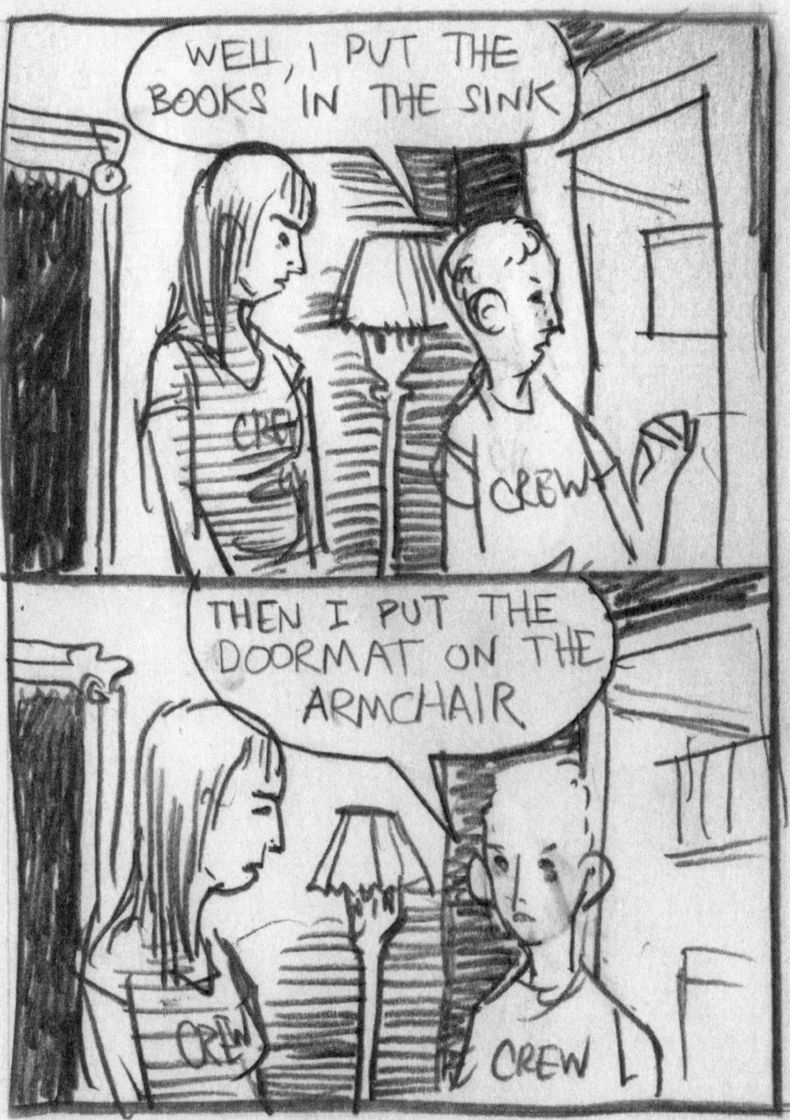
WELL, I PUT THE BOOKS IN THE SINK
CREW
CREW
THEN I PUT THE DOORMAT ON THE ARMCHAIR
CREW
CREW

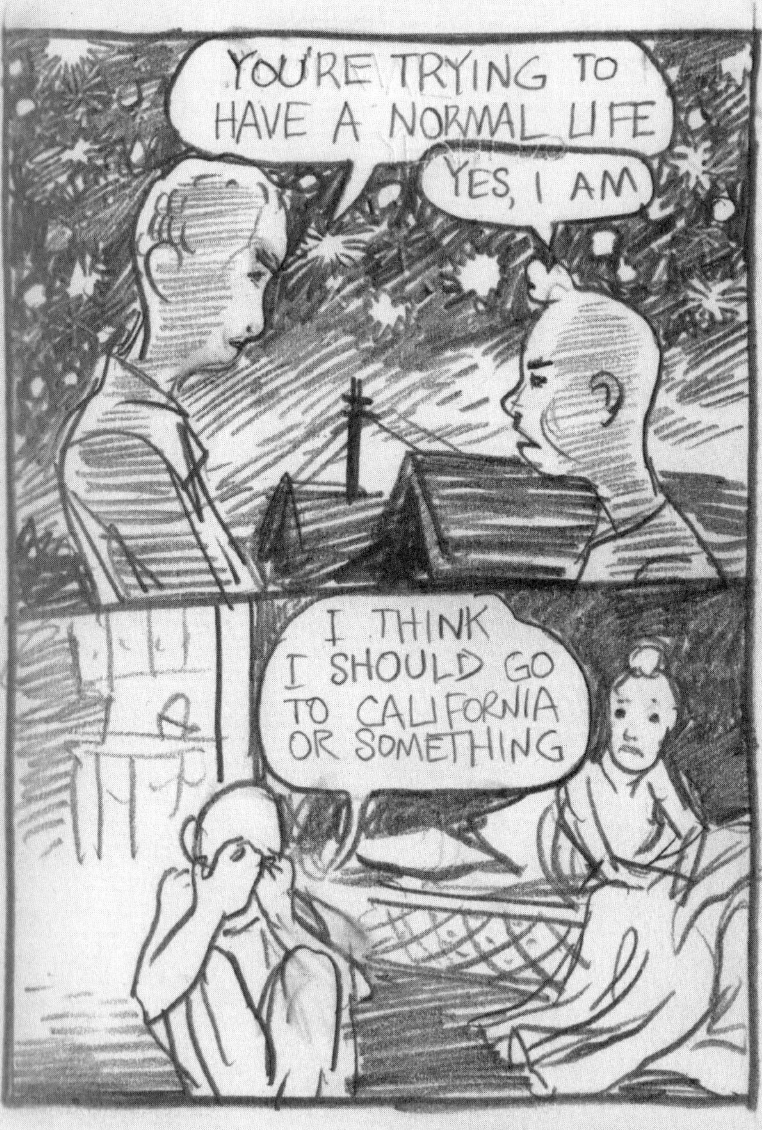
YOU'RE TRYING TO HAVE A NORMAL LIFE
YES, I AM
I THINK I SHOULD GO TO CALIFORNIA OR SOMETHING

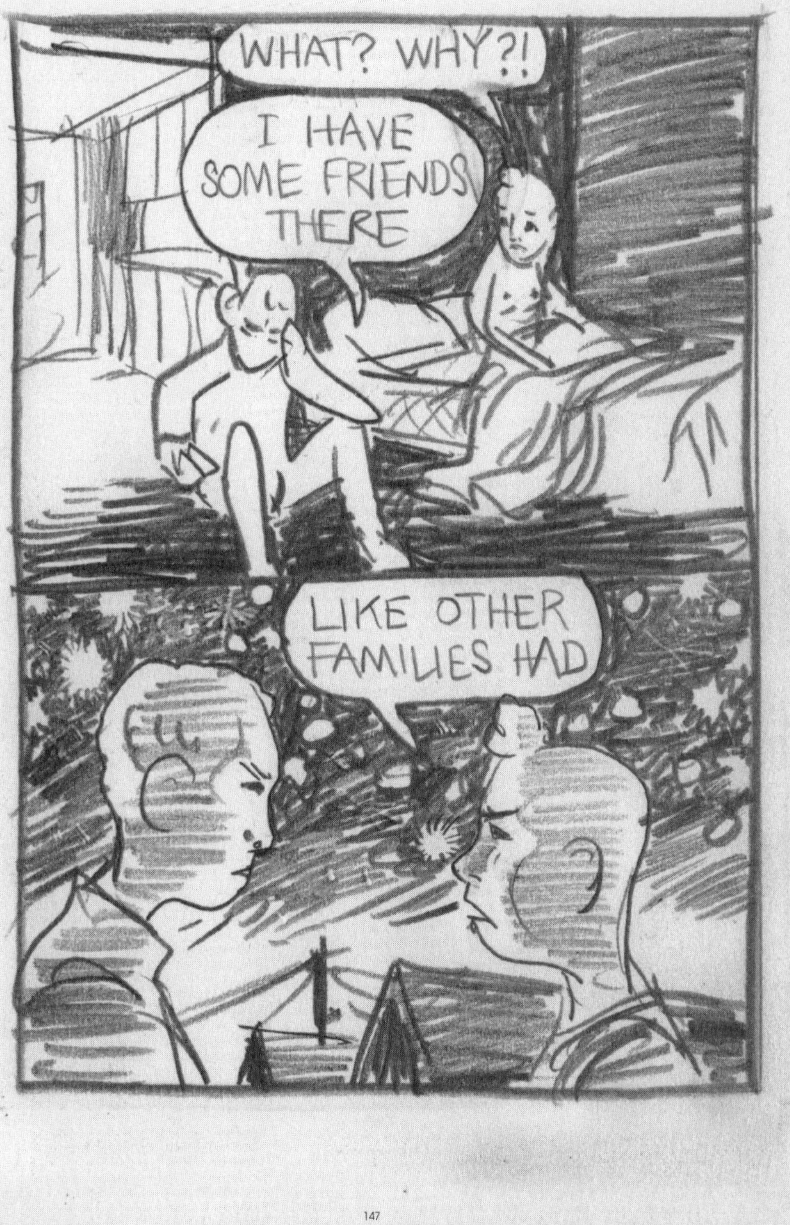
WHAT? WHY?!
I HAVE SOME FRIENDS THERE
LIKE OTHER FAMILIES HAD

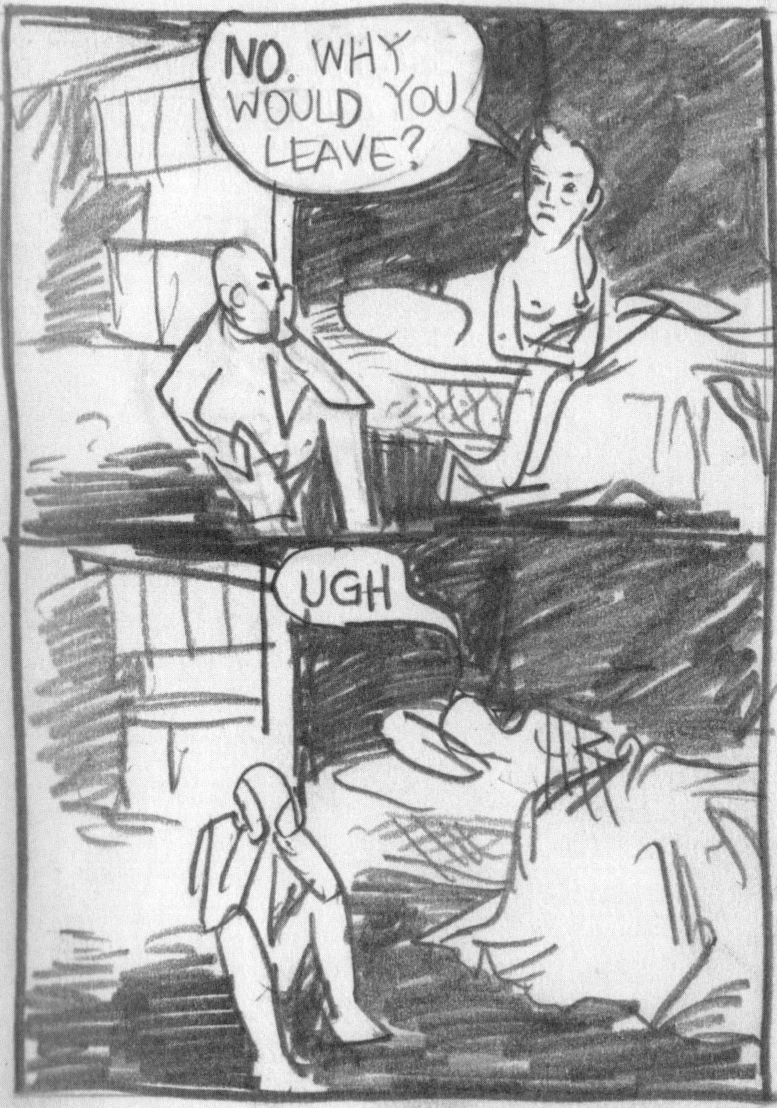
NO. WHY WOULD YOU LEAVE?
UGH

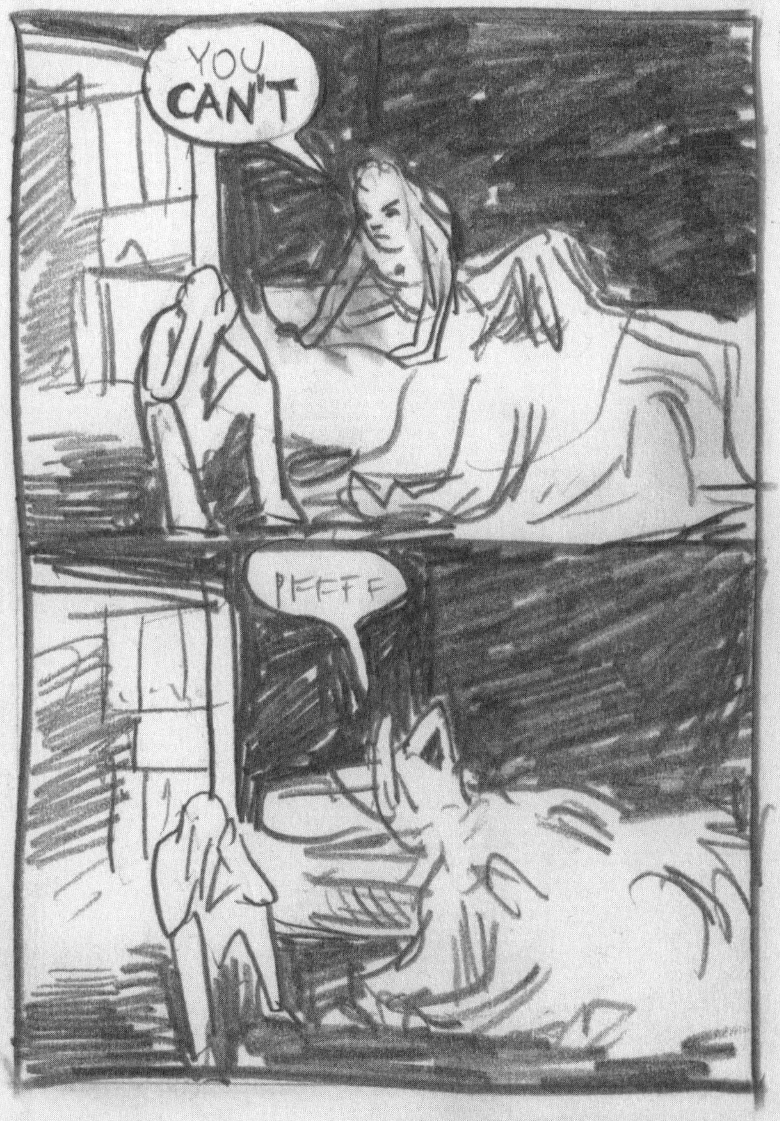
YOU CAN'T
PFFFF

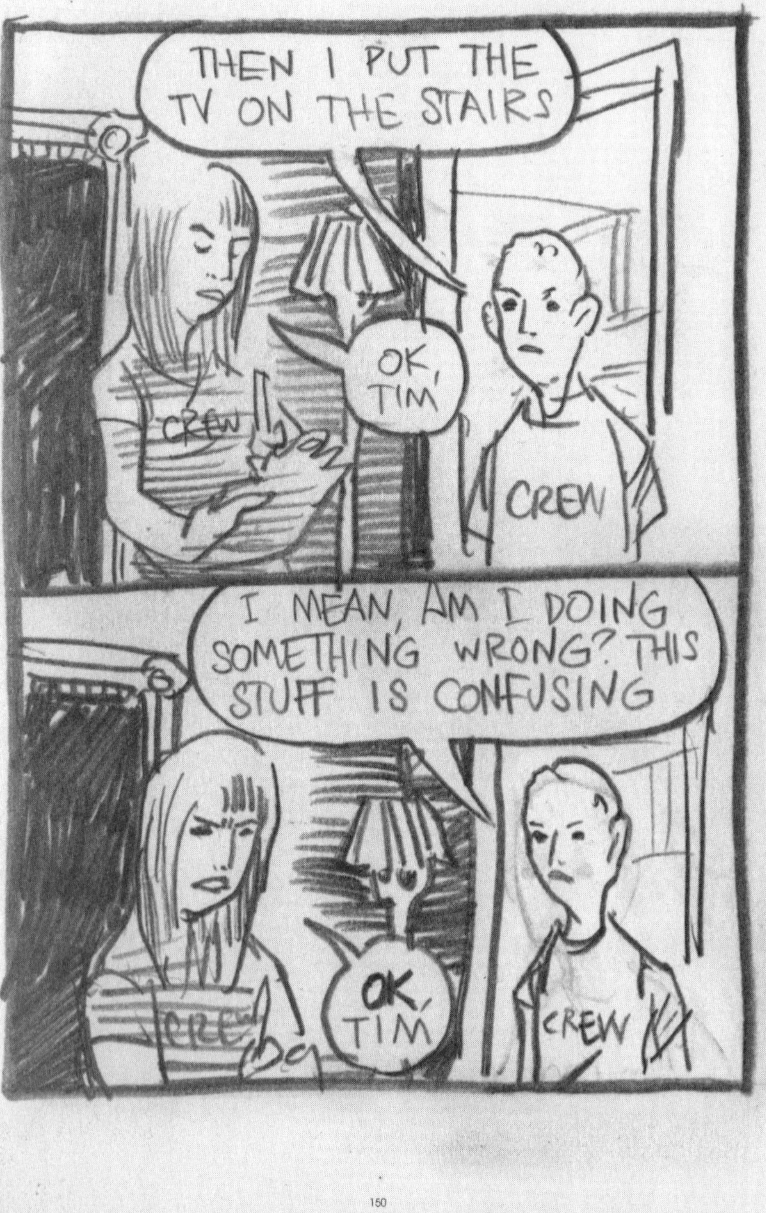
THEN I PUT THE TV ON THE STAIRS
CREW
OK, TIM
CREW
I MEAN, AM I DOING SOMETHING WRONG? THIS STUFF IS CONFUSING
OK, TIM
CREW

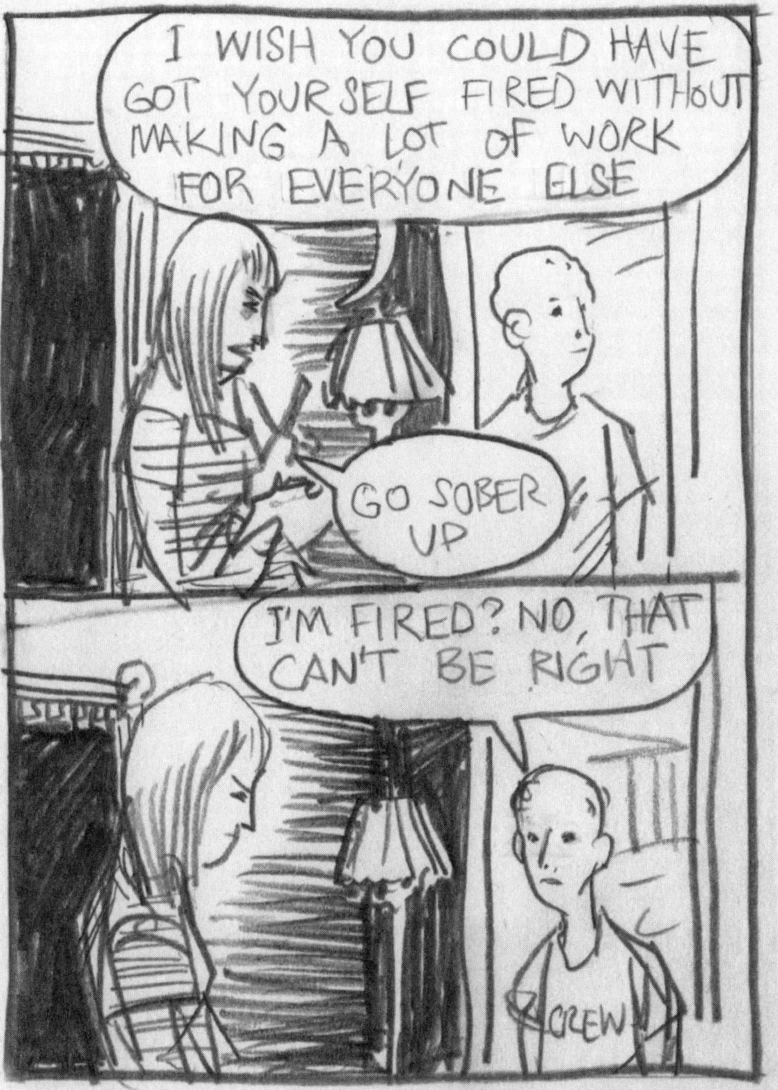
I WISH YOU COULD HAVE GOT YOURSELF FIRED WITHOUT MAKING A LOT OF WORK FOR EVERYONE ELSE
GO SOBER UP
I'M FIRED? NO, THAT CAN'T BE RIGHT
CREW

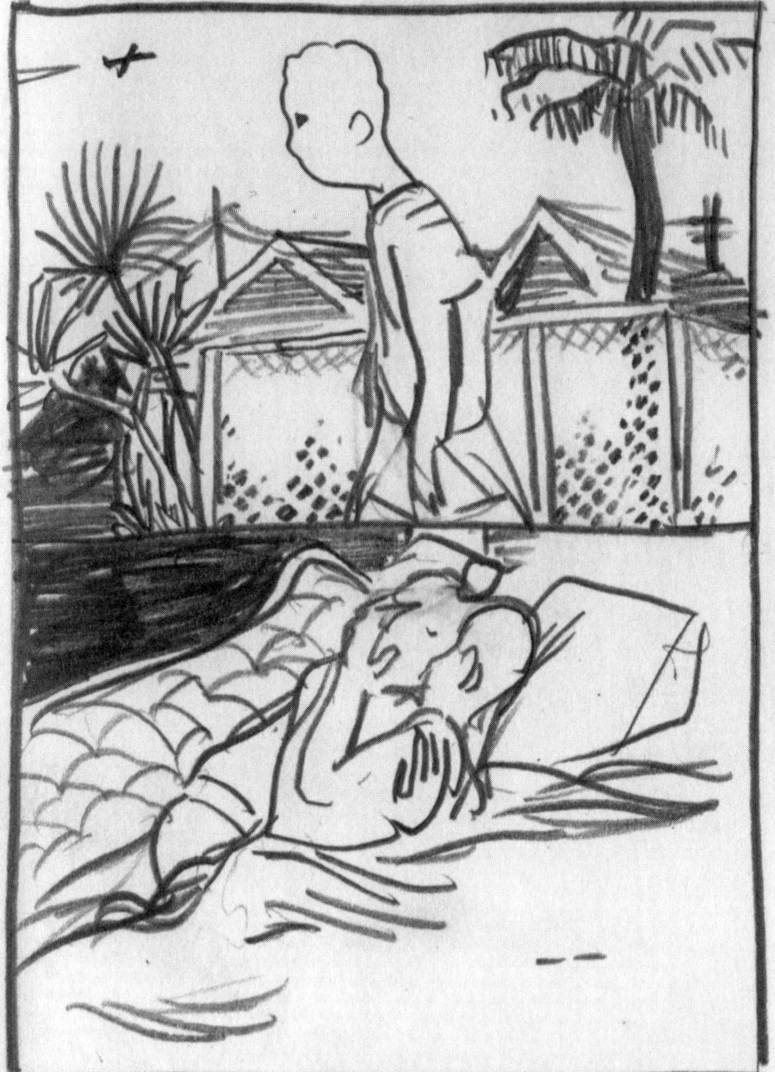

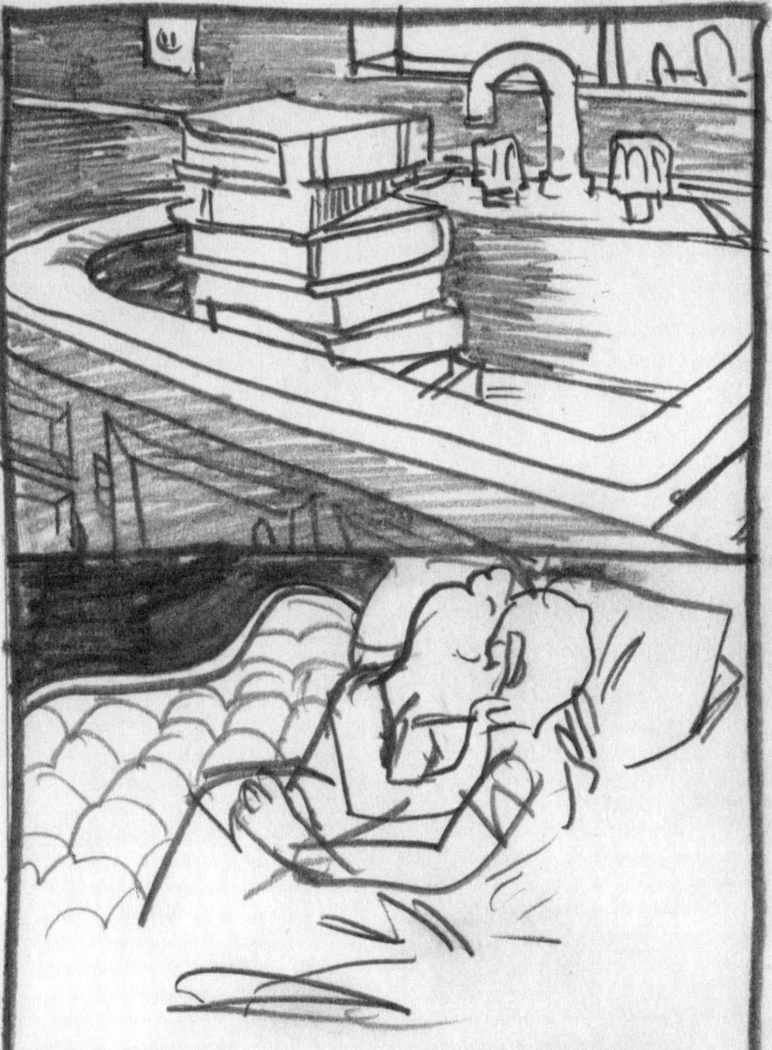

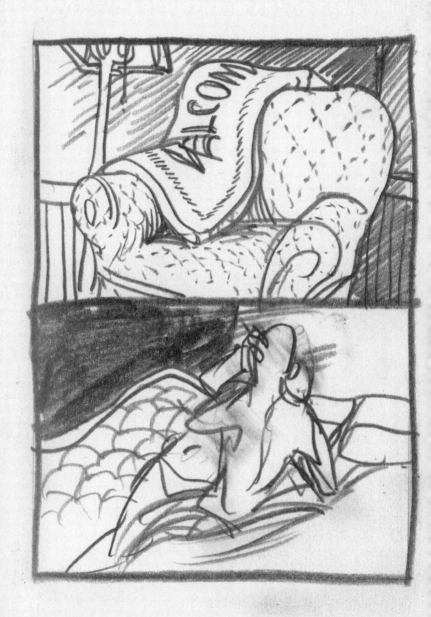

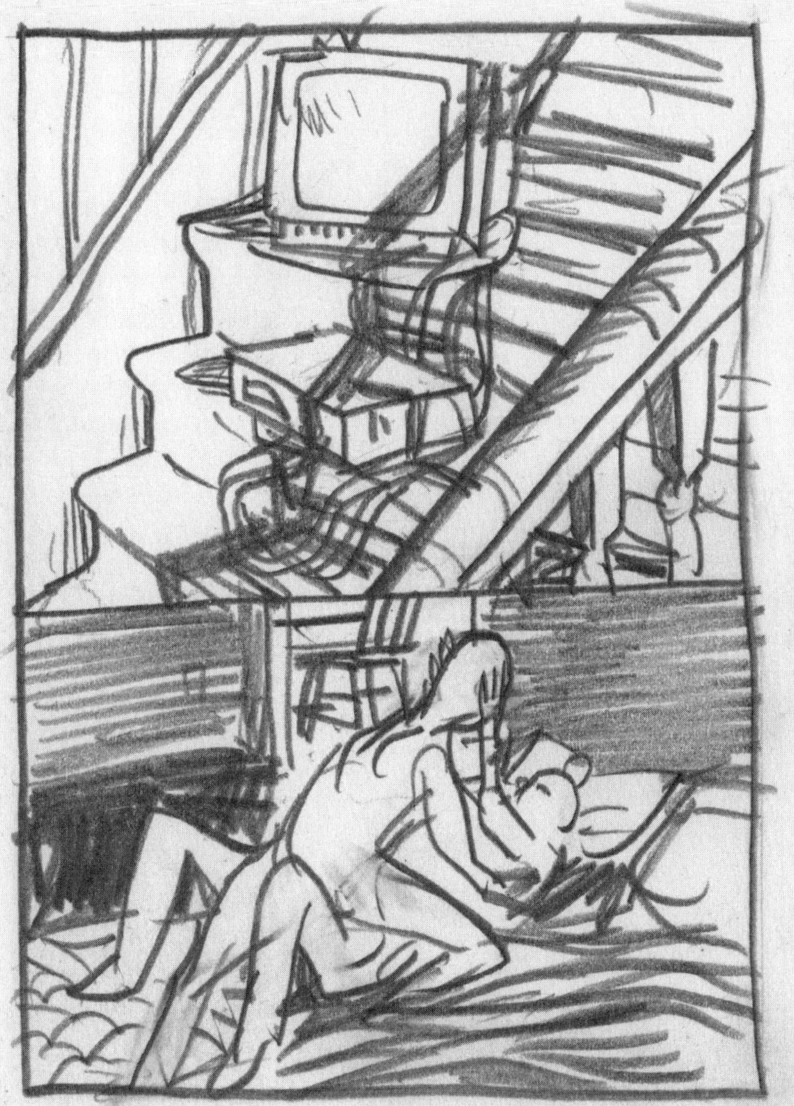

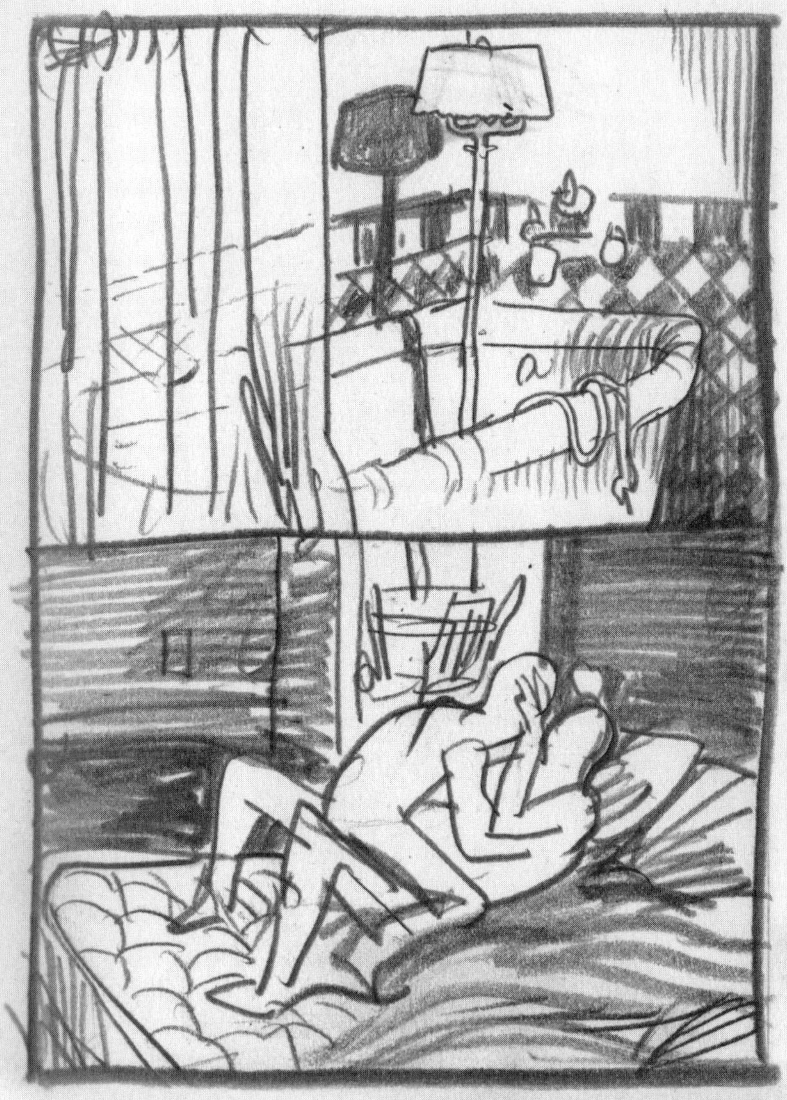

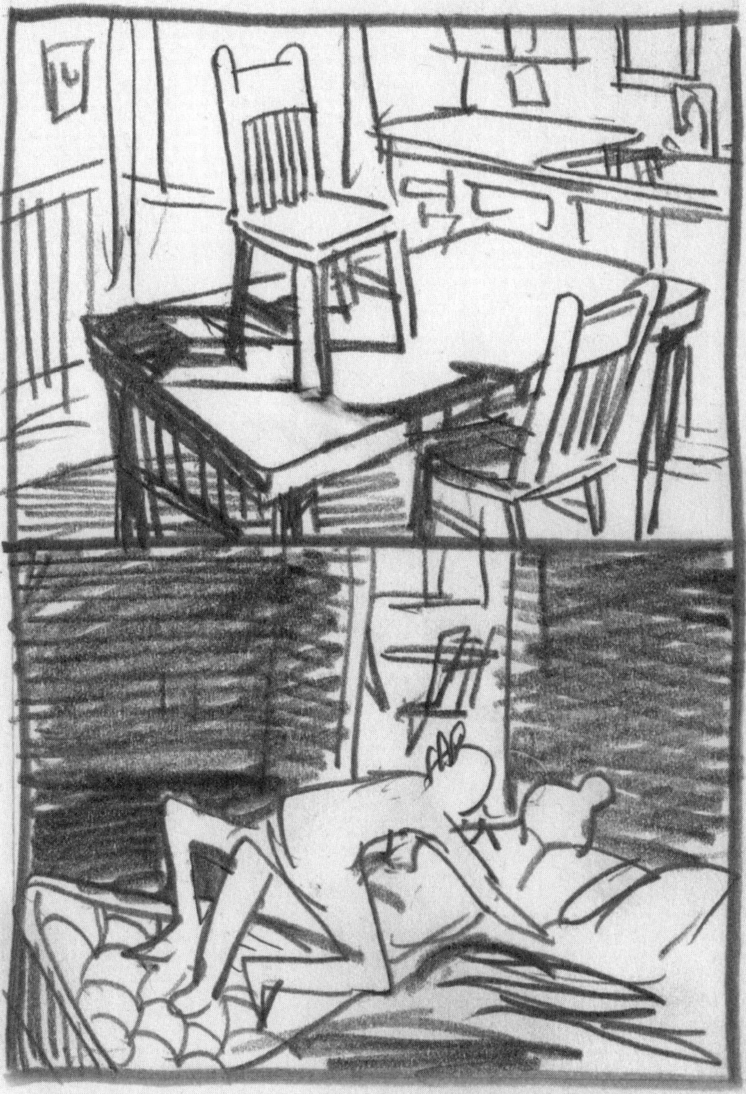

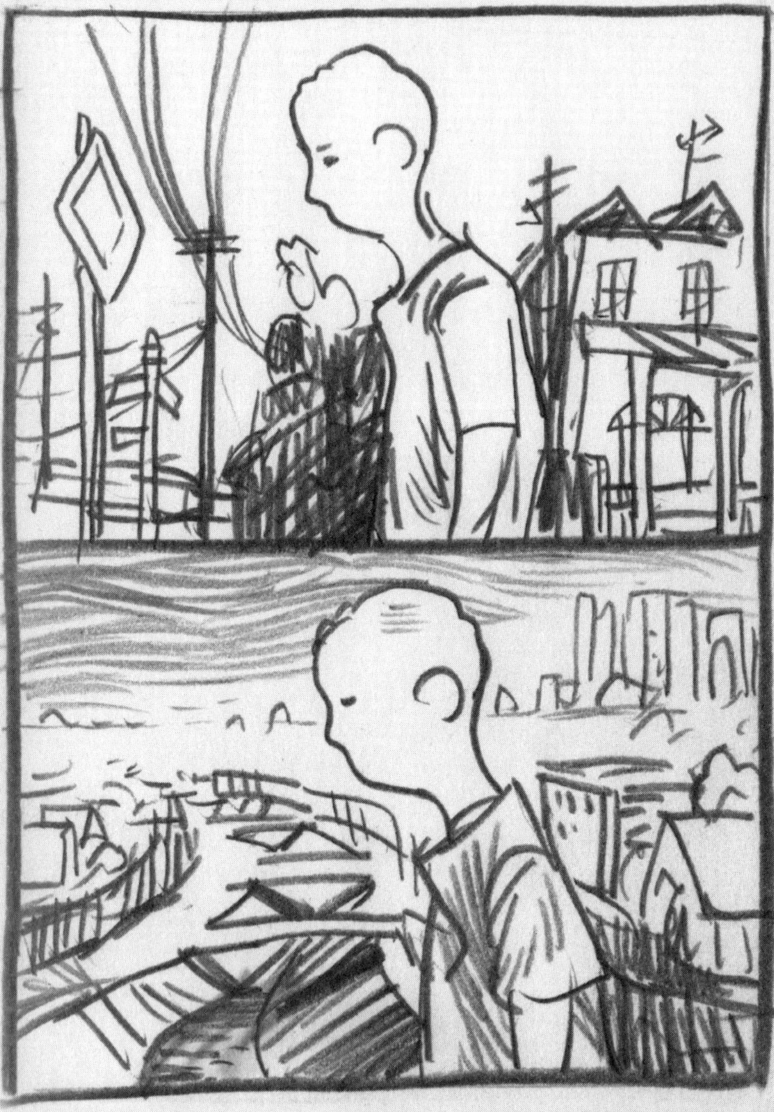

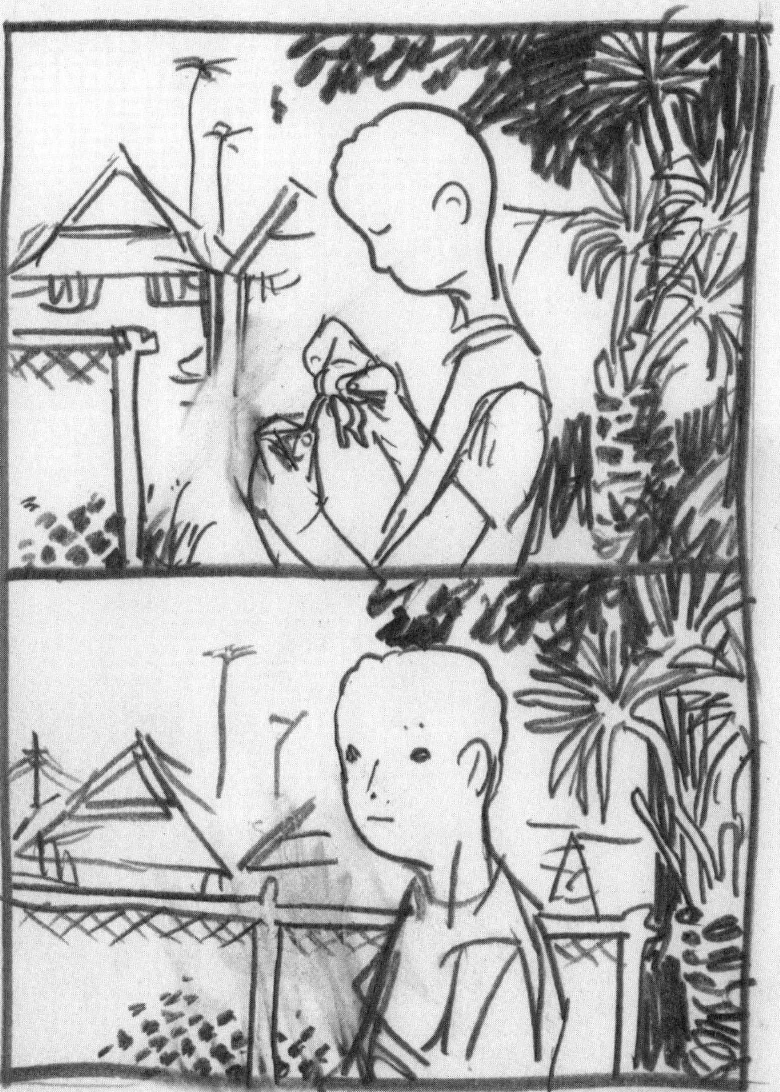

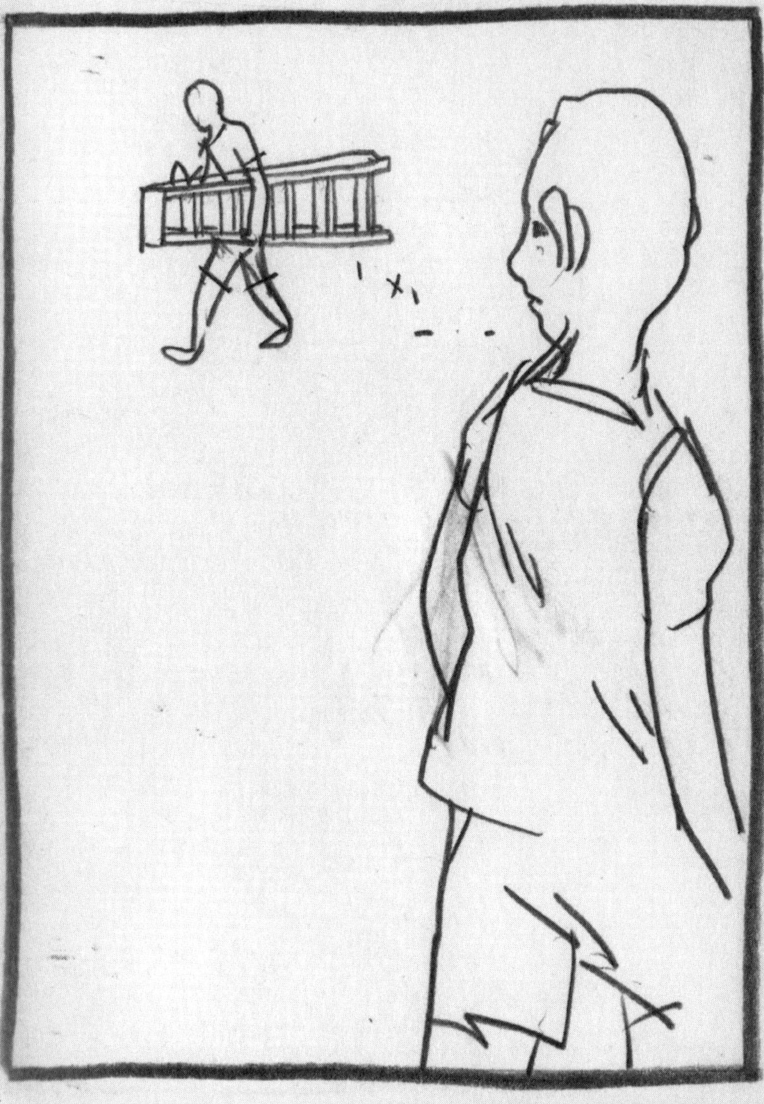

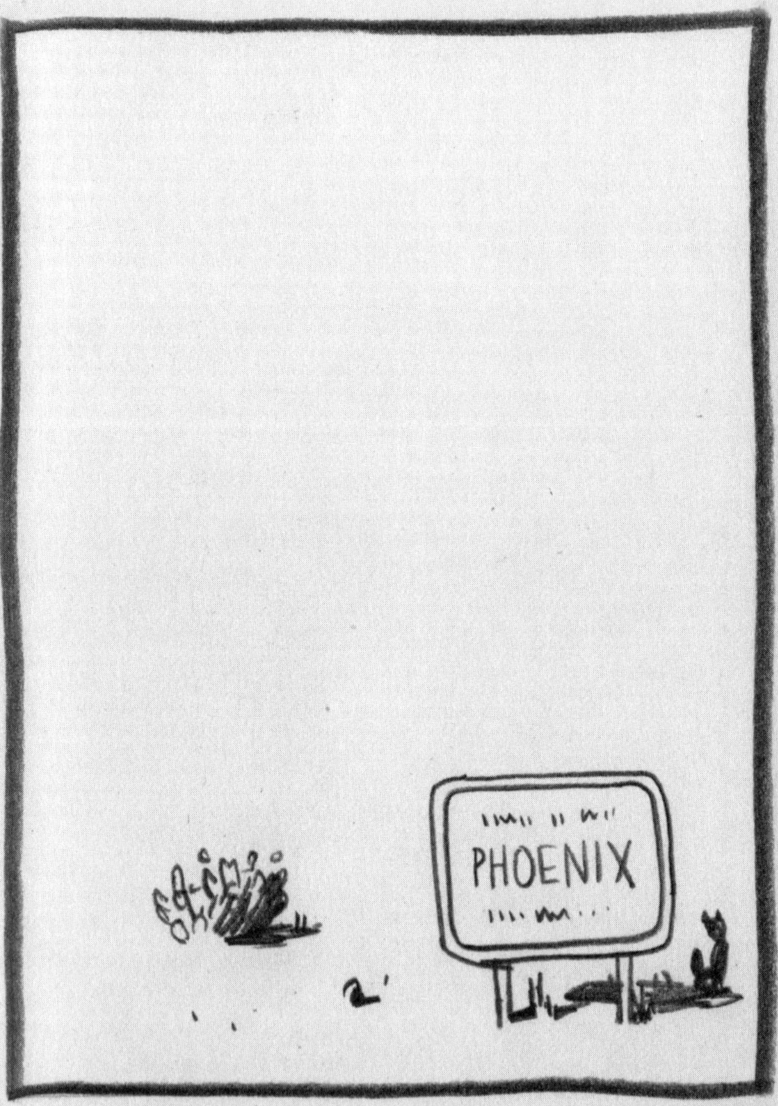
PHOENIX

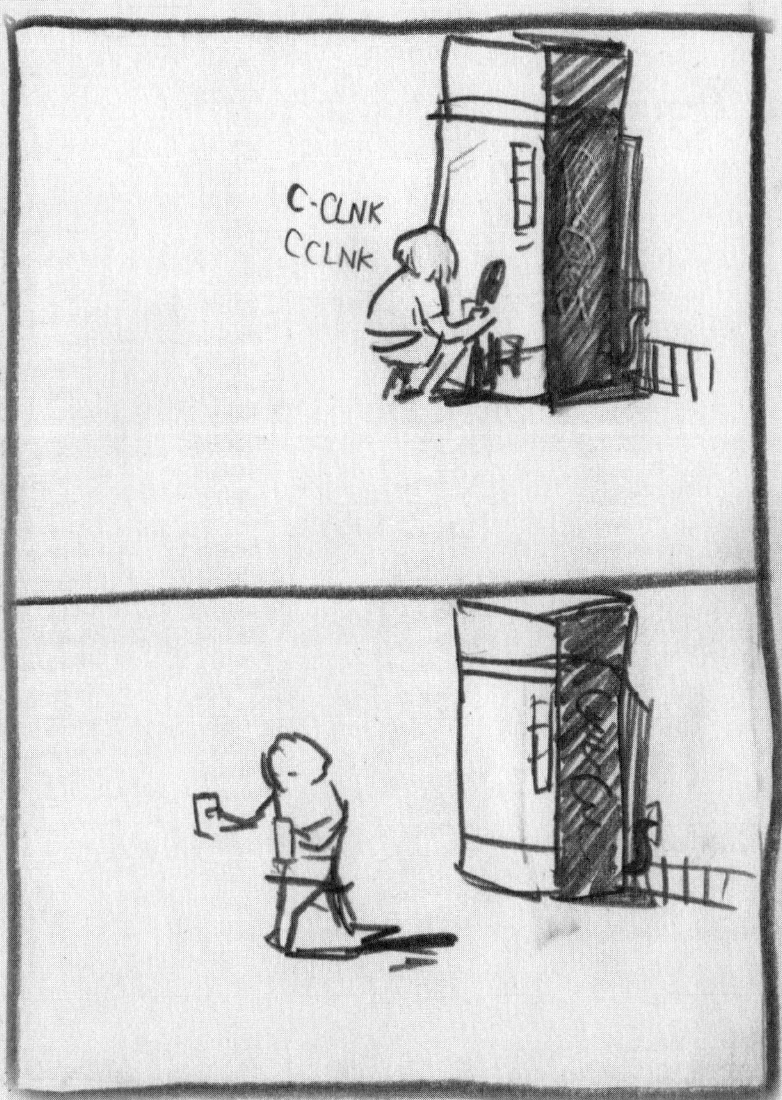
C-CLNK
CCLNK

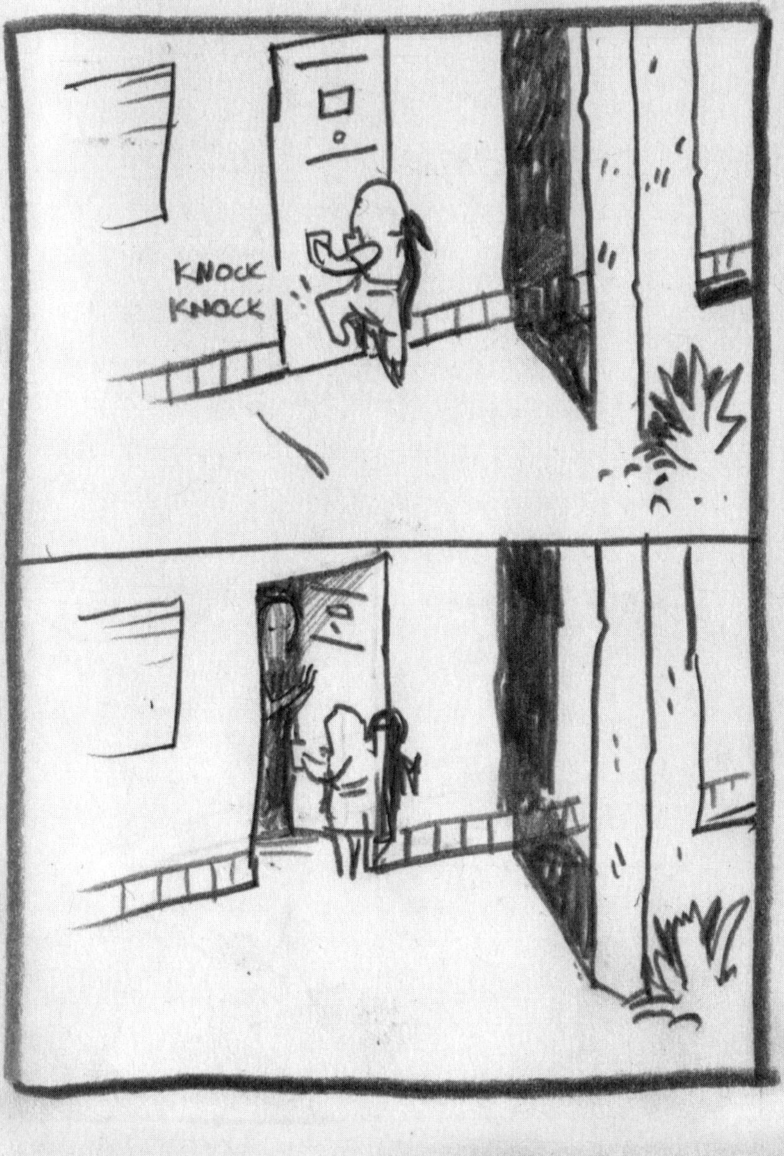
KNOCK
KNOCK

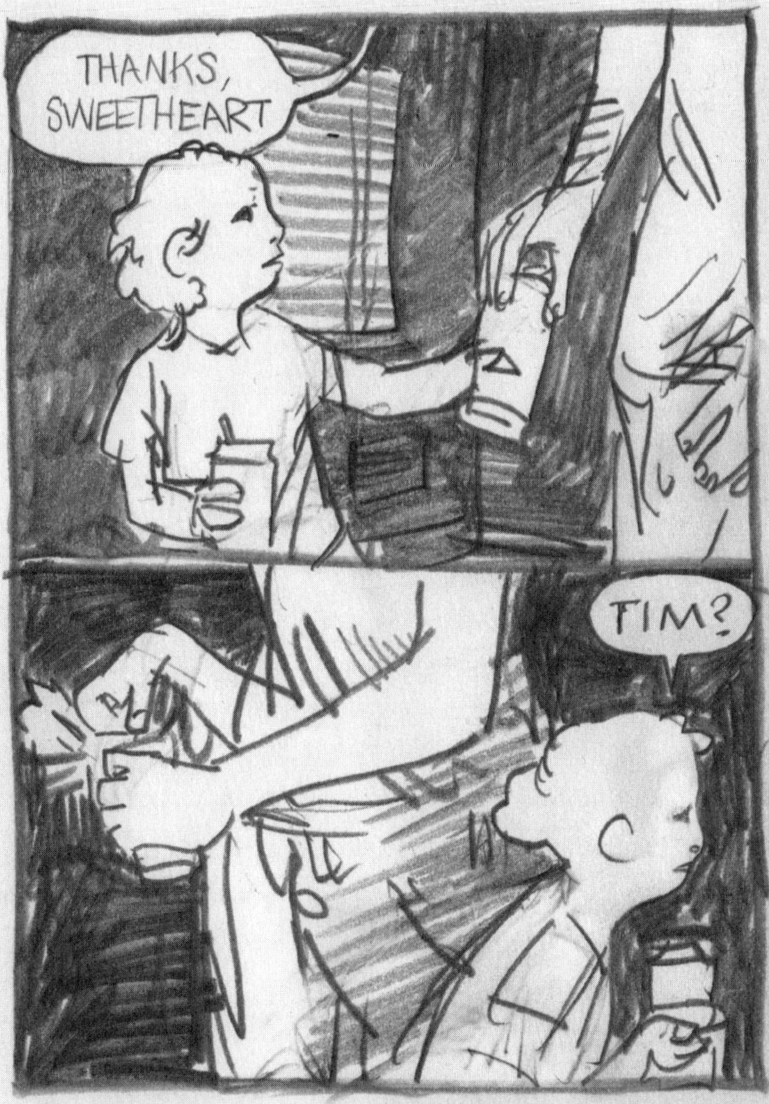
THANKS, SWEETHEART
TIM?

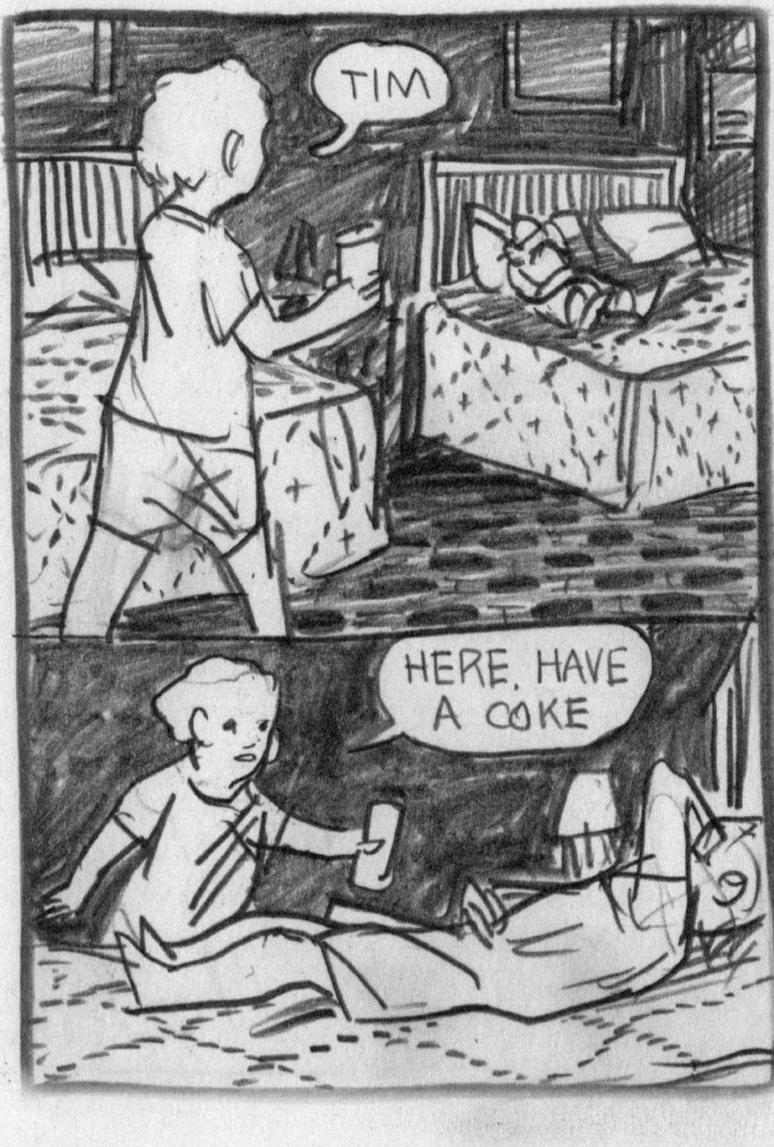
TIM
HERE, HAVE A COKE

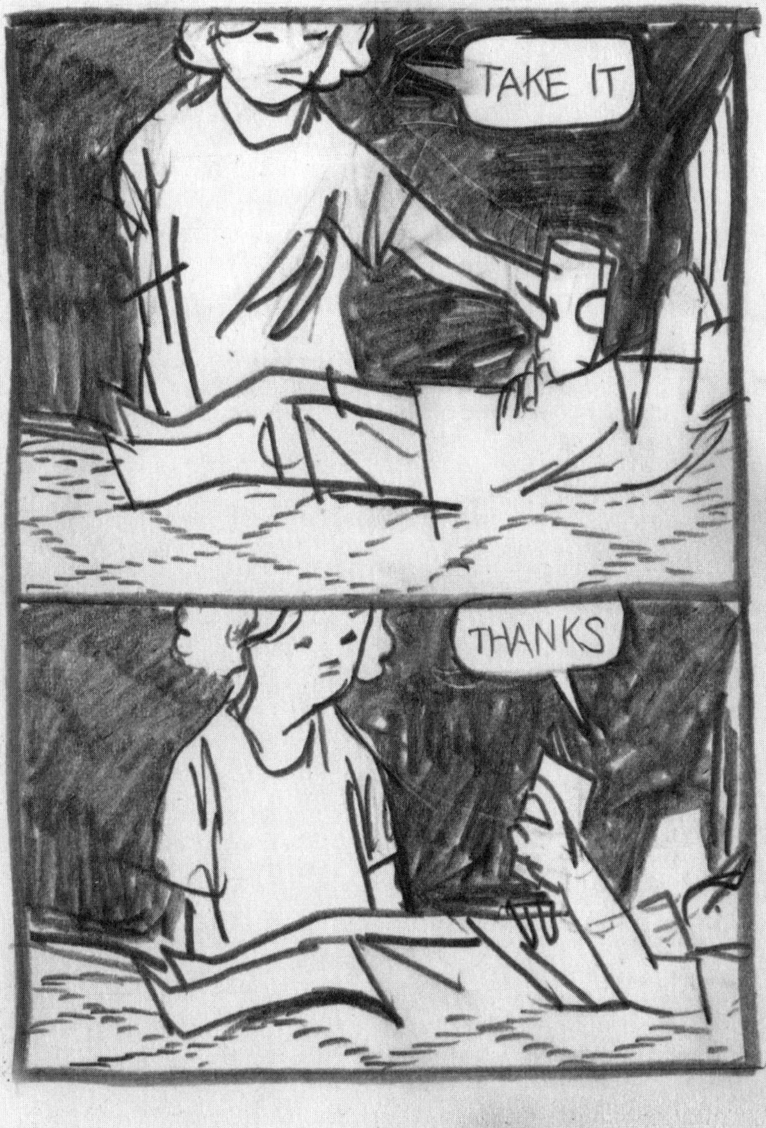
TAKE IT
THANKS

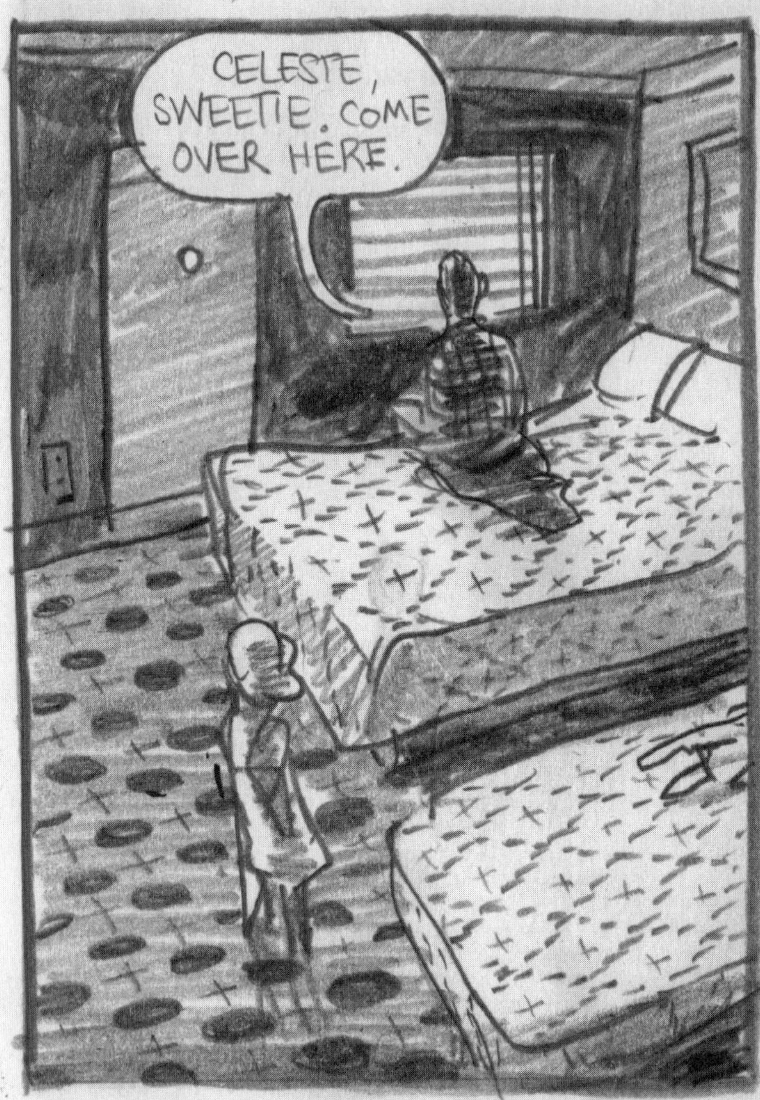
CELESTE, SWEETIE. COME OVER HERE.

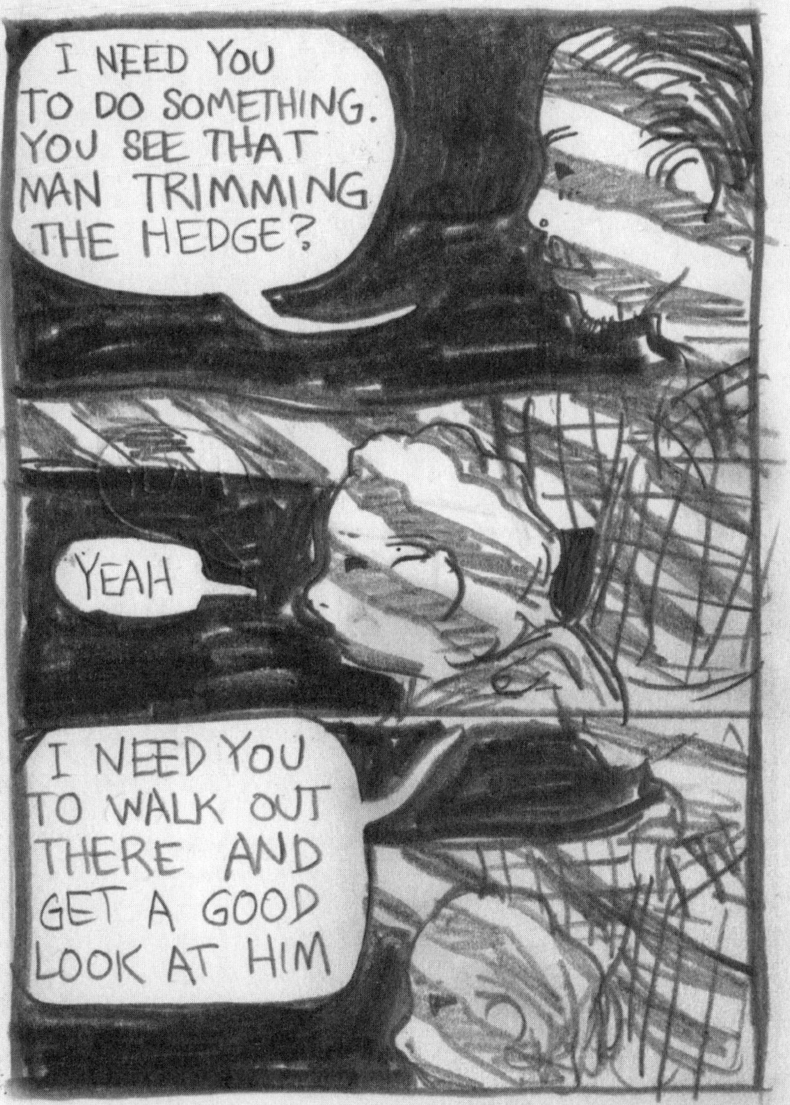
I NEED YOU TO DO SOMETHING. YOU SEE THAT MAN TRIMMING THE HEDGE?
YEAH
I NEED YOU TO WALK OUT THERE AND GET A GOOD LOOK AT HIM

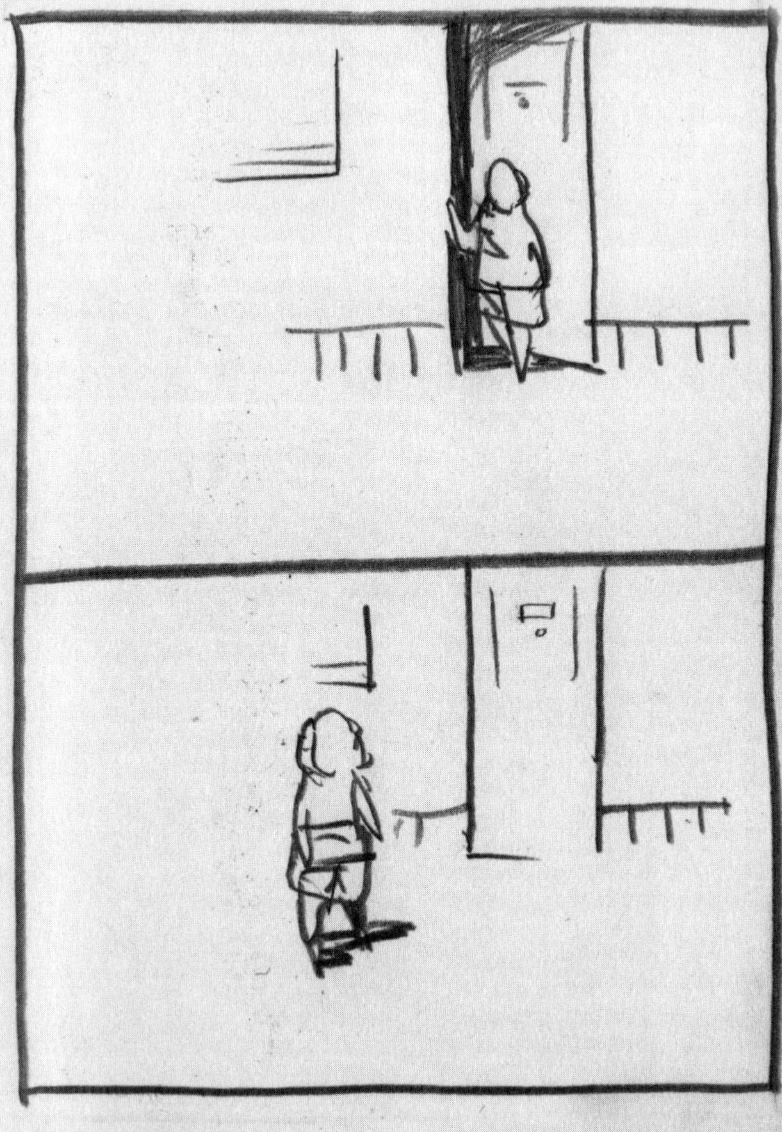

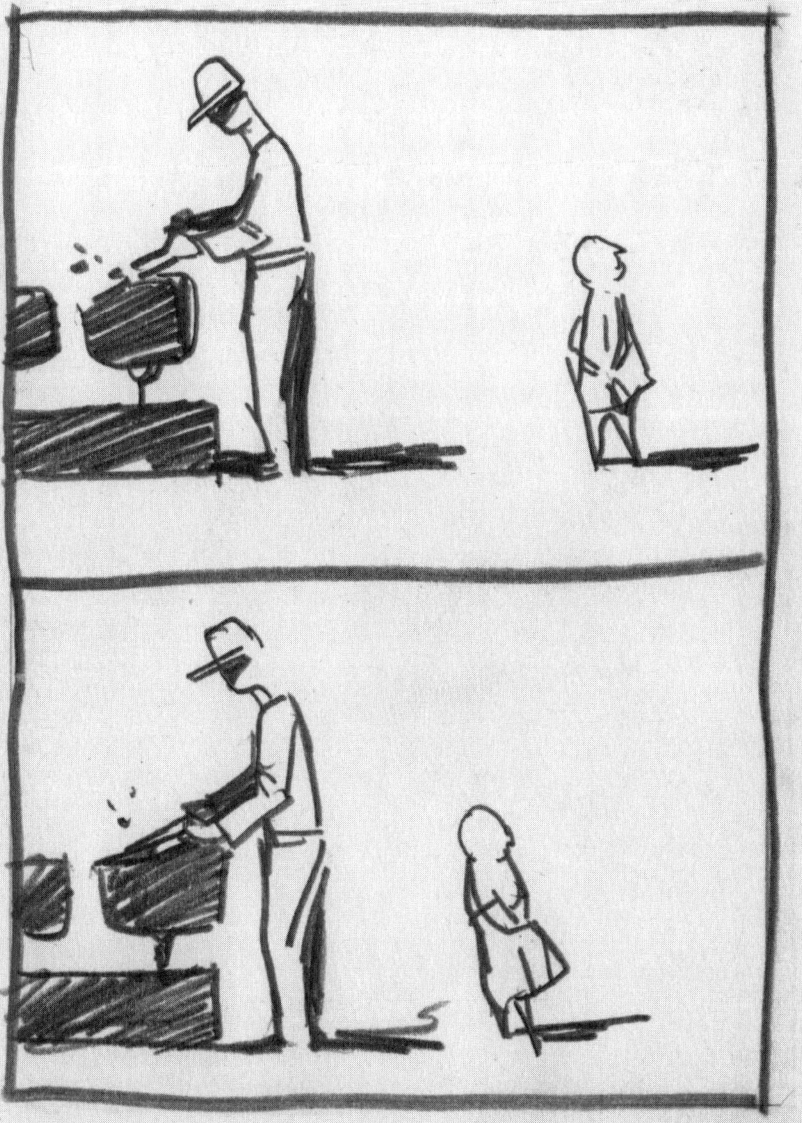

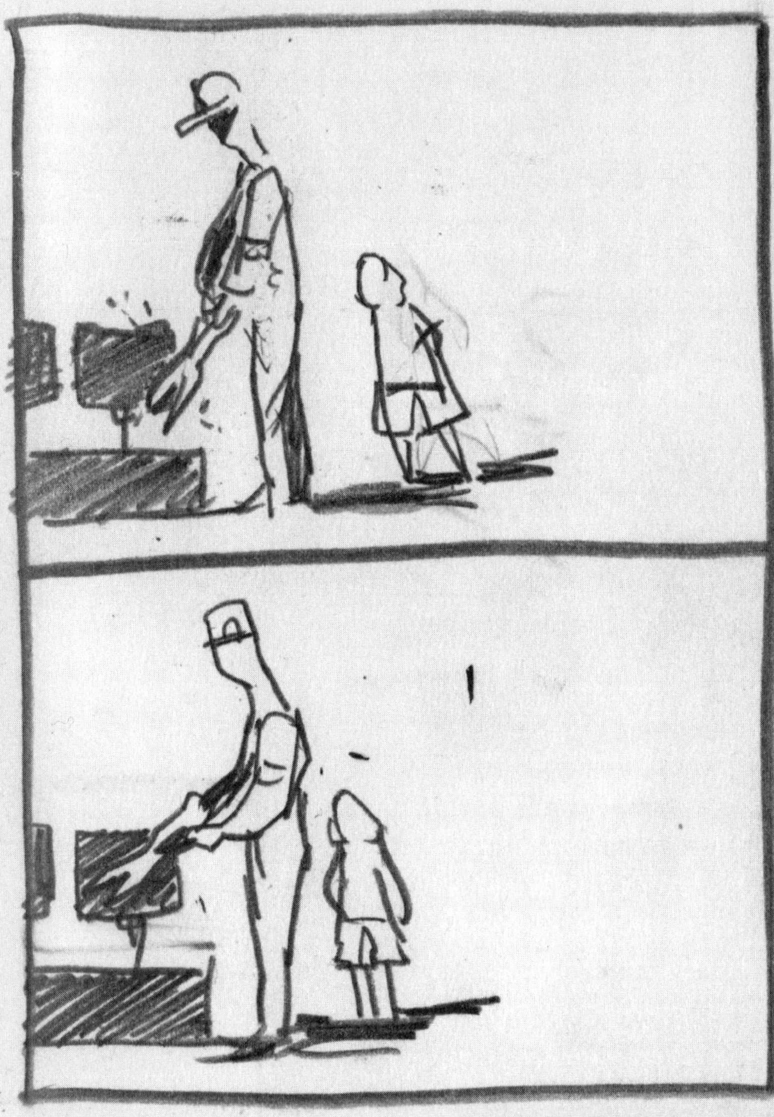

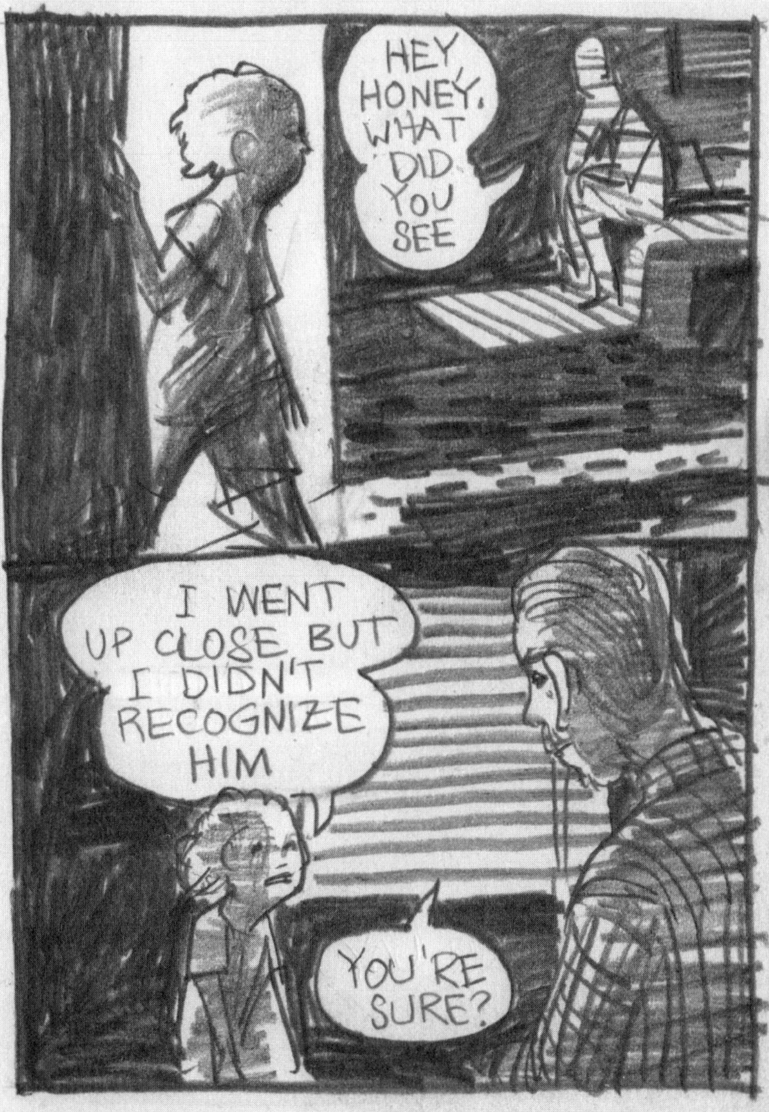
HEY, HONEY, WHAT DID YOU SEE
I WENT UP CLOSE BUT I DIDN'T RECOGNIZE HIM
YOU'RE SURE?

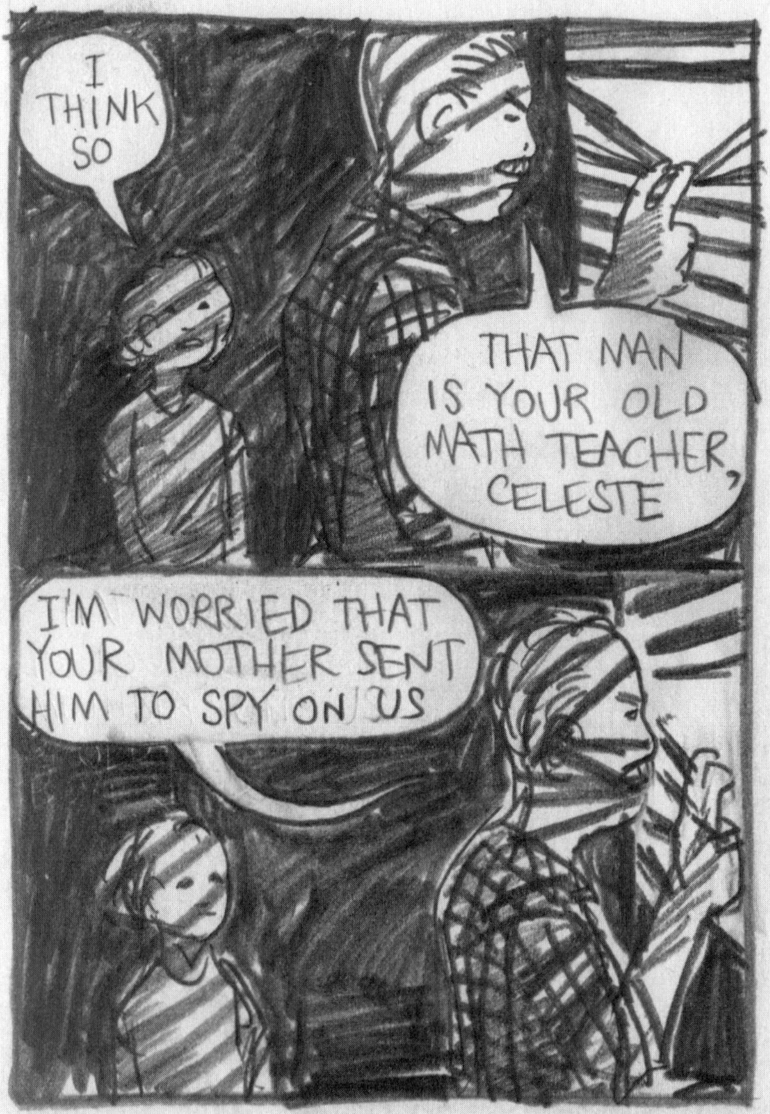
I THINK SO
THAT MAN IS YOUR OLD MATH TEACHER, CELESTE
I'M WORRIED THAT YOUR MOTHER SENT HIM TO SPY ON US

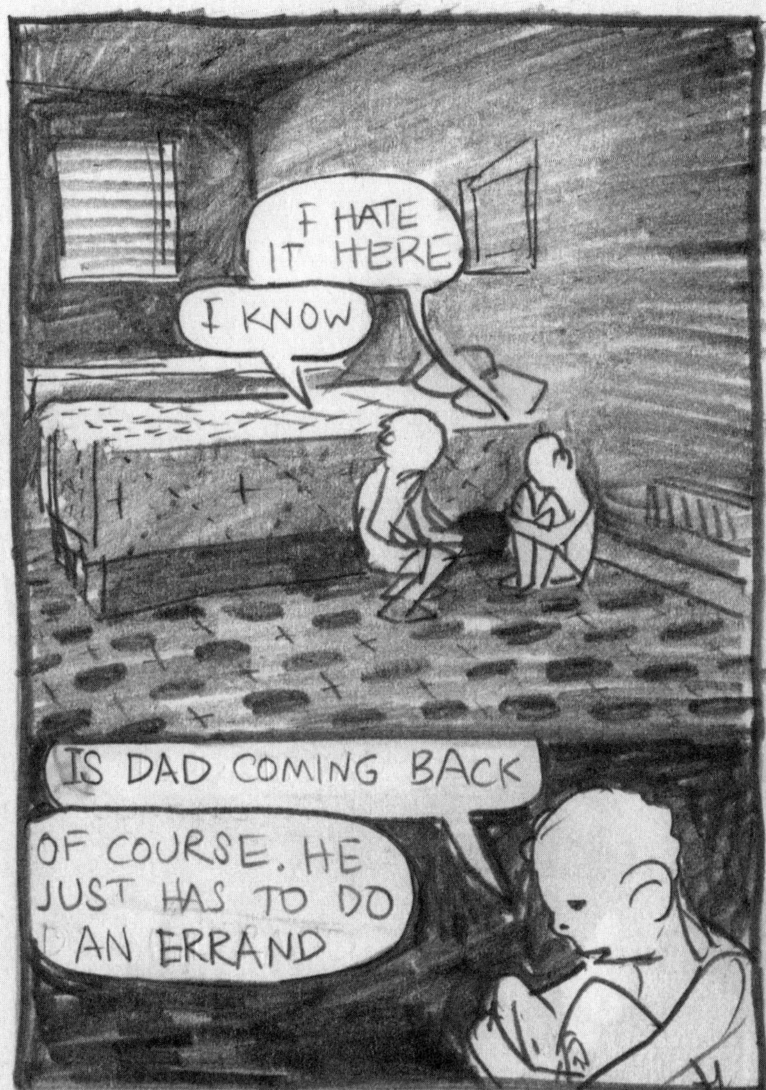
I HATE IT HERE
I KNOW
IS DAD COMING BACK
OF COURSE. HE JUST HAS TO DO AN ERRAND

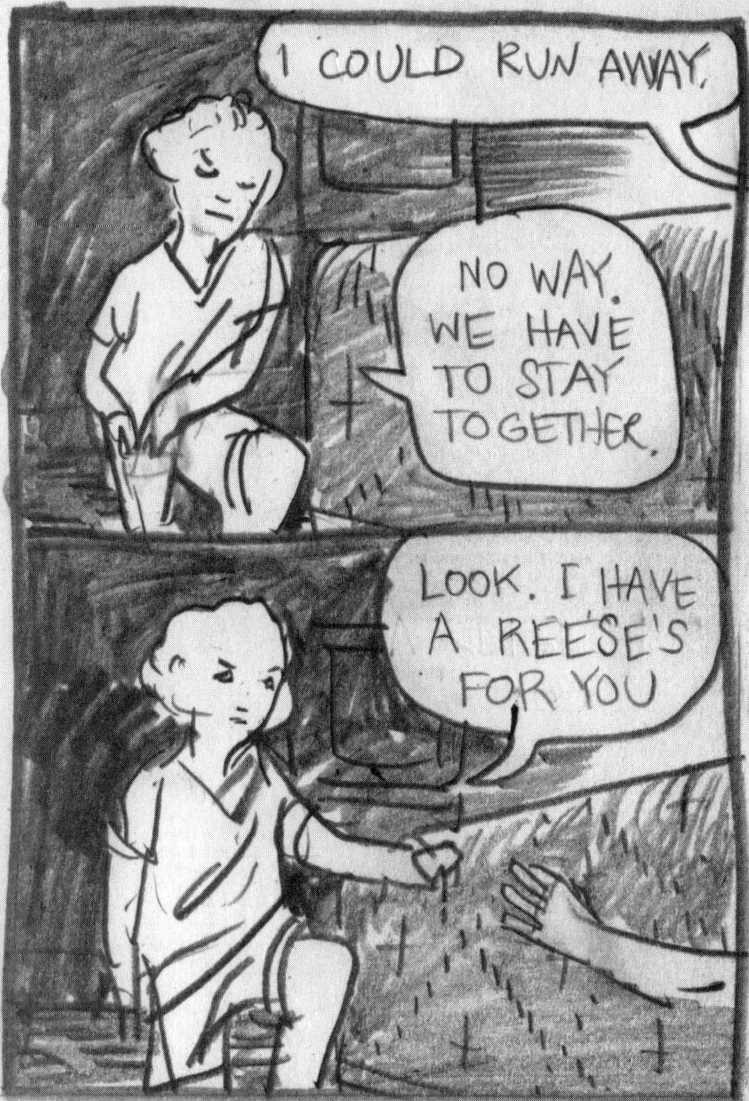
I COULD RUN AWAY.
NO WAY. WE HAVE TO STAY TOGETHER.
LOOK. I HAVE A REESE'S FOR YOU

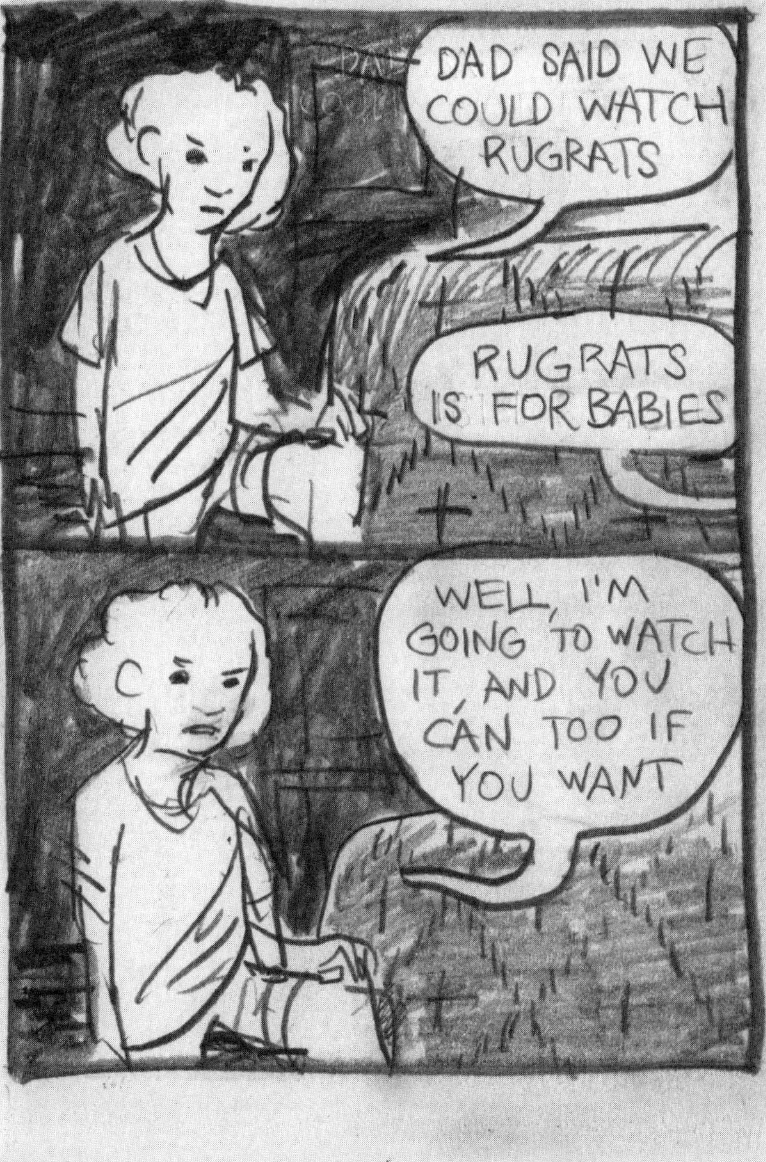
DAD SAID WE COULD WATCH RUGRATS
RUGRATS IS FOR BABIES
WELL, I'M GOING TO WATCH IT, AND YOU CAN TOO IF YOU WANT

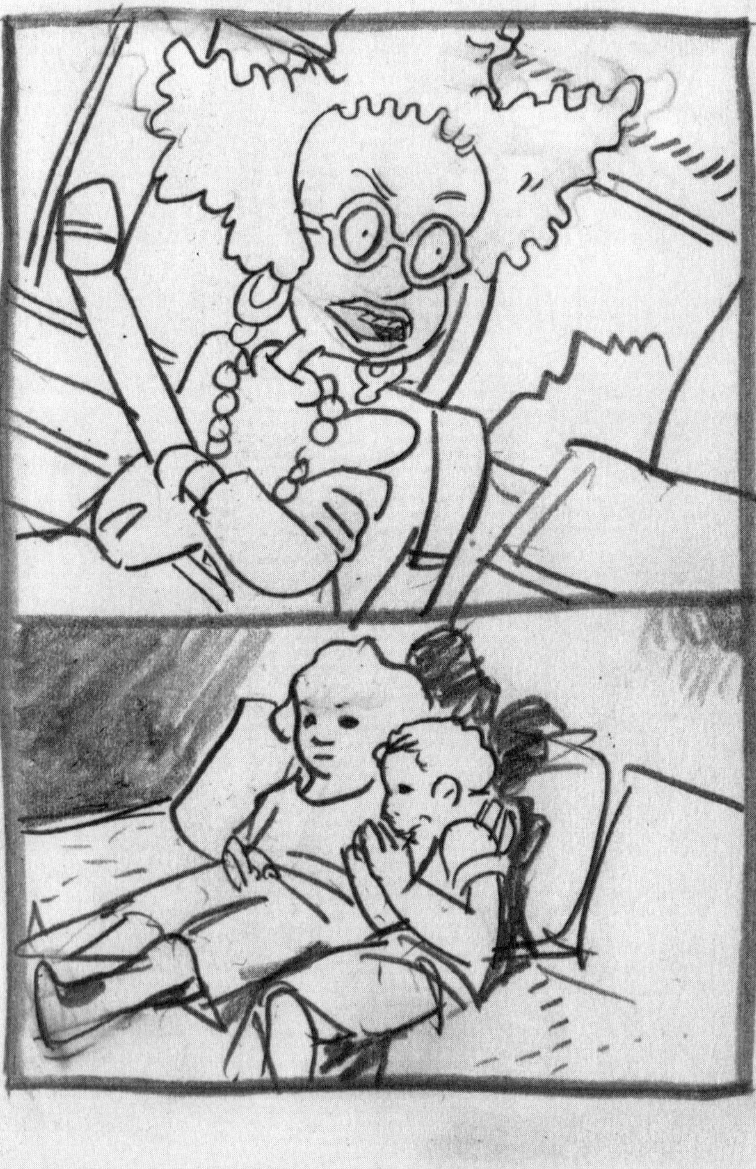

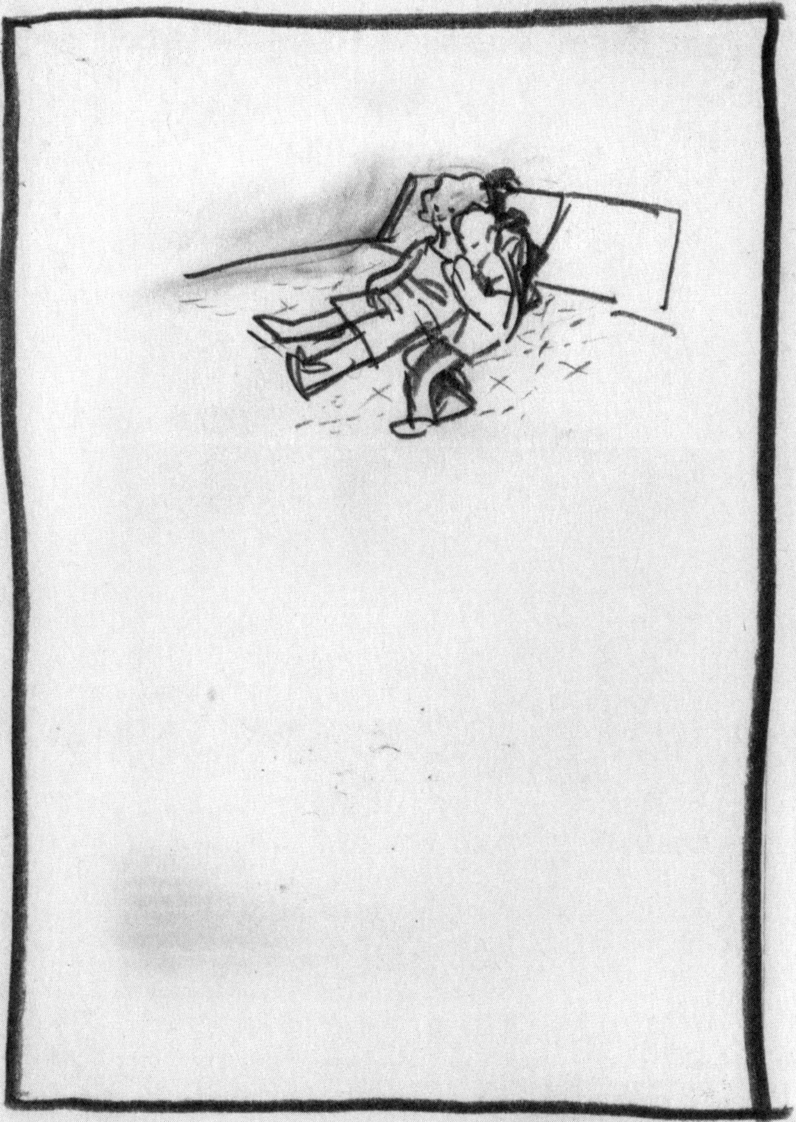

THANKS: SOPHIE YANOW, VINCENT GIARD, RACHEL MILLMAN, TOM KACZYNSKI, ALEC BERRY, SCOTT LONGO, MICHAEL DeFORGE, OLIVIA HORVATH, CATHY JOHNSON, SARA DRAKE, DARRYL AYO, TOBY ALDEN, BEN URKOWITZ, JEREMY SORESE, MELISSA TVETAN, HAILEY McCARTHEY, ALEX SUTHERN, ANNIE KOYAMA, SOPHIE JOHNSON, ULLI LUST, + MY PARENTS

SAM ALDEN WAS BORN
IN 1988 AND GREW UP IN
PORTLAND OR. HE IS A
2-TIME RECIPIENT OF THE
IGNATZ AWARD AND
CURRENTLY WORKS ON THE
CARTOON NETWORK SHOW
ADVENTURE TIME. HE LIVES
IN LOS ANGELES.

UNCIVILIZED CATALOGUE

INCIDENTS IN THE NIGHT by David B.; Translated by Brian Evenson

THE VOYEURS by Gabrielle Bell

TRUTH IS FRAGMENTARY by Gabrielle Bell

AN IRANIAN METAMORPHOSIS by Mana Neyestani

WAR OF STREETS AND HOUSES by Sophie Yanow

AMAZING FACTS & BEYOND by Kevin Huizenga & Dan Zettwoc

SAMMY THE MOUSE by ZAK SALLY

TRUE SWAMP by Jon Lewis

POST YORK by James Romberger & Crosby

EEL MANSIONS by Derek Van Gieson

OVER THE WALL by Peter Wartman

ED VS. YUMMY FUR by Brian Evenson

UNCIVILIZEDBOOKS.COM